A Dream Deferred

A DREAM DEFERRED

The Art and Activism of
Edwin Augustus Harleston

M. AKUA McDANIEL

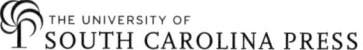

THE UNIVERSITY OF
SOUTH CAROLINA PRESS

© 2026 University of South Carolina

Published by the University of South Carolina Press
Columbia, South Carolina 29208

uscpress.com

Printed in the United States of America

Library of Congress Cataloging-in-Publication Data can be found at
http://catalog.loc.gov/.

ISBN: 978-1-64336-559-6 (hardcover)
ISBN: 978-1-64336-604-3 (ebook)

For my late parents,
Frank F. and Thelma W. McDaniel,
on whose love and support the foundation
of my life has been built

What happens to a dream deferred?

Does it dry up
like a raisin in the sun?
Or fester like a sore—
And then run?
Does it stink like rotten meat?
Or crust and sugar over—
like a syrupy sweet?

Maybe it just sags
like a heavy load.

Or does it explode?

—Langston Hughes, "Harlem"

CONTENTS

LIST OF ILLUSTRATIONS

PREFACE

IN THE THIRTY-SEVEN YEARS between the opening of New York's Studio Museum exhibition, "Harlem Renaissance: Art of Black America" in 1987, and "Harlem Renaissance and Transatlantic Modernism," which debuted at the Metropolitan Museum of Art in 2024, art scholars, critics, and cultural historians have continued to explore the rich aesthetic legacy bequeathed to us by these talented artists. Yet, there is still very little information about the artists who lived and worked beyond the rim of Harlem's creative circle in the 1920s. The Harmon Foundation exhibitions have provided insight into the aesthetic vision of some of these artists including Chicago artists such as William E. Scott, William M. Farrow, Charles C. Dawson, along with Indianapolis artists Hale Woodruff and John Wesley Hardrick. But with the exception of Woodruff, none of these Midwestern artists held a prominent place among those associated with Harlem's burgeoning renaissance. However, I did find one exception, Edwin Augustus Harleston, a South Carolina artist whose name not only appears several times in the Harmon catalogue, but also in exhibitions held at the 135th Street Branch of the New York Public Library, and in an announcement for a solo exhibition held at Paul Lawrence Dunbar High School, an important center for African American arts and culture from the 1920s through the 1950s in Washington, DC.

The work of this artist first came to my attention while reading James A. Porter's groundbreaking book, *Modern Negro Art*, a pioneering survey of African American art, published in 1943 and reissued in 1969. As I read and reviewed every page, it came as a shocking revelation that the names and works of so many Black artists had been excluded from the annals of American art. I was familiar with the artwork of Henry O. Tanner, and I knew of sculptor Meta Warrick Fuller because her grandson lived in my hometown, but the majority of the late nineteenth- and early twentieth-century visual artists included in this text were new to me. Edwin Harleston's profile stood out because he was one of the few artists discussed in

Porter's book who continued to live and work in the South at the turn of the twentieth century, but because his artworks bore titles such as *The Bible Student* and *The Old Servant*, he was of no interest to me. The Afrocentric haze of the 1970s Black Arts Movement, which placed strong emphasis on cultural nationalism, had blinded me to the possibility that Harleston's artwork had any sociopolitical value, therefore, I dismissed his work without giving it a second thought.

Fortunately, I was given a second opportunity to learn about Edwin Harleston in 1990 when I was introduced to the artist's niece Edwina Augusta Harleston Whitlock (aka Gussie Louise Harleston) by Dr. Richard A. Long, a nationally recognized African American arts and culture scholar, author, and professor at Clark Atlanta and Emory Universities. Mrs. Whitlock's vivid memories of Harleston family history and her willingness to give me unfettered access to the artist's personal letters and papers, sent me on a quest to uncover the social constraints and aesthetic challenges he faced as a Black artist living in Charleston during the 1920s. As I began combing through these documents and examining his paintings, I speculated about his reasons for remaining in the South at a time when thousands of others were joining the northern exodus known as the Great Migration. But as I dug deeper into Harleston's life, the amazing story of his career as an artist and his accomplishments as a civil rights activist began to surface. With this in mind, I decided to explore the life of Edwin Augustus Harleston so that others would more accurately comprehend and accept his aesthetic choices and appreciate the sacrifices he made for his family, community, and the race.

Much has been written about African American artists of the 1920s and 1930s who lived and worked in Harlem, yet little is known about those who worked outside the creative borders of the Northeast. Edwin Augustus Harleston's story will shed new light on the triumphs and tragedies of being a southern artist and instill in each reader a deeper appreciation for his ability to defy the odds to pursue his dream of becoming an artist.

1

THE BLACK BRANCH

EDWIN AUGUSTUS HARLESTON sat staring at the white linen canvas on his easel as if he were a writer nervously confronting the blank page. He had painted a dozen or more portraits over the last few years, but for some reason the task of capturing his own image seemed daunting. To reassure himself, he pulled out a sepia-toned photograph he had taken a year or so before and attached it to the top of his easel. Harleston studied the smooth, clean-shaven face of the young man in the picture by following the line of his jaw and the contour of his head with his eyes. He then focused his attention on the blank canvas and began mapping out these areas using a small brush as if it were a pencil. When he finished drawing the contour lines of his face, head, and upper torso, he stepped back, squinted his eyes, then looked at his work for a moment to make sure the proportions were accurate. Once he was satisfied, Edwin Harleston opted to use a larger brush and began applying layers of brown and beige oil paint onto the canvas to make the skin tones look realistic. With each layer, his image began to slowly emerge as if it had always been there, hidden beneath the linen fibers.

Since leaving Boston's School of the Museum of Fine Arts in 1912, opportunities to paint had become almost nonexistent, not only because of time constraints associated with his family's business, but mainly due to the lack of models willing to pose for a Black artist working in Charleston, South Carolina. As a result, he was left with the most available and willing subject he had at his disposal—himself. In his informal *Self-Portrait*, completed in 1916, Edwin Harleston presents himself as a handsome, youthful-looking thirty-three-year-old man who wears a white shirt and black bow tie. He has placed himself in a three-quarter pose against a background of soft gray tones infused with warm, rose-colored accents that suggest an Impressionist influence. The air of contentment that radiates from his brown face is reinforced by the slightly upturned corners of his mouth, but this pleasant outward appearance is somewhat neutralized by the sad dullness of his eyes.

Critics often describe the act of creating a self-portrait as an exercise in self-examination, while others have compared this type of painting to a mask that presents only what the artists wants the viewer to see.[1] In Harleston's case he seems, at first glance, to be taking physical inventory of himself, but in studying his face more closely, especially around the eyes, a psychological portrait emerges that is sheathed in an atmosphere of melancholy. Perhaps this disconsolate air is reflective of his frustration at being an academically trained African American artist who has been forced to return to Charleston, a city which he thought of as a cultural wasteland, void of the museums and galleries he had often frequented in Boston. Or it may have been the realization that after years of living a relatively carefree life in the North, he was back in the oppressive Jim Crow South working in the family funeral business under the firm control of his demanding father. This was not the life he had envisioned for himself but like most African Americans at the turn of the century, the boundaries of his life had been predetermined by those who were convinced that formerly enslaved people and their offsprings were inferior and therefore deserved to be permanently relegated to the margins of society. This idea would impact his life in ways he could have never imagined.

————

EDWIN AUGUSTUS HARLESTON, the third child of Edwin Gaillard and Louise Moultrie Harleston, was born on March 14, 1882, in a two-story

Charleston-style frame house at 28 Laurel Street (now 51 Ashe Street). After nearly twenty years of freedom, his parents were living examples of what African Americans could achieve if they were allowed to plan the course of their own lives. Before coming to the city, Edwin Gaillard had lived his entire life on a plantation in St. John's Berkeley Parish owned by one of the wealthiest members of South Carolina's elite planter class, William H. Harleston, his father. William was a distinguished looking man who stood six feet tall with dark hair, a high forehead, light blue eyes, smooth face, and a florid complexion.[2] His success as a gentleman farmer could be attributed to the more than one hundred enslaved people of African descent who worked his fields, tended his livestock, harvested the rice and other crops during his plantation's peak years.[3] Edwin Gaillard's mother, Kate, was one of these workers. She was four years old when she was purchased for $900 at a Charleston slave auction in 1829, along with her parents Anthony and Sarah Wilson. By 1843, when he was nearly forty, William Harleston fathered the first of eight children (four boys and four girls) with Kate, who was about eighteen years of age at the time.[4] Edwin Gaillard, born in 1854, would be the fifth in this line of biracial Harleston children. Enslaved people were considered chattel with no rights or protection under the law and as a result, fell prey to the demands of their owners. Black women were particularly vulnerable for it was understood that all white males were imbued with a sense of sexual entitlement when it came to the bodies of Black women. Therefore, it is difficult to determine the nature of their relationship, but a family historian for the white Harleston branch discovered that despite the family's urging, William never married and continued to live openly with Kate. As a result, he was shunned by most of his family, friends, and members of Charleston society, but Kate seems to have been accepting and comfortable with their relationship.[5]

The couple continued to live in quiet isolation on the Berkeley County plantation, known as The Hut, throughout the Civil War. In the aftermath of this conflict, President Lincoln signed the Emancipation Proclamation in 1863, freeing nearly four million enslaved people of African descent. This declaration became law when the Thirteenth Amendment was ratified and passed by Congress in January 1865. Three months later, the

Bureau of Refugees, Freedmen and Abandon Lands, better known as the "Freedmen's Bureau," was established to assist white war refugees and the formerly enslaved with basic needs such as food, clothing, and shelter. But the agency soon took on the larger mission of providing education, legal assistance, and work placement services when it became clear that more assistance was needed to meet the goal of a "biracial, free-labor society based on national citizenship."[6] With the assassination of Lincoln in April of 1865, this vision was placed in jeopardy.

Now that Kate and her children were no longer William Harleston's legal property, the decision was made to purchase the house on Laurel Street in Charleston to guarantee their safety. News of the growing reign of terror brought on by the rise of the Ku Klux Klan in surrounding counties had not only instilled fear in the Harleston clan, but many other formerly enslaved families were also seeking the protection of the city's urban environment.[7] During the decade between 1860 and 1870, the African American population increased from 16,660 or 41 percent to 26,173 or 53 percent.[8] This surge in Black residents during this period was unsettling to white people not only in Charleston, but throughout the South. Lincoln's successor, Andrew Johnson, opposed all efforts to protect or assist African Americans and as a result, laws known as Black Codes were passed in 1865 to maintain "the vestiges of antebellum legal and judicial control" over a group of people who were deemed unworthy of independence.[9] These laws restricted freedmen economically, politically, and socially by limiting their job opportunities, property rights, voting rights, and imposing strict vagrancy laws that carried the threat of imprisonment for unemployment. High taxes in addition to licensing and other fees were disproportionally levied on Black businesses, and firearm possession as well as interracial marriages were strictly forbidden.[10]

These draconian rules were quickly repealed and, in 1867 the Congressional Reconstruction Acts implemented military rule in the South to prevent white supremacists from seizing power. The following year, Republicans were able to secure passage of the Fourteenth Amendment to the Constitution, which guaranteed freedmen full rights as citizens and equal protection under the law.

The 1868 election of Republican Robert Kingston Scott as South Carolina's governor was made possible by the newly franchised African American majority and their white allies. Scott, a native of Ohio, who had been an officer in the Union army and an assistant commissioner of the Freedmen's Bureau during Reconstruction, won a second term in 1870 but the win had not been easy. Members of his party had hoped this would be "the year of the happy deliverance," however, outraged white people were openly hostile to Scott's administration.[11] To underscore their displeasure, members of South Carolina's newly formed Klan intimidated Black people and supportive white Republicans who had successfully installed an inclusive civil government. Acts of physical violence, which included beating, whipping, maiming, and lynching, along with the destruction of property during midnight raids, became common occurrences. One Ku Klux Klan member even went so far as to threaten the governor by ensuring "him a free ticket to Hell Station on the Devil's R.R." if he didn't remove Black local officials and white sympathizers from office. Their goal was the destruction of the "radical" Republican party and the killing or banishment of its leaders and supporters.[12]

A few years after Kate and her children had settled into the house on Laurel Street, William Harleston, who continued to live in St. John's Berkeley Parish, died at his plantation home. The cause of his death is unknown, but in his will, dated July 17, 1873, William Harleston generously provided for Kate and their eight children. His final decree stated:

> I desire that all my debts shall be paid. I give to the colored woman Kate (formerly my slave) my bed and all my bedding. The rest and residue of My estate which I now or may here after [sic] possess, I give and bequeath To my brother John Harleston and to the colored woman Kate (formerly my slave) to be divided between them share and share alike and for their sole and separate use forever.[13]

It is unlikely that he would have given his personal belongings and half of all that he possessed, including nearly $2,000 in cash, $1,000 in South Carolina Railroad mortgage bonds, and $2,210 in City of Charleston stock, to a mere servant.[14] John Harleston, William's only living sibling, was executor of the estate and carried out all the decedent's requests without contesting the will. He even continued to provide some financial support for a few years after his brother's death, which confirms that William and Kate shared a caring relationship.[15] In addition to monetary support, William Harleston secured his family's future by purchasing the house on Laurel Street. This residence, according to family history, could not be sold until the last offspring and their heirs had died.[16]

While John dutifully carried out his brother's directives, other members of the white Harleston family were incensed and humiliated with the knowledge that this "colored woman" would be the beneficiary of such a substantial estate. To remedy this perceived injustice, William's nephew, Benjamin Huger, a prominent Charleston lawyer, devised a scheme to take Kate's bequest for himself. Huger arranged a meeting with Kate to offer his services as her financial manager and assured her that he would take care of all her family's monetary needs and obligations. Kate was illiterate and reluctant to question white authority so without consulting John Harleston or her children, she affixed her X to the power of attorney Huger placed before her. Once signed, he left knowing that Kate had forfeited her rights to any further compensation thereby leaving the family with only a small fraction of the money she would have inherited.[17] Fortunately, the Laurel Street house had been willed to Kate and her heirs in a separate agreement, so the roof over the family's head was safe.

While the Harleston household was adjusting to urban life, sixteen-year-old Edwin Gaillard Harleston was looking for work. According to the 1870 US Census, he found a job as a phosphate miner in St. James Goose Creek Parish, not far from the Harleston plantation.[18] New technology and the discovery of rich veins of phosphorus created a market for inexpensive plant fertilizers which were then sold to local farmers in coastal South Carolina and throughout the South. Edwin Gaillard and many other newly freed African Americans found employment in these mines and nearby fertilizer production plants.[19] However, the backbreaking work associated with this type of manual labor may have been too much for Edwin Gaillard because after leaving his job in mining, he focused his attention on rice farming for a while but eventually settled on the cargo transport business. There were several mills, factories, and foundries in the Charleston area that could have provided employment, yet only 25 percent of the city's income came from these industries. Most of the region's revenue came from the sale of farm produce.[20] Selling fruits, vegetables, and rice had been profitable for many recently emancipated Black people in the region and the prospect of being an independent business owner greatly appealed to Edwin Gaillard for he was a proud, sometimes difficult, yet confident man with a strong entrepreneurial spirit. For several years he worked as a boatman until he was able to buy his own small vessel, the *Dorothea*, to haul rice, cotton, and produce along the Carolina and Georgia coasts.[21] The success of this business allowed him to buy a large schooner, the *Beulah Benton*, which earned him the moniker, "Captain" and for nearly twenty years he transported goods along the Southeastern coast. Unfortunately, his career as a seaman came to an end after an accident involving another boat. Because of this incident, Captain Harleston was forced to defend himself in court, but he lost the case and as a result, he also lost his boat and shipping business. Unable to raise enough money to purchase a new vessel, Captain Harleston brought his produce business ashore and began selling fruits and vegetables in and around the City of Charleston.[22]

During the early phase of his shipping business, Captain Harleston married Louisa Ann Moultrie in 1877. The circumstances of their meeting are unknown, but South Carolina records show there was a campaign organized by the Freedmen's Bureau to encourage young African American couples to marry. The Missions and Marriage Relations Department was supervised by Mansfield French, a Lowcountry missionary, who wrote a set of rules designed to encourage formerly enslaved individuals to enter a legally sanctioned marriage to "correct as far as possible one of the most cruel wrongs inflicted by slavery," forced procreation and the separation of families. In this document, a lawfully sanctioned union was presented as the pinnacle of manhood and womanhood as well as a benefit to the larger community. African American churches continued to play a key role in promoting this concept long after the Freedmen's Bureau closed its doors in 1872.[23] Captain Harleston had probably been exposed to some of these ideas, which may have motivated him to finally marry when he was twenty-three years old, but whatever the reason, Harleston had shrewdly chosen a wife whose family connections and respect in the Black community would strengthen his own status.

Edwin Gaillard had been born enslaved and labored as a field hand while Louisa's family was comprised of enterprising African Americans who had been free for nearly four generations. Louisa's great-grand-mother, Lucy Wilkinson, purchased her own freedom and that of her young daughter, Flora, for $420 in 1804.[24] Although no one knows exactly how Louisa's family earned a living, free African Americans living in Charleston before emancipation owned and operated a wide range of service-oriented businesses. Women dominated the laundry and skilled sewing professions while free men generally worked as artisans, mechanics, boatmen or fishermen.[25] A year after their marriage, Captain and Louisa Harleston had their first child, Katherine (aka Kitty, 1878), followed by John Moultrie (1879), then Edwin Augustus (1882), Eloise (aka Ella, 1883), and finally Robert Othello (1889).

The decade between 1865 and 1875 had been marked by unparalleled progress for many African Americans. With the Thirteenth, Fourteenth, and Fifteenth Amendments written into the Constitution of the United States, the Black citizens of Charleston were now able to send their children to public schools, build and attend their own churches, develop businesses, organize trade workers, exercise the right to vote and enjoy equal access to the city's street cars.[26] As a member of this upwardly mobile community, Captain Harleston was certain his produce business would provide a good income for his growing family. But the loss of Republican control in state government and the election of former Confederate general and Democratic Party leader Wade Hampton as governor in 1876, placed the promise of continued prosperity for Black people in jeopardy. Between 1877 and 1895, a time known as the period of "redemption" for white citizens, large numbers of African Americans were warned against participating in local and national politics, threatened by a hostile city police force, and restricted by those who were determined to thwart the financial and social advances of the race.

As South Carolina moved to enact policies that would make efforts to disenfranchise African American citizens legal, Black Republican congressman Thomas E. Miller tried to persuade members of the state's constitutional convention that such measures would be detrimental to the state's progress. In his convention address, Miller stated, "We were eight years in power. We had built schoolhouses, established charitable institutions, built and maintained the penitentiary system, provided for the education of the deaf and dumb, rebuilt the ferries. In short, we had reconstructed the State and placed it upon the road to prosperity." But white delegates, who represented a majority in the convention hall if not in the state, were fearful that the majority Black population in South Carolina would "Africanize" the state if they continued to follow the path of inclusive civil government laid out during Reconstruction with the help of Black legislators, therefore, Miller's plea was rejected.[27]

Captain Harleston soon realized that the doors of opportunity for African Americans were rapidly closing. In an effort to provide the best opportunity for his children's success, he and his wife, Louisa, enrolled them in the nearby public school. The Morris Street School, renamed "Charles H. Simonton" in 1891, was originally operated by the Freedmen's Bureau and later became the first public school in the City of Charleston for children of African descent.[28] Designed for grades one through nine, the school's basic curriculum consisted of arithmetic, reading, drawing on slates and blackboards, and writing instruction.[29] The teaching of drawing had been a regular part of the public-school curriculum since the late 1870s, but by the end of the nineteenth century, the function of this type of art education in public schools had expanded beyond its initial purpose, that of creating in students a greater appreciation for the industrial arts. Now, the development of drawing skills was seen as a means to improve the gross and fine muscle coordination necessary for good penmanship, rather than a way to encourage the imagination.[30] This method of teaching drawing originated with the Swiss education reformer, Johann Heinrich Pestalozzi (1746–1827), who believed that when drawing precedes writing, flexibility develops in the hand and arm that makes it much easier to introduce the concept of writing as a linear form of drawing that has a "fixed direction of its form."[31] In these penmanship-associated drawing lessons, children were taught to differentiate between vertical, horizontal, oblique, and parallel lines; between right, acute, and obtuse angles and to study the properties of the human figure. As a result of being exposed to the Pestalozzi method of drawing, educators concluded that students would be able to acquire an exactness of thought that was otherwise difficult to attain.[32]

Edwin Augustus Harleston, who was called "Teddy" by his family and friends, was extraordinarily adept at combining the components of this approach in his drawings. However, this talent did not originate in the classroom. From his earliest memories, Teddy had always enjoyed sketching, and with his mother's encouragement, his skills continued to improve once he entered school.[33] Unfortunately, his artistic potential was not fully appreciated by the all-white teaching staff at the school. According to family lore, Harleston proudly showed his teacher a drawing of a horse he had completed for a school assignment. Instead of praising his artistic accomplishment and seeing him as an up-and-coming artist, Harleston's teacher saw the drawing as an indication that his future career would likely be that of a stableboy.[34] Teddy's parents interpreted the teacher's response as a veiled insult, and for them, this incident underscored the failure of the public school system to encourage talented Black students such as their son.[35]

To ensure that their son's talents were recognized and nurtured, Captain and Lousia Harleston decided to withdraw Teddy from public school and enroll him in Avery Normal Institute, a private school for African American children. Avery was founded in 1865 by the American Missionary Association (AMA), under the auspices of the Congregational Church.[36] Because of the inferior education Black children were receiving in the public school system, the AMA, with the help of the Freedmen's Bureau, acquired the State Normal School building (now the Memminger School) for the site of their privately funded institution.[37] Staffed by northern white missionaries and members of Charleston's free Black community, the support for the new school was so overwhelming that enrollment increased to more than one thousand students, forcing the school to be temporarily housed in Charleston's Military Hall.[38] In 1868, the school moved into its permanent facility which was named for Charles Avery, a Wesleyan minister and Pittsburgh philanthropist whose estate provided much of the funding for this private, nondenominational Christian school.[39]

The first principal of Avery was Francis Lewis Cardozo, the first African American to hold an elected office in South Carolina and one of the most outstanding teachers of the Reconstruction era. Trained in the free schools of Charleston and in Europe, Cardozo believed that a good education had to be rooted in the classics and philosophy. As in the public schools, this classically oriented curriculum was structured around the philosophy of Pestalozzi, who believed that "all knowledge which an individual gains is obtained through the five senses."[40] Therefore, an experienced-based curriculum, using sound (language), numbers (arithmetic), and form (drawing) as the major elements of instruction, was the primary teaching method used in the school.[41] The ultimate goal of this type of education was to make the students better prepared to reach their full potential and to improve life in their communities.[42]

The school's basic program, which included three years of primary education (including kindergarten), three years of intermediate studies and three years of grammar, was taught by an integrated staff, a third of whom were African American.[43] Art classes, using *Prang's Brief Course in Drawing* was a primary text, were also a part of the curriculum.[44] A three-year advanced program prepared students for positions in primary teaching, while the four-year classical program equipped them for intermediate and high school teaching. Pupils such as Teddy Harleston, who were planning for a high school or college teaching career, took college preparatory classes, including three years of Latin and two years of Greek, French or German.[45]

Although the AMA and Avery's administration believed that a solid classical education was the only way to advance the race, there were those who felt that providing instruction that would ensure economic security had to be incorporated into the curriculum as well. This thinking was espoused by Booker T. Washington, the famous educator and advisor, who believed that people of African descent would have a greater opportunity to prosper by learning "to dignify and glorify common labor . . . [by putting] brains and skill into the common occupations of life."[46] However, most of Avery's parents rejected the administration's efforts to include technical training courses because they did not want their children following in their footsteps, even though many of them came from a long line of respected Charleston-area artisans and domestic workers. Eventually, industrial arts classes became a requirement for all Avery students. The parents and the alumni association, however, resisted any effort on the part of the administration to downgrade the school's curriculum in favor of the industrial arts program because their goal was to produce well-educated community leaders who would unite with other progressive groups in southern society to reform public institutions, especially the school system.[47]

To make the AMA's hope a reality, the tuition at Avery was relatively low in order to accommodate as many children as possible. Each student was required to pay approximately $1.75 per month for college preparatory classes and $1.00 for primary, intermediate, and normal courses.[48] Needy students were usually provided financial assistance through the Daniel Hand Fund, a community-based support program funded by Charleston's most successful African American citizens, while academically gifted students, like Teddy Harleston, were awarded academic scholarships.[49] This community support gave him the type of intellectual and social experiences he needed to flourish at a high academic level—a level he could never have achieved had he remained in public school. Harleston was a popular student who became a leader in many school organizations, his exceptional singing voice garnered him solos in choral productions, his athletic ability made him the first choice of any sports activity, and he was often called upon by various clubs and school committees to utilize his artistic skills.[50] These experiences transformed a quiet, sensitive child into an outgoing, dynamic young man.

While Teddy was thriving at Avery, his mother, who had always been considered a hardy woman, became seriously ill during the winter of 1897.[51] The birth of her fourth child, Eloise (Ella) and the fifth child,

Robert, had not been problematic but after the stillbirth of her sixth baby, Louisa was diagnosed with albuminuria, which is the first sign of diabetic kidney disease. Because medical care in the African American community was inadequate and access to a hospital nearly impossible, Louisa's condition went untreated for nearly a year. The official death certificate, dated February 28, 1897, identified the cause of death as renal failure.[52] She was forty years old. The life of fifteen-year-old Teddy Harleston would be forever changed without the care and support of his mother. So, too, would the lives of his four siblings, Kitty, John Moultrie, Ella, and Robert. To cushion the blow of this immeasurable loss, Captain Harleston wrote to his sister Susan and her husband, John Singleton, who lived in Beaufort, South Carolina, asking them to move to Charleston to help him with the children. "Sister Sue," who has been described as a strong, domineering woman, willingly took charge of the Harleston household and made every effort to return their family life to a state of normalcy.[53] But as far as Teddy was concerned, no one could replace his mother, the only person who understood and encouraged his creative desires. Three years later, on a Wednesday afternoon in June of 1900, Edwin Augustus Harleston, along with twenty-two of his fellow classmates, entered Zion Presbyterian Church for Avery Normal Institute's graduation exercises.

During the ceremony, Edwin presented one of his drawings, *Lincoln and His Cabinet*, as a gift to the incoming Senior Class of 1901.[54] The drawing was probably not an original work. More than likely, it was a copy of a popular lithograph, *President Lincoln and His Cabinet, Reading of the Emancipation Proclamation*, by Edward Herline.[55] This subject held special meaning for Americans of African descent because Abraham Lincoln was the embodiment of freedom and the Emancipation Proclamation the manifestation of his benevolent power. In Black communities across the nation, emancipation, or the Day of Jubilee, was celebrated on the first day of the year. Charleston's African American citizens annually marked the occasion with a parade featuring prominent civic leaders and social organizations riding in decorated wagons and carriages. This festive event usually culminated at the Battery with speeches intended to inspire and uplift the race.[56] Historical prints of this type were often produced in large

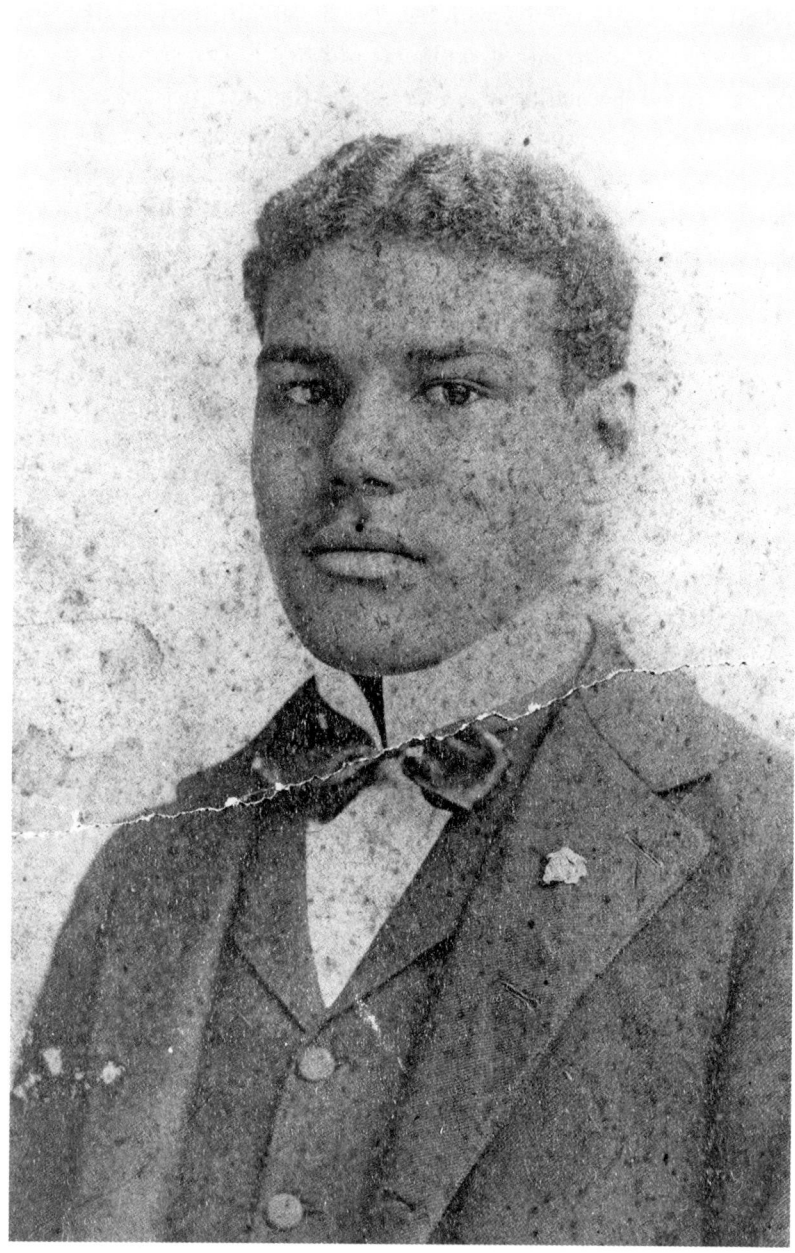

Edwin Augustus Harleston, photograph, ca. 1900. Edwin A. Harleston and Edwina Harleston Whitlock Family Papers, Stuart A. Rose Manuscript, Archives, and Rare Book Library, Emory University.

numbers to fulfill the public's insatiable desire for real and reimagined images of important events.[57] In the 1866 Herline print, Lincoln is seen in a library-like setting at the left end of a table located in the center of the room. Seven cabinet members, who are either sitting or standing around the table, listen attentively as Lincoln reads the Emancipation Proclamation aloud. Although the background has been skillfully rendered, Lincoln and the other figures seem flat, stiff, and lacking in proper proportion, giving the print a naïve quality. Because prints produced during this time were drawn by draftsmen of varying skill, rather than by one or two master artists, the images often seemed technically deficient. Yet, faults in the execution of narrative images of this type were more readily accepted by the public if the subject matter was of national importance.[58] There is no way to judge the quality of Harleston's version of this print because his drawing was destroyed in the Avery fire of 1945. But his attempt to duplicate such a popular subject and present it publicly at graduation indicates that his artwork was well above average. Harleston's selection of an image containing so many identifiable figures may have also been one of the earliest indications that he was interested in the art of portraiture.

At the end of graduation exercises, Edwin shook hands with his teachers and waved goodbye to his classmates. Although several of his friends were going on to college, he was the only one who would be attending school in Georgia. For the first time in his life, Teddy Harleston would be traveling to Atlanta, the "Gate City of the New South."

2

GATE CITY OF THE NEW SOUTH

EDWIN HARLESTON ARRIVED in Atlanta on one of the hottest September days on record. With temperatures nearing one hundred degrees, he must have been overwhelmed by the oppressive heat, the smell of horses pulling wagons loaded with farm produce, and the sound of trolley cars moving along the city's main streets. To get to the school, Harleston was instructed to board the car marked "Atlanta University" at the corner of Marietta and Broad Streets which would take him to the campus gate.[1]

When he exited the trolley, Harleston saw tree-lined walkways leading to several large brick buildings perched on a grassy knoll. At the center stood Stone Hall (now Fountain Hall on the campus of Morris Brown College), a High Victorian Gothic-style edifice with contrasting bands of decorative masonry crowned by a tall, narrow pyramid-shaped clock tower that rose above the surrounding structures. Built in 1882, this building housed the administrative offices, classrooms, lecture halls, a library, printing office, science laboratories and the chapel.[2] It was here that Harleston paid his tuition totaling $2 per month and his boarding fee, which included fuel, lights, and washing at $10 per month.[3]

The stateliness of Stone Hall reflected the high esteem with which Atlanta University was held in the Black community for it was considered one of the most important African American institutions of higher learning in the country. Founded in 1865 by two formerly enslaved men, James Tate and Grandison Daniels, the school quickly grew under the guidance of the AMA, which installed Edmund A. Ware as the university's first president two years after the school opened. By the time Edwin Harleston arrived, Dr. Horace Bumstead (1888–1907), known as "the most consistent champion of higher education for the Negro," had become head of the university.[4] His mission was to provide a quality liberal arts education for the African American population so they could become accomplished, upstanding citizens who would then go out into the world to help others.[5] In the beginning, college courses and degrees were offered in several professional areas, but the administration soon realized that a broader range of educational support from kindergarten through college preparatory classes was needed to adequately serve the community's thirst for knowledge at every level.

Unfortunately, the educational needs of Black citizens were not shared by the white community. The dark cloud of political and social disfranchisement that covered South Carolina, now hung over the entire southern United States. In the case of Atlanta University, disapproval of African Americans seeking higher education led to the loss of the school's annual appropriation from the Georgia state legislature and a decline in individual philanthropic gifts. This trend has been attributed, in part, to Booker T. Washington, a powerful proponent of industrial education, which he believed would lead to economic independence for the race. To reenforce his ideas, Washington used his platform as president of Tuskegee Normal and Technical Institute (now Tuskegee University) to influence wealthy donors, such as Andrew Carnegie and Robert C. Ogden, two men who often consulted with him about the distribution of monetary contributions. On several occasions, Washington discouraged the giving of monies to schools he deemed unworthy or institutions whose faculty members had openly disagreed with him.[6] A vocal critic of Booker T. Washington's philosophy was Atlanta University professor, Dr. W. E. B. Du Bois. By the turn of the century, Du Bois had become one of the country's most important Black intellectuals. He argued that education was the only way African Americans would gain equality and to deny its importance would permanently relegate them to second-class citizenship. As a result of Du Bois's unwillingness to support Washington's stance on industrial versus liberal arts education, Atlanta University suffered losses to its endowment.[7]

Although worrisome, these financial woes did not affect the school's national reputation. In an 1895 letter supporting Bumstead's effort to raise money, Dr. Timothy Dwight, president of Yale University, wrote that Atlanta University was an important institution to people of color in the South because it had accomplished much, and its sphere of influence was widening. During the same year, President E. Benjamin Andrews of Brown University stated that Atlanta University was "one of the most useful and well managed educational institutions in all the South."[8] Yet, the southern press, particularly *The Atlanta Journal*, reacted negatively to the efforts of Bumstead and his northern supporters. In response to a discussion concerning African American higher education, one editor wrote that "the Negro needs to be educated but he must be educated to make a useful citizen and an industrious member of the community in which he lives . . . Bumstead and his proposed friends in the North need to be educated to understand that no member of the community is so utterly helpless and impotent as he who has been given merely a book education."[9] Ironically, the editor's comments were in line with Booker T. Washington's viewpoint, which supported the development of practical skills over the need for higher education. But the flaw in this thinking was the failure to realize that there was a need in American society for schools such as Atlanta University. It was this type of institution that supplied teachers to public as well as industrial schools, thus allowing them to keep their doors open. Bumstead understood the need for a liberal arts education because it gave students the kind of well-rounded, morally based education they would need to lift up others once they left the institution.[10]

To achieve the objectives of intellectual and moral excellence, the university put rules in place that were designed to inspire students to strive for academic merit and encourage high ethical standards. Nondenominational church services were a requirement, and each student was asked to bring a Bible for church, classroom, and personal use. Students were encouraged not to travel or receive guests on Sunday so that they could concentrate on their spiritual aspirations. To further lessen distractions from the material world, the administration asked students to wear clothes made of inexpensive material such as gingham and plain worsted wool rather than showy garments made of silk or velvet. Restrictions were also placed on receiving extra clothing, food, fruit, and candy from family or friends. Of course, the use of tobacco and consumption of alcohol was strictly forbidden.[11]

A twenty-two-member faculty composed primarily of white New England missionaries trained in Northeastern schools was in charge of educating and shaping the character of these students. The college curriculum for first-year students included the study of Greek and Roman literature, mathematics, ancient history, and elocution. The elocution teacher, Mrs. Adrienne McNeil Herndon, was one of three African American instructors who would play a significant role in the life of Edwin Harleston during his time at Atlanta University and in the years that followed. Adrienne Herndon, a small, slender woman who carried herself with an air of sophistication, received her training at the Boston School of Dramatic Arts and New York City's American Academy of Dramatic Arts. She began her career by teaching elocution classes and later became the director of Atlanta University's Department of Elocution and Dramatics.[12] It was because of her encouragement that Harleston entered the annual elocution contest in the spring of 1901. The student newspaper, *The Scroll*, does not list the subjects presented by the participants in this event, but it does identify Edwin Harleston as the second-place winner of the competition.[13] Mrs. Herndon directed *Class Night*, a college-wide variety show and was well known for her Shakespearean productions. In 1903, she wrote and produced a play for an athletic association benefit entitled *The Shadow*. The script has been lost but according to a review in *The Scroll*, the production focused on Nam-Bok, a Native American man who lived in the Pacific Northwest. Harleston was chosen to play the lead character, not only because of his outstanding performances in Herndon's elocution classes, but his small frame, reddish-brown complexion, high cheekbones, keen features, and straight dark hair made him an excellent choice for the part. The student paper must have agreed because Edwin Harleston was given a favorable review for his acting ability and the play was described as "a grand success."[14] It is difficult to determine whether this production marked the beginning of Harleston's interest in theater, but throughout his life, he would occasionally write plays and perform on stage.

At the time of the production, the head of the athletic department was George A. Towns, an Atlanta University graduate (1894) who had recently returned from Harvard University where he earned a second bachelor of arts degree. Although his primary responsibility was teaching English and pedagogy, Towns also became the coach of the football team, the debating team, and faculty advisor for *The Scroll*. Football was established on the Atlanta University campus in 1893, but enthusiasm for the sport was not widespread because of a sporadic playing season and uneven coaching. But in 1900, the team was undefeated under the leadership of Coach Towns. Shortly after Harleston joined the team in 1902, he became the team's captain and star halfback.[15] One of his best friends, Truman K. Gibson, was the team manager. Another good friend, Julius Westmoreland, the athletic editor of the student paper, wrote vivid accounts of Edwin Harleston's winning maneuvers on the gridiron, thus heightening his popularity on and off the field.[16] However, it was under Coach Towns's direction that he learned the fundamentals of the game, but more importantly, he discovered the power of leadership.

College sports occupied much of Harleston's free time, but his studies always came first. The classical background he had acquired at Avery had sufficiently prepared him for his college courses in Greek and Roman history and literature. However, during his senior year Harleston showed a particular interest in sociology, which may have been inspired by the presence of Dr. W. E. B. Du Bois. His groundbreaking sociological study of Philadelphia's African American community caught the attention of the university's board of trustees who extended an invitation to Du Bois to join the Atlanta University faculty in 1896. Soon after arriving on campus, Du Bois was asked by the administration to develop a sociology program and assist in expanding the university's curriculum. The board and his colleagues supported Du Bois's efforts but winning over students was another matter.

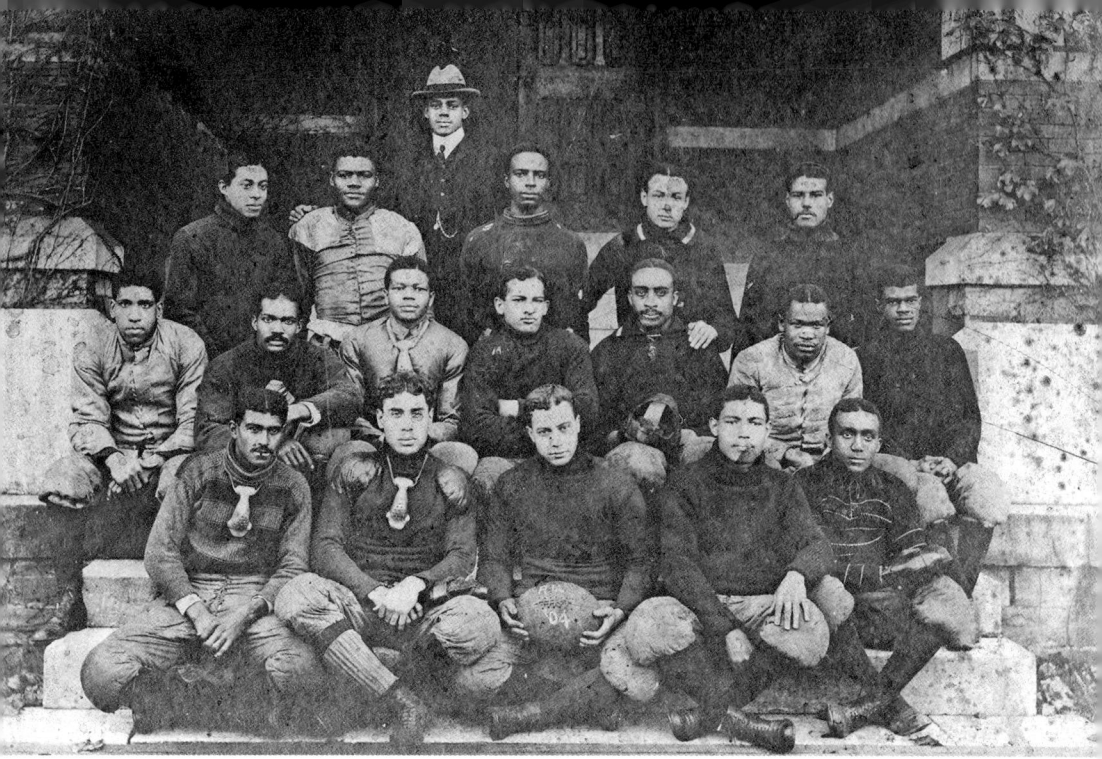

Atlanta University football team, photograph, ca. 1902. Atlanta University Photograph Collection, Atlanta University Center Robert W. Woodruff Library.

Initially, the undergraduates saw him as aloof because his habit of wearing gloves and carrying a cane made him appear pretentious.[17] He also had a reputation for being a demanding teacher, but all these perceived drawbacks were met with respect and admiration by members of Harleston's class. This change in attitude may have occurred, in part, because of Du Bois's attempt to go beyond class lectures and share some personal cultural experiences with his students. In the spring of 1904, he gave a lecture on the subject of "Art and Art Galleries in Europe."[18] In his talk he gave a brief overview of ten great European collections and showed examples of major works by artists such as Michelangelo, Titian, Rembrandt, and Velázquez. But the main purpose of the lecture was to ignite in his students the desire to seek out and appreciate beauty. Du Bois stated that "three things in life beckon the human soul: the Good, the True and the Beautiful . . . Goodness is a matter of the Will power, Truth, a matter with which the mind deals; The heart and the emotions deal with the Beautiful . . . the Beautiful is one of the great ends of life and we can train ourselves to appreciate the beautiful things in life and even discover beauties hidden to untrained hearts."[19] Du Bois urged his audience to visit art galleries in Chicago, New York, Philadelphia, and Boston, for he knew the search for this kind of beauty would be impossible in Atlanta, even though the city was considered the most important center for the visual arts in the South.

Atlanta's reputation as a cultural capital developed as a result of the important art exhibitions mounted during the Cotton States and International Exposition of 1895. Organized by Horace Bradley, the show included works by such artists as Winslow Homer, William Merritt Chase, Thomas Eakins, Thomas Hovenden, Mary Cassatt, Eastman Johnson, Child Hassam, and Henry O. Tanner.[20] The exposition's success made real the possibility of creating an art school, art league, and an academy of fine arts in the city. To keep public interest in the arts alive until one or more of these institutions could be established, the Atlanta Women's Club and the Atlanta Art Association sponsored art exhibitions, art history lectures, and art classes.[21] However, none of these activities were open to art lovers in the Black community.

Unfortunately, officials at Atlanta University showed little interest in the visual arts. The only painting on view at the college was an oil painting of Dr. Bumstead by Marie Danforth Page, a graduate of the Boston Museum School of Fine Arts and student of the well-known American artist Edmund Tarbell.[22] The painting was unveiled and presented to the president at the close of commencement exercises by the Class of 1902. Aside from this portrait, reproductions of Henry Tanner's religious paintings were the only other visual images displayed on the campus.[23] Despite the general lack of interest in the visual arts at Atlanta University, administrators at Morris Brown College, a neighboring institution supported by the African Methodist Episcopal Church, opened a Department of Fine Arts in the fall of 1900. John Henry Adams Jr., a returning native of the state, was selected to head this new department. Trained at the Drexel Institute of Art, Science and Industry in Philadelphia, Adams had great hopes of pursuing his artistic career in Atlanta, but when this did not occur, he concentrated his efforts on teaching art, organizing annual art exhibitions, and occasionally creating illustrations for African American literary periodicals such as *Voice of the Negro*.[24] There is no indication that Harleston participated in any of these shows and none of his works exist from this period, but letters from classmates indicate that he did create sketches while at the university.[25]

Teddy Harleston was an exceedingly popular student. Not only was he the school's star football player, but he also led the university's baseball team to victory as its pitcher. In addition to being an outstanding athlete, Teddy also possessed a beautiful singing voice, thus making him a standout in the school's glee club.[26] Because he was smart, handsome, and talented, the ladies on campus found him irresistible. Letters from these classmates, written over summer vacations, are filled with informative tidbits about mutual friends, teasingly romantic banter, expressions of admiration, and rejection. One young lady offered a subtle warning that she would enter a convent in Baltimore if she did not receive a letter from him soon. The note closes with a promise that she will send a photograph in her next letter in exchange for one of him. Another classmate confessed that she had loved him since their first meeting in Mrs. Herndon's elocution class.[27] But not all of these communications were amorous. At some point, Teddy had conveyed his romantic feelings to Mamie Cole, a classmate from Aiken, South Carolina, but in her response to him, she expresses surprise and confesses that she thought of him as a friend and nothing more. Mamie's rebuff must have come as a shock to Teddy, but he took her closing words to heart by "look[ing] forward with hope to the future" and moving on with his life.[28]

———

WHILE TEDDY WAS AWAY AT SCHOOL, Captain Harleston began searching for a more lucrative source of income. The produce business had not been as successful as he had hoped and the cost of supporting his family was a constant worry. Captain's older sister Hannah had married into the well-respected Mickey family whose patriarch, Reverend Edward Charles Mickey, pastored a large congregation and had served in the South Carolina state legislature during Reconstruction.[29] His son, Edward Henry

Mickey, was the highly regarded owner of a thriving undertaking business, which had been in operation since 1894.[30] Captain Harleston saw this relationship as an opportunity to be affiliated with the kind of successful business he had always wanted for himself. Therefore, he decided to work part-time for his brother-in-law and sister to learn the trade.

The modern funeral industry that the Mickeys were now a part of did not exist before the Civil War. Prior to that time, most Americans died at home, the deceased was sorrowfully mourned for a brief period of time, then the body was prepared for burial by relatives. This somber period of grieving began with the body being washed, dressed, and laid out in the parlor for a day or two in a roughly honed handmade coffin or one bought at the general store. For the enslaved, the practice was similar, yet different in a variety of ways. For them, death was a victory to be celebrated; it was not seen as a loss but as an escape from the oppressive life the deceased had been forced to endure. Because many of the people of African descent who worked on South Carolina's plantations and farms came from West and Central Africa, including the Congo and Angola regions, they followed some of their indigenous burial rituals thereby insuring the safe passage of the deceased into the next world.[31] As in most funeral ceremonies, the enslaved washed the body, wrapped it in a shroud or sheets but before being placed in a coffin, the corpse was laid out on what was called a "cooling board" or special wooden plank, while the coffin was being made. Family and friends would then conduct a wake or "settin' up vigil" where mourners would gather to sing, tell stories about the deceased, or just sit quietly with the body through the night until it was time to process to the grave site. At the place of burial, whether it was at the edge of a field, deep in the woods, or at an assigned cemetery plot on the plantation, a baby was usually passed over the coffin two or three times in an effort to safeguard the infant from harm and to divert the spirit's attention away from the living. An integral part of the ceremony was the sermon delivered by a Black preacher who either lived on the plantation or traveled the area. It was thought that the spirit of the deceased could not be at peace and free to move on to the next world until the home-going sermon was delivered. If the preacher could not preside on the day of the burial or important family members could not attend, a second funeral was often held weeks, months, or even a year after interment.[32]

Among the Bakongo people, it was customary to decorate the grave after burial with some of the last objects the deceased may have touched: a cup, bowl, pitcher, especially white vessels, seashells, or other domestic objects. All of these items were associated with water which, according to Bakongo cosmology, represented the ocean separating the world of the living from that of the dead. Parts of this tradition were also practiced among African Americans in South Carolina and other parts of the Southeast for it was thought that the spirit would be satisfied and not wonder about if a few of their personal possessions were intentionally cracked or broken and placed on top of the grave so the spirit could ascend unincumbered.[33]

If the deceased were displeased with the manner of burial, or disturbed in any way, the spirit could return with the ability to do harm to

African American grave site, photograph, ca. 1910. The John Bennett Papers, 1875–1976, Coll. No. 1176.00, South Carolina Historical Society.

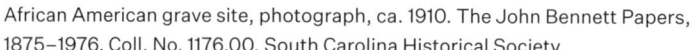

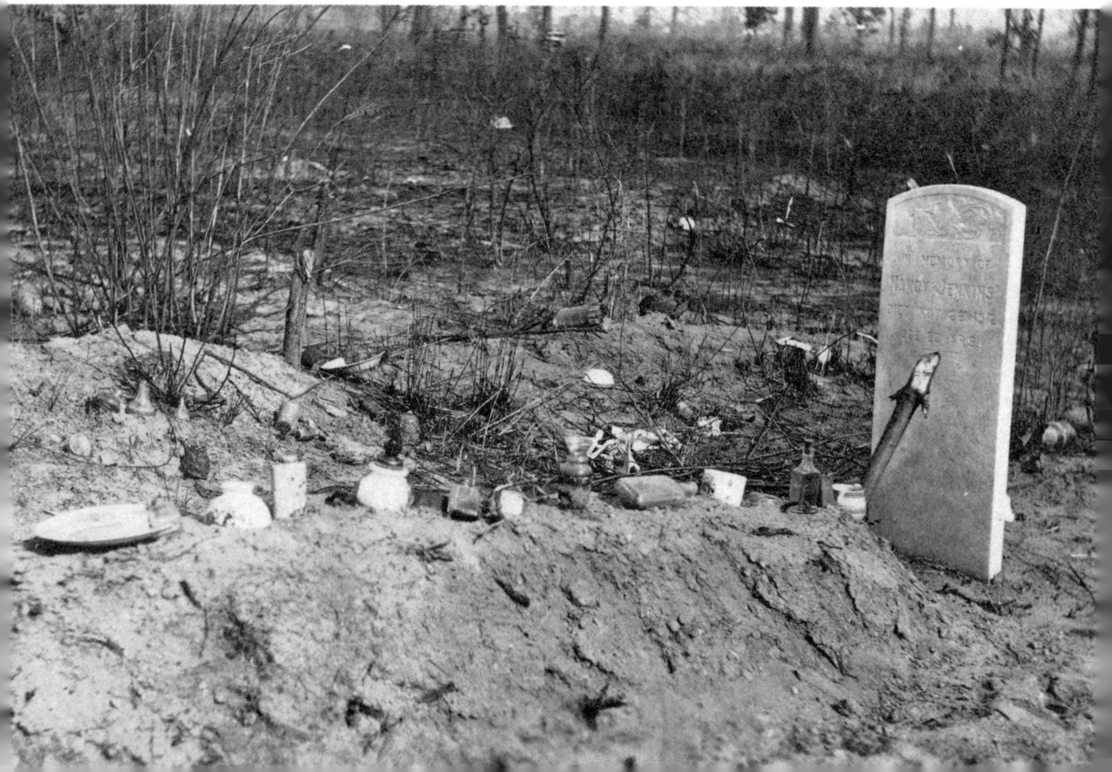

the living. The final event, after the graveside ceremony, was a burial feast, known as the repast.

The practice of embalming became standardized during the Civil War when necessity required the bodies of fallen soldiers be preserved for the long journey home. Before this time, using chemicals to conserve a corpse was performed almost exclusively by doctors and scientists for study purposes. While simple burials were still standard practice in rural areas, by the late 1880s, those who lived in cities preferred to have the preparation and interment of their loved ones overseen by the local funeral home with the undertaker managing all aspects of the service. The evolution of the funeral business from a modest trade before the Civil War to a highly lucrative business at the end of the nineteenth century underscores the seismic shift that occurred in the United States, especially in urban areas, and among members of a rising middle class. In the African American community, funeral directing offered economic security and the social respect that other professions had denied them.[34] Consequently, Captain Harleston dedicated himself to learning as much as he possibly could about the business of death at the Mickey Funeral Home.

In the fall of 1899, Edward H. Mickey died unexpectedly leaving Hannah with the responsibility of running their funeral business on her own. The comfortable life she had come to enjoy was now in jeopardy because their customers expected the reassuring presence of a male undertaker in their time of grief, not a woman.[35] As a result, Hannah temporarily closed Mickey Funeral Home, located at 259 Meeting Street, and in 1901, Captain Harleston established his own funeral business, at 255 Meeting Street, with the help of his older brother, Robert. When the Harleston Brothers Funeral Home opened its doors, the task of embalming and making all the arrangements for burial was Captain's responsibility while his brother, who was a tailor, prepared the deceased for viewing. Because they could not agree on how the business should be managed, Robert left less than a year later. Shortly after his departure, Hannah's oldest son, Edward Crum Mickey, joined Harleston Funeral Home to learn the business under the tutelage of his uncle. At the beginning of his apprenticeship, Edward was seventeen years of age but by the time he was nineteen, he had become a clerk at the Harleston business. Two years later Edward C. Mickey was listed as an undertaker in the *Charleston City Directory* and in 1904, the Harleston & Mickey Funeral Home, was established.[36]

———

IN THE SPRING OF THAT SAME YEAR, Edwin Augustus Harleston graduated from Atlanta University. Commencement ceremonies normally mark the end of a college career, but for Harleston it represented an extension. At graduation, he received one of the two fellowships given each year to graduates interested in advanced study; consequently, he would be returning for the 1904–5 academic year as a sociology and chemistry fellow.[37] Harleston's duties would include teaching several undergraduate courses

Atlanta University graduating class of 1904, photograph. Atlanta University Photograph Collection, Atlanta University Center Robert W. Woodruff Library.

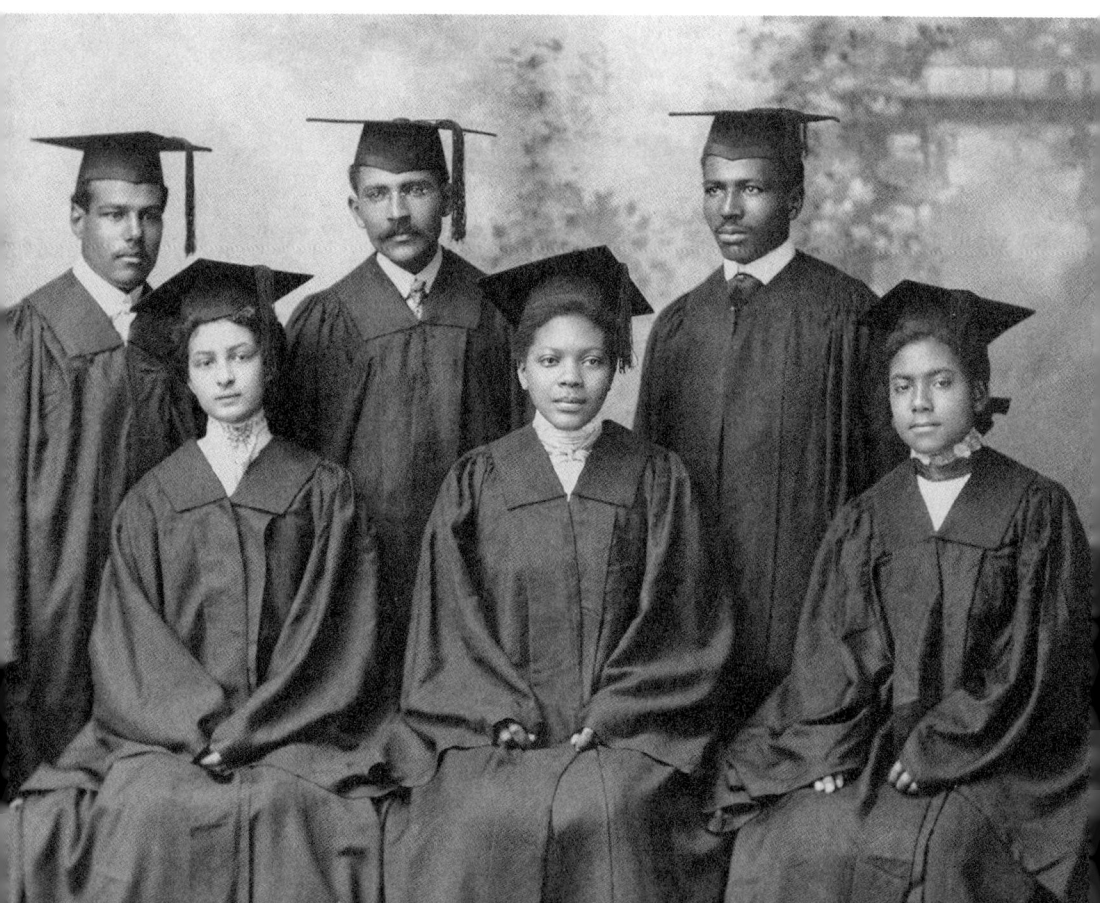

and serving as a teaching assistant; therefore, it is likely that he worked closely with Du Bois.

The fact that Harleston remained at Atlanta University an additional year suggests that he may have been preparing for a career in teaching. His classical course of study in high school and college had been designed to prepare students for that profession, a field in which 61.4 percent of Atlanta University's graduates had already entered.[38] When his fellowship ended, Harleston, like his mentors Du Bois and Towns before him, applied and was accepted into the junior class of Harvard University in 1905.[39] The thought of attending this Ivy League school was undoubtedly exciting to Harleston for he had experienced life in the North while working on the Hudson River Day Line, a premier steamboat company, during summer vacations to earn money for his school tuition.[40] But now he would be traveling to Boston to begin his studies at the most prestigious university in the country, Harvard.

3

BOSTON AND THE SCHOOL
OF THE MUSEUM OF FINE ARTS

In 1906, Boston was a fast-moving city of more than a half million residents from all walks of life.[1] To a young man who had become accustomed to the slower southern pace of Charleston, South Carolina, and Atlanta, Georgia, this unfamiliar environment must have been exhilarating. As Edwin Harleston made his way through the city's streets, he could hear accents swirling around him from Irish, Eastern European, and West Indian immigrants, mixed in with Boston natives. Being in Massachusetts, home of the abolitionist movement and the site of so much American history, must have strengthened his sense of freedom and independence for Harleston had arrived in this city a changed man. Harvard was no longer his destination, instead, he had decided to enter art school. In the year following his fellowship at Atlanta University, Harleston's desire to become a teacher had been eclipsed by his long-felt passion to become an artist.[2] His creative talent had always been encouraged by his mother, teachers, and school friends but being an artist was an inconceivable vocation for him, especially as a Black man. Yet, a deep desire to go beyond the limits others had set for him had awakened in Edwin Harleston, and to test the boundaries of what his future could be, he decided to enroll in the Boston

School of the Museum of Fine Arts (SMFA, Museum School) to pursue his fascination with portraiture.

The plan to attend Harvard may have been abandoned because their fine arts program focused almost exclusively on art history and theory. In the college catalogue, only one studio course was offered, Principles of Delineation, Color and Chiaroscuro, and even that class had required lectures with "collateral reading."[3] Moreover, the school was admitting him as a junior, not a graduate student, which meant he would have to repeat the courses he had successfully completed at Atlanta University. At twenty-three years of age, Edwin Harleston was unwilling to waste valuable time developing skills that might not lead to gainful employment or economic independence; therefore, he set his sights on the School of the Museum of Fine Arts. Local artists often boasted that the SMFA was the best art school in the country.[4] But most artists outside the Boston area considered the SMFA too provincial and conservative to have any lasting impact on aesthetic trends in American art, despite its high standards.[5] If this was the attitude of artists across the country, why did Harleston come to Boston and abandon Harvard in favor of the Museum School when other more progressive institutions, such as those in New York City or Chicago, would have accepted him?

One of the reasons for Harleston's decision may have been connected to the fact that Boston had enjoyed the reputation of being the center of American portraiture since the mid-eighteenth century but by the 1820s, the city's reputation began to fade.[6] It was rehabilitated, however, when John Singer Sargent adopted Boston as his New England home in the late 1880s. Sargent represented a new breed of American portrait painters. His training was deeply rooted in the French academic tradition and his style was heavily influenced by seventeenth-century Dutch masters, Rembrandt, and Hals, along with the Spanish artist Velázquez.[7] Sargent was known for exhibiting "a certain bravura in the method of brushstroke" and his extraordinary ability to capture the spirit of his subjects.[8] Because of these attributes, he became the most sought-after portrait painter in the United States. Since Sargent spent only short periods of time in Boston, the overwhelming demand for portraits by Boston's elite had to be met by local artists. Two of the most successful were Edmund Charles Tarbell and Frank Weston Benson, both of whom joined the SMFA faculty in 1889. By 1906, both men had become widely recognized for their teaching abilities, and both had received national acclaim for their work as portrait painters.

Harleston may have become familiar with the reputations of Benson and Tarbell while he was a student at Atlanta University. During the 1902 graduation exercises, Marie Danforth Page, a New England aristocrat, who was a member of the Boston School of Painting and former student at the SMFA, presented the university with a portrait of President Bumstead.[9] Since Harleston's artistic abilities were well known on campus, he may have had an opportunity to meet Page during her visit to the school. If such an encounter did occur, Page may have discussed her career and her training under Benson and Tarbell and thus sparked Harleston's interest in studying portrait painting in Boston. When he decided to enter the SMFA, it is possible that Page may have served as his reference, since each applicant was required to give the name and address of a person who could assure the admissions committee that the applicant was worthy of consideration.[10] The submission of her name would have carried considerable influence, not only because of her association with the SMFA, but because of her prominence in Boston society.

A more likely reason for Harleston's choice, however, was the strong connection that existed between the city of Boston, Harvard, and Atlanta Universities. For many years, Harvard served as a mentor to Atlanta University students and faculty. The teachers with whom Harleston had close working relationships, George Towns and W. E. B. Du Bois, had both attended Harvard. But the most compelling factor was the substantial number of Atlanta University graduates and supporters who were living in the Boston area, including his best friends and college classmates, Truman K. Gibson and Julius Westmoreland, who were both attending Harvard Business School. The prospect of being reunited with Atlanta University classmates and alumni probably influenced Harleston's decision to relocate to Boston more than any of the other considerations. Once word of Edwin Harleston's plans to continue his studies in Boston had circulated among the alumni who knew him, several friends stepped forward to offer their homes for residency. But after some thought, he decided to accept lodging in the spacious brick townhouse at 16 Wellington Street, the family home of Julius C. Westmoreland.[11]

The School of the Museum of Fine Arts, located just a short walk from the Westmoreland's residence, was in the basement of the Italian Gothic-style Museum of Fine Arts on Copley Square. Designed in 1876, the red brick building decorated with ornate terracotta trimmings imported from England, initially included the art collection of the Boston Athenaeum, an engravings collection, and a group of architectural casts from the Massachusetts Institute of Technology. An impressive collection of Early American and European paintings, Japanese art, Egyptian artifacts, and classical antiques was also included in its holdings.[12] A year after the Museum opened its doors, the SMFA was given space in the building, but it was not considered a part of the museum.

Sharing accommodations with the SMFA had been encouraged by the museum board because of the overwhelming need for an institution that provided formal fine-arts training. Over the years, a few schools had offered art instruction, but the curriculum had been designed for amateur artists. With the help of wealthy Bostonians and well-established artists, the SMFA grew to become the most important art institution in the city and by 1906, it had gained national recognition. Evidence of its prominence could be measured by the 232 students who arrived on October 1 to pay the forty-five-dollar registration fee.[13] More than two-thirds of the student body came from the Boston area; the remaining class members came from across the country, and a few came from as far away as Hawaii and Mexico. Most of these young artists were between the ages of eighteen and twenty-one; however, there were some older students, the majority of whom were women.[14] Although this first-year class was composed of young men and women of varying backgrounds, Harleston was the only African American student. This was not unusual since two-thirds of the Black population were still living on farms in the South with little opportunity for any type of education. But even in the North, Black residents struggled for survival in urban areas where they faced cramped, substandard housing, unsafe work conditions, and the lowest possible wage.

As an African American college graduate, Edwin Harleston belonged to a privileged group representing three-tenths of 1 percent of his race, and the number of professionally trained African American artists was even smaller.[15] However, this fact did not discourage him from believing that he could become a successful artist.

A week after registration, the SMFA Department of Design held a luncheon and reception for the school's newcomers and faculty. As part of first-year student initiation, each class member was required to wear a hand-decorated bib during lunch. At the end of the meal the instructors and the class presidents greeted the students and wished them success in the coming year.[16] This gathering offered Harleston his first opportunity to meet the members of the drawing and painting faculty, which included William MacGregor Paxton, Philip Leslie Hale, Frank Benson, and Edmund Tarbell, who served as the unofficial department chair. These artists were members of Boston's elite society who believed that the preservation of shared Eurocentric cultural values held precedence over any artistic risks. Because of this belief, the style and subject matter of their work reflected the reserved and rigid moral code of upper-class Boston Brahmans.[17] This aesthetic philosophy, however, cannot be attributed entirely to Boston artists. During the mid-nineteenth and early twentieth centuries the standards of art in America were controlled by the National Academy of Design, founded in New York in 1825. Although conservative in their views, the academy membership (which included some of Boston's best artists) represented a microcosmic profile of the larger society. Based on the standards set by art institutions in Europe, such as the École des Beaux-Arts in Paris and the Royal Academy in London, the National Academy was dedicated to the preservation of a conservative cultural tradition, thereby setting the standard for art in America. This prototype was maintained by cultivating a particular stylistic approach that emphasized drawing as the foundation for painting rather than expressive color.

The academy also promoted a certain ideological approach to art. These tenets stressed eternal moral values that applied not only to personal conduct but also to aesthetic choices as well. As a result, the institution upheld a nineteenth-century belief that it was the artist's responsibility to produce artwork that was morally uplifting for the viewer. This visualization of moral truth no longer took the form of history painting but was now associated with the concept of beauty as it related to nature. Unfortunately, this approach often produced sentimental, mediocre works of art. Despite the weakness of this academic tenant, institutional arbitrators expanded upon the idea of the artist as a partner in shaping an ethical society. Progress in the world, which included artistic development, was guided by moral truth that was often reflected in the artist's choice of subject matter. The final aspect of the academic credo charged its members with maintaining the cultural tradition established by the National Academy of Design.[18] This inflexible philosophy was embraced by Boston artists and sanctioned by those who supported them. It was in this atmosphere of social and artistic conservatism that Edwin Harleston was officially introduced to the Boston arts community.

One of the most prominent standard bearers of this academic tradition was Edmund Tarbell, who was also known as the leader of a regional painting style known as the Boston School. This precise style, which combined techniques of the old masters and French Barbizon painting, originated with Boston portraitist William Morris Hunt and the SMFA's first painting instructor, Otto Grundmann. While studying in Düsseldorf, Germany, Hunt learned how to masterfully use restricted color schemes and dynamic value contrasts.[19] While studying with Thomas Couture and Jean-François Millet in Paris, he added the skill of infusing his subjects with a vibrant, lifelike appearance. When Hunt arrived in Boston in the fall of 1862, he was already well known for his abilities as a portraitist and teacher, prompting some critics to proclaim him "the most vital factor in the development of American art."[20] Because of his status as a national figure in the arts, Hunt was able to develop a large student following. His marriage to Louisa Dumaresq Perkins, granddaughter of wealthy merchant Thomas H. Perkins, gave him considerable influence over the aesthetic taste of those in Boston's highest social circles. Hunt's status among local artists and the city's wealthy patrons earned him the distinction of being recognized as "the fountain head of art-feeling and thought in Boston."[21]

Otto Grundmann, a German artist known for his figure studies, portraits and dark genre scenes, succeeded Hunt in his role of influencing local art trends. Although Grundmann was not included among Boston's cultural elite, he did have dominion over one particularly important group, the SMFA students. Trained at the Dresden Academy and at the Antwerp Academy, Grundmann was considered a master of figure painting and "fat painting," or "la belle peinture," a Dutch painting technique that had been used for more than four centuries.[22] His student, Edmund Tarbell, stated that this method, like a mosaic, was designed to give each little area its own paint, its own hue and the right value.[23] The combination of Grundmann's subdued genre scenes with underlying linear structure and Hunt's vigorous brushwork, muted Tonalist color, and soft use of light and shade became the foundation for the Boston School of Painting.[24]

To receive a diploma in drawing and painting from the SMFA, all students were expected to successfully complete a rigorous twenty-one terms (seven years) of study based on the Boston School as well as the French academic model for studio art. Beginning courses started with linear exercises and copying reproductions. The next level included drawing simple objects such as plaster geometric forms and models of body parts using light and shade to create the illusion of volume. Once the concept of rendering was mastered, students were allowed to study the head and body, as a whole, from plaster casts. Finally, after these skills were perfected, students were then permitted to work from live models.[25] One of Edwin Harleston's first classes was Perspective, taught by Anson Kent Cross. The course introduced the students to eighteenth- and nineteenth-century theories of perspective in conjunction with problem-solving exercises.[26] During the term, Harleston successfully completed more than 164 of these perspective problems, which included drawing everything from single geometric shapes to rooms filled with objects of varying sizes. Although Edwin Harleston received a passing grade in his perspective course, his first notable academic success occurred in the Antique Drawing class. The practice of drawing from plaster casts was considered a crucial step in academic training and had been a part of the European academic tradition since the sixteenth century. The objective of drawing from casts was to acquire a thorough knowledge of the ideal human body in order to develop an appreciation for the classical beauty of its form.[27] Casts were preferred during the preliminary stages of figure study because they were composed of simplified shapes and the light and dark planes of the body were more clearly defined than those of a live model. In addition, they did not move as live models were apt to do, thus allowing students to examine various aspects of the figure indefinitely without fear of having their concentration disrupted due to a shift in pose.[28] The Museum of Fine Art's collection of classical casts (which filled the entire first floor and half of the exhibition space) provided SMFA students with a variety of stances and body types from which to draw.[29] This is how Edwin Harleston's teacher, William McGregor Paxton, had been trained; therefore, he continued this traditional approach to figure study in his SMFA classroom.

Paxton began his art studies in Boston and later entered the École des Beaux-Arts and the Académie Julian in Paris. When he returned to the United States in 1893, Paxton supported himself by painting portraits and drawing posters for the *Boston Herald* until he accepted a teaching position at the SMFA in 1906.[30] Paxton, who many described as a cultured intellectual, was a solidly built man whose thinning hair and pleasant face, adorned by gold-rimmed spectacles, made him look more like the family doctor than an artist. Although his outward appearance seemed warm and approachable, those who knew him considered Paxton to be arrogant and contentious.[31] Yet, the forty students who enrolled in his class that year found him to be a good instructor who was always willing to help them.[32] Though none of Harleston's work from this course has been found, he finished near the top of his class. The SMFA *Thirty-first Annual Report* for the 1906–1907 academic year states that Harleston received honorable mention for his work in Paxton's class. Receiving this recognition is a clear indication that this young artist's talents were being recognized and rewarded by his teachers.[33]

The third course Harleston took during his first year at the school was Artistic Anatomy, a class that studied the human figure using live models.[34] His instructor was Philip Hale, a portrait, figure, and landscape specialist, who came from an established Boston family whose lineage included luminaries such as Revolutionary War hero Nathan Hale and author Harriet Beecher Stowe. Hale had studied at the SMFA and The Art Students League of New York and like his fellow instructors, he also spent time at the École des Beaux-Arts and the Académie Julian in Paris. In 1893, Hale joined the SMFA faculty and during his tenure he proved to be a dedicated teacher and capable artist. In a letter to a friend, Frank Benson remarked that Hale was "a great teacher and he loved to teach to the detriment of his work—that is he gave too much time to teaching but his heart was in it and younger people got the benefit."[35] However, his students probably would have preferred less attention from Hale since it was his custom to fail most of his beginning anatomy students. Even with a reputation for being difficult, Hale managed to earn the admiration and respect of his students because of his skills as an artist and teacher.[36]

In the back of Harleston's 1906 perspective notebook there are two anatomical sketches that indicated he was having difficulty mastering the human figure.[37] The first drawing is a lower-body muscle study of a male seen from a rear view. Only traces of the person's left profile can be seen. The left leg is slightly bent to support the figure's weight, and the right leg extends from the body at a forty-five-degree angle. In this drawing, Harleston has made one of the most common mistakes for beginning anatomy students, that of inaccurately proportioning the figure. The torso is slightly elongated, and the thigh is disproportionately long in comparison to the calf and foot. Despite these miscalculations and the stiff appearance of his subject, Harleston has accurately placed and identified each muscle, especially those in the lower body. This meticulous attention to human anatomy demonstrates his earnest attempt to discover how this system influences the body's shape. The second study is a three-quarter action figure with the male model posed like a runner who has just crossed the finish line. The subject's arms are raised in a gesture of jubilation and his legs extend into the foreground and background in positions usually associated with rapid movement. Proportion is still a problem in this study; however, it is minor when compared to the previous sketch. What has changed dramatically is his fluid use of line. In the second drawing Harleston is no longer interested in the precise placement of muscles;

an accurate depiction of motion is the main objective for this drawing. Because the goal has changed, the detailed rendering in the muscle study has been replaced with a more graceful linear approach. This drawing shows the substantial growth Harleston experienced in his effort to render the human figure. But unfortunately, it was not enough to pass the course.

Even though Harleston received a failing mark in anatomy, he considered his first year at the SMFA to be a success. He had adjusted to his surroundings, made new friends, and achieved substantial progress in his studies. Notwithstanding his achievements, finding money to cover the increasing cost of his education was difficult and his father had little to spare for he was putting all of his resources into creating his own funeral enterprise. Katherine, Harleston's oldest sister, sent what she could afford whenever she could, but it was not enough. In an attempt to relieve this monetary burden, Edwin Harleston became a partner in a small postcard business owned by Julius Westmoreland and T. K. Gibson. The Westmoreland Company produced postcards designed to educate and encourage the next generation of artists and business leaders by featuring photographs of successful African Americans such as poets Paul Lawrence Dunbar and Phillis Wheatley and musician Samuel Coleridge Taylor. The Gate City Drug Store, The People's Shoe Store and W. E. Braswell's dental office in Macon, Georgia, were some of the businesses featured on these cards. Unfortunately, the $13.83 Harleston collected from this venture was not nearly enough to cover the cost of tuition, art supplies, and living expenses.[38] As a result, Harleston dropped out of school, and in the fall of 1907, he became a crew member aboard the Kamden, a cargo ship that made regular trips between Boston Harbor and the port city of St. John, in New Brunswick, Canada.[39] There are no letters, postcards, or diary notations about his time at sea, but a fellow classmate, Philip Adams, would later capture Harleston's seafaring image in a portrait entitled *The Sailor*. Adams portrays Edwin in a three-quarter pose wearing a dark casual shirt that is slightly askew and open to the chest, exposing his neck and collarbone. His smooth, handsome face displays the introspective gaze that was often depicted in portraits of this period. The success of this painting and the artist's ability to capture the individuality of the sitter led to

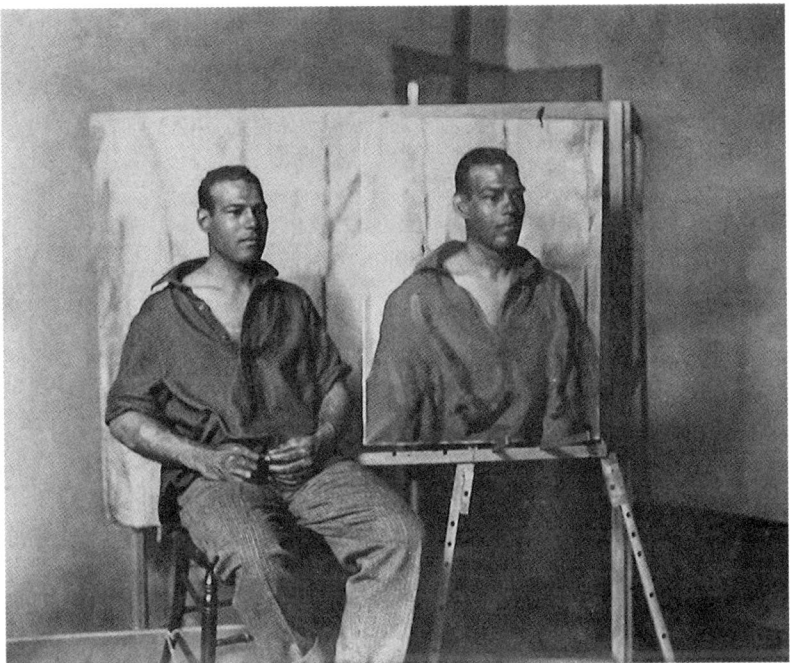

The Sailor, photograph, ca. 1910. Collection of Mae Whitlock Gentry.

The Boston Post newspaper publishing a photograph of Edwin Harleston seated next to his portrait by Adams. Unfortunately, only the photograph of this artistic endeavor has survived.[40]

When Harleston returned to Boston in the fall of 1908, he was able to pay tuition for the year and secure housing in a three-story brick apartment building at 23 Berwick Street.[41] This section of town, known as the "Lower Broadway of Boston," included the largest African American community in the city. At one time, Lower Broadway housed "colored folks of the better class," but with the opening of the Back Bay train station in 1899, followed by the establishment of the city's only hotel for people of color in 1906, this part of Boston soon became a stopping-off point for Pullman porters and other railway employees. The infusion of transients transformed the area from a quiet residential neighborhood into a gathering place for the "sporting set."[42] As a resident of this neighborhood,

Edwin Harleston was able to break through the confines of his small Atlanta University and SMFA circle of friends and connect with the broader African American community.

Lower Broadway had a robust Black population, in part, because of the city's historic association with the abolitionist movement. During the Civil War and Reconstruction, Boston was a model for racial relations in America. The state lifted the ban on interracial marriage in 1843, desegregated public schools in 1855, and established African American male suffrage in the nineteenth century, making both the state and its largest city northern leaders on issues of race. However, racial discrimination remained widespread in the city. By the turn of the century, racial tolerance declined as the African American population grew by 50 percent after the Civil War. As a result, there was a growing concern among New Englanders that they had unleashed upon themselves a group of uncivilized people whose rude manners and uncouth behavior made them unqualified to manage the responsibility of full citizenship.[43] These ideas were reinforced by a flood of propaganda found in speeches, books, and articles written by southern Democrats such as Henry Grady, managing editor of *The Atlanta Constitution* newspaper.[44] By 1908, Bostonians had adopted many southern racial views, leading to restrictions on some public amusements and accommodations. However, African Americans refused to passively accept their deteriorating position in the Boston community. Members of political organizations such as the Wendell Phillips Club and the National Independent Equal Rights League continued to confront issues concerning racial discrimination by challenging them in court.[45] While *The Guardian*, an African American newspaper owned by William Monroe Trotter and George W. Forbes, openly contested the ideas of those who supported the abandonment of their privileges as citizens and kept the community informed on issues concerning the state of Black America on a national level.

The clouds of racial tension that were gathering over Boston did not affect Harleston's return to the SMFA. School records from that period are incomplete. But if he followed the normal course of study, Harleston took two courses under Philip Hale, Life Drawing and Anatomy. The class began with a series of short poses known as gesture drawings. In this exercise, detail was not an objective; the goal was to encourage spontaneity and facilitate the student's ability in rapidly capturing the essence of the human figure. After warming up with the rapid poses, the students concentrated on one long pose, which usually took a week or more to complete. Models for life class were selected for their beautiful form and strong lines. They usually posed on a raised platform under a skylight so that the students could easily see variations of light and shade on the figure.[46] In order to effectively create a sense of volume through the gradation of tone, charcoal was the preferred medium for long studies. Harleston's drawings improved and by the end of the semester, he had successfully completed the Life Drawing class and received a passing mark in Anatomy on the second try. This meant that Harleston was no longer a beginner, he was now an advanced student.

———

THIS ELEVATION IN STATUS was paralleled by improved accommodations at the SMFA. During the last five years the Museum of Fine Art had been planning a new building and in January of 1909 it was finally completed. The facility, located on Huntington Avenue near Fenway Parkway and Museum Road, was more than three times the size of the old building, providing more room for the museum's new acquisitions and permanent collection. Adjacent to the museum was the new art school, which was intended to be revolutionary in its design, altering forever the atmosphere of the school but not its character.

The SMFA was to be located in a low rectangular temporary building, which would later be replaced by a building similar in style to the new museum. Yet, the temporary status of this structure did not discourage *The Boston Globe* from describing the new facility as "the most complete art school in America, if not the world."[47] Designed by Guy Lowell and built by J. W. Bishop & Co. (the same architect-builder team that conceived the new museum), the building was constructed of reinforced concrete with two open courts that eventually were to be glassed over.[48] There was no attempt at ornamentation. The large, airy studio-classrooms were painted silver gray and illuminated by skylights that faced north, making an excellent background for models or casts. These specific features made the SMFA unique in comparison to other American art schools.

The official day for moving from the old museum on Copley Square to the new location on Huntington Avenue was set for February 3, 1909. In preparation for the move the following notice was placed on the school's bulletin board: "Farewell parade this afternoon 1 o'clock sharp. Everybody come in appropriate costume."[49] The students began to gather in the main hall in front of the museum entrance at 12:30 PM. What started out to be a sad farewell quickly became a festive parade as the procession began to move through the corridors of the building precisely at one o'clock. More than two hundred students dressed in all sorts of artistic costumes marched through the vacant rooms of the museum with banners and placards that bid the old school farewell. The chief marshal of the parade was dressed in a scalloped cocked hat and carried a sign that read "MOVING DAY."[50] He was followed by members of Philip Hale's Life Drawing class who held aloft banners reading "Hale's Conquering Heroes Come," followed by a pair of "Paxton Sunbeams." Another student displayed a sign with the following tribute:

> Here's to our much-loved anatomist Hale,
> Who flunks us our first year without fail,
> and turns a deaf ear to our despairing
> wails,
> He says he believes we're depicting a
> whale.
> Or a red and blue chimpanzee minus his
> tail.
> And tells us our picture will ner'er go on
> sale.
> But three cheers for Philip—hail!

Anson Cross, an instructor of drawing and painting, was represented in the parade by a student carrying a tall wand with a paper cross attached to

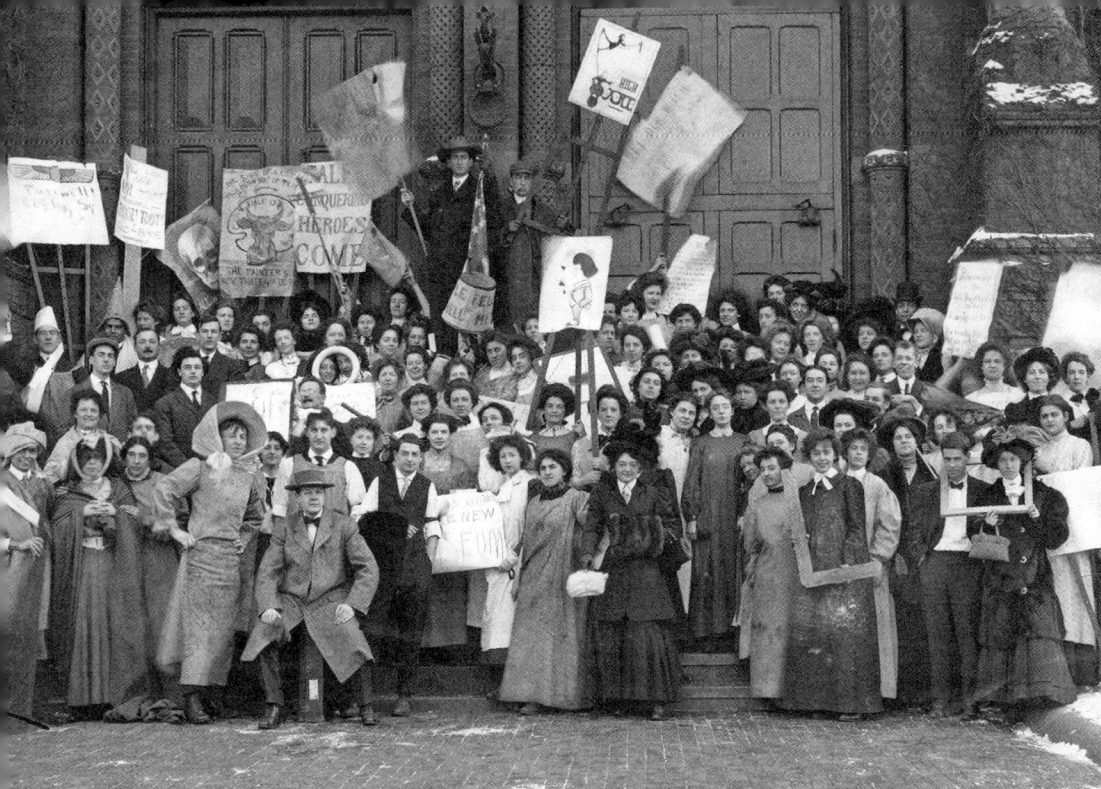

Moving Day: School of the Museum of Fine Arts, photograph, 1909. Tufts University, Tufts University Archival Research Center, Medford, MA.

the top that bore the inscription "I am A. Cross."[51] Closing out the procession was a group of students from the antiques class, who carried a replica of the new museum made from the erasers they had been using all year.[52]

The parade wound its way throughout the building and finally ended on the steps of the museum where a photograph was taken of the participants. Edwin Harleston can be seen in the fifth row on the far left, wearing a pointed paper hat, holding aloft a "Farewell Copley Sq" poster, decorated with the image of an ancient Egyptian falcon and attached to the legs of an old easel. After the picture was taken, Harleston and the other students gave the teachers and staff a rousing cheer, sang a few choruses of "Good Night Ladies" and "Auld Lang Syne," then went their separate ways.[53]

4

FROM AMATEUR TO FINE ARTIST

THE NEW SCHOOL OPENED without fanfare. Instead of parades, exotic outfits, and banners, students simply assembled in their assigned class-rooms for instruction. However, three weeks into the semester the SMFA held a costume housewarming party replete with decorations and refresh-ments. When the crowd of students who were dressed as Native Ameri-cans, Spanish dancers, kings, and clowns had gathered, they danced the waltz and two-stepped to music provided by a local musician.[1] At the end of the festivities, students and faculty posed for group photographs but Edwin Harleston does not appear in any of these pictures. He may have decided not to attend because he was still the only student of color at the institution and this type of socializing may have been uncomfortable for him. His absence could have also been related to the fact that two class-mates decided to come to the party in blackface dressed as mammy and pickaninny characters. Their costume choice reflected the popular, yet disturbing attitude that it was perfectly acceptable to openly mock Afri-can Americans.[2]

The movement to publicly denigrate, socially isolate, and politically disenfranchise citizens of African descent had grown into a well-defined national campaign affecting every aspect of society. The result of these political and intellectual attacks manifested itself in the form of increased violence against members of the Black community. Physical attacks, especially lynching occurred with such regularity that it was sometimes described as "a hybrid of sports-vengeance."[3] It was not unusual during this period for a lynching to be advertised in local community newspapers across the country so that those who were officiating would be assured of a crowd. Between 1890 and 1909 more than 1,600 African Americans were lynched for alleged crimes ranging from rape to failure to address a white man as "mister."[4] However, Boston's Black citizens were never confronted with this level of violence because of its abolitionist history, but job and housing discrimination were routine occurrences. In reaction to these acts of human degradation, a group of concerned citizens met in February of 1909 in Springfield, Illinois, the home of Lincoln, to discuss the state of the race. Well-known community leaders including Ida B. Wells, Monroe Trotter, Jane Addams, Garrison Villard, James Dewy, William Dean Howells and W. E. B. Du Bois presented scholarly papers and discussed issues concerning the vote, education, segregation, and the rise of violence against African Americans. As a result of this conference, a biracial committee of forty members was organized for the purpose of forming a permanent organization. The following year, the National Association for the Advancement of Colored People (NAACP) came into existence.

Although Harleston was immersed in his studies during this period, he was not oblivious to the problems facing those of his race. On December 2, 1909, he attended the "Celebration of the Fiftieth Anniversary of the Public Murder of John Brown," sponsored by the New England Suffrage League and the National Independent Political League at Faneuil Hall.[5] Reverend C. Ransom, pastor of St. Charles AME Church and the main orator for the evening session, was known for his passionate speeches concerning John Brown. In his address, Ransom reminded the audience that "like the ghost of Hamlet's father the spirit of John Brown beckons us to arise and seek the recovery of our rights, which our enemy . . . has sought forever to destroy."[6] The substance of these words would later spur Edwin Harleston to take up the challenge in his hometown of Charleston, South Carolina, more than a decade later.

During the 1909–10 academic year Harleston began to develop his painting skills under the guidance of Frank Benson. A native of Massachusetts, Benson entered the SMFA in 1880 and studied painting with Otto Grundmann. Three years later Benson and his classmate Edmund Tarbell left Boston to continue their studies in Paris. When they arrived, they immediately enrolled in the Académie Julian classes taught by Gustave Clarence Rodolphe Boulanger, a French neo-Greek painter, and Jules Joseph Lefebvre, an artist who specialized in the nude figure.[7] As students, Benson and Tarbell learned the Impressionist technique of creating light-filled atmospheres through the use of color. Their success in mastering this style was furthered by William T. Dannat, and American expatriate who helped to develop their "sensual perception" of light and color.[8] While in Paris, Benson and Tarbell also visited the Luxembourg and Louvre Museums to study the painting techniques of masters such as Rubens, Rembrandt, Hals, Goya, V Velázquez, Vermeer, and David.[9] Both artists were impressed by these experiences and later incorporated some of the methods used by this diverse group of masters, especially those dealing with light, into their own paintings. When they came back to the United States, Benson in 1885, followed by Tarbell in 1886, they returned with a cumulative body of aesthetic knowledge that not only enhanced their artistic talents but also prepared them for teaching.

Frank Benson's ability to pass his knowledge of oil painting on to his intermediate students can be seen in Harleston's *Nude Female Study*, completed around 1910. The model in this painting stands in front of a dark gray background with her back toward the viewer, allowing only a three-quarter view of her body. The subject's stance indicates that her weight is evenly distributed because her shoulders and hips appear to be parallel. To add some interest to this pose, the model's head is slightly tilted upward with her face turned away from the viewer in an apparent effort to preserve her modesty. Harleston's skill as a draftsman is evident in this painting. The hours spent meticulously drawing and redrawing the human figure in Hale's life class, as seen in his charcoal drawing, *Seated Female Nude*, ca. 1910, allowed him to construct this figure with broad, smooth, carefully placed brushstrokes. Yet, the overly modeled shoulder

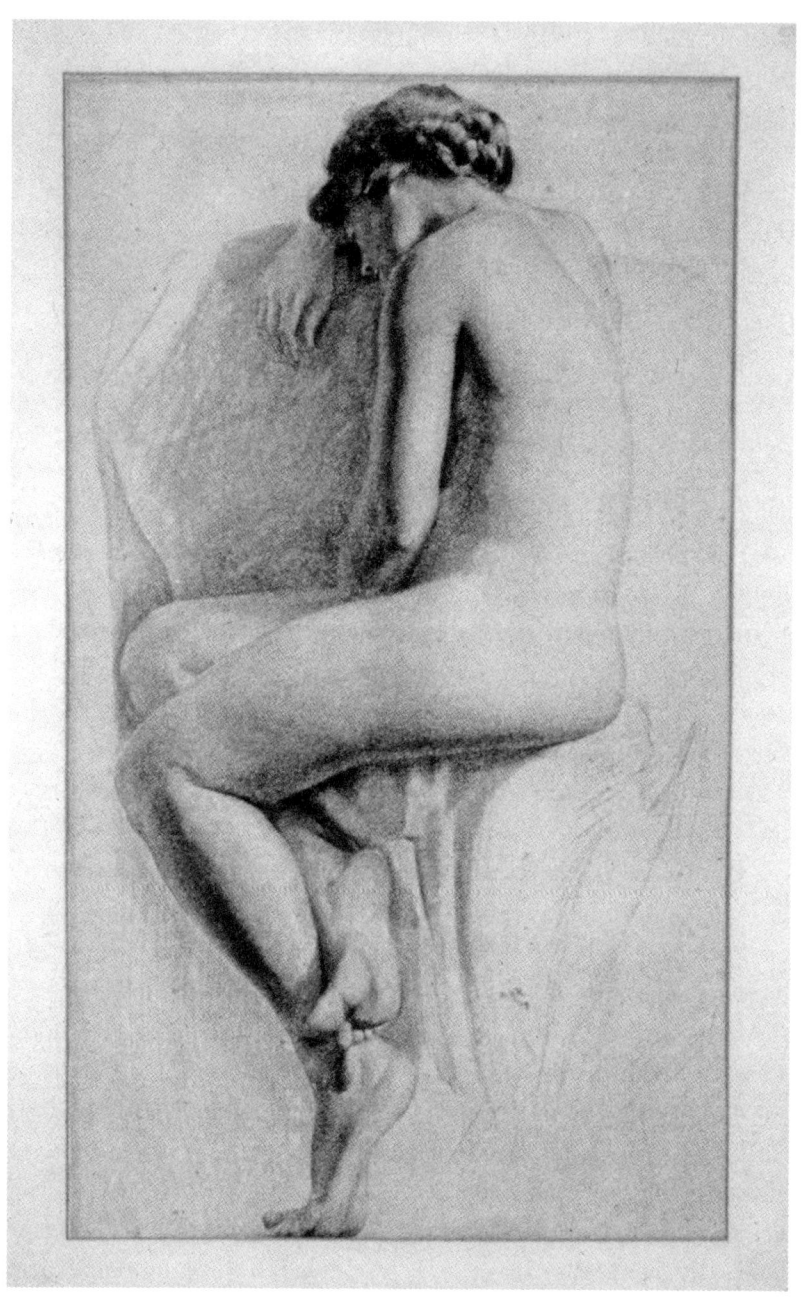

Edwin Augustus Harleston, *Seated Female Nude*, charcoal on paper, ca. 1910, whereabouts unknown.

blades, neck muscles, and vertebrae in tandem with the sharp contour of the body suggest that at this stage in his development Harleston had not fully made the transition from drawing to painting. Instead of interpreting the figure in a loose, painterly manner, he used his brush with the draftsman-like precision of a drawing implement in an effort to ensure correctness. Because of this approach, his work takes on the appearance of a careful anatomical study by a student rather than the painterly work of a professional artist.

However, Harleston shows a high level of skill in his handling of the light bathing on the left side of the model, revealing the suppleness of her form. The high key areas of the torso are heightened by contrasting dark shadows and hard edges found in the area of her left arm, back, and a portion of the right arm. Harleston has attempted to give these shadows and edges warmth by structuring them with flecks of red, blue, and violet. But instead of producing the desired effect, the shadows take on the appearance of dull, flat shapes with limited tonal gradation, making it difficult to

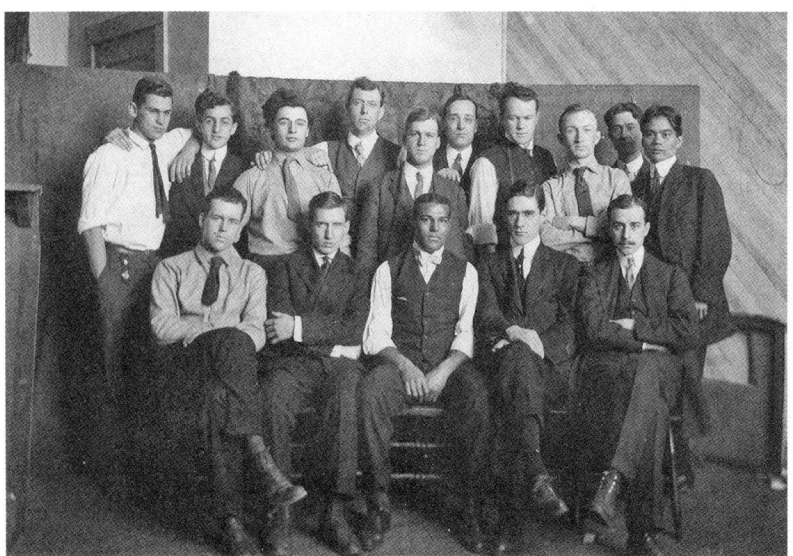

Men's Life Drawing Class, photograph, 1910. Tufts University, Tufts University Archival Research Center, Medford, MA.

see the figure underneath.[10] Despite his heavy-handed treatment of these shadows, Harleston was able to balance them by delicately highlighting the model's hair. A single speck of white, probably intended to represent a hairpin of some sort, appears on the left side of her head. This small but dramatic ornamentation successfully draws the viewer's attention away from the torso and upward to this area. No doubt this pose tested Harleston's ability to render a well-proportioned figure and satisfactorily render the form through the use of color, light, and shade. Even though his canvas had technical problems, his potential to become a successful figure painter was undeniable.

Harleston was making outstanding progress in his coursework, and he was well liked by his teachers, but financial pressures proved to be a constant distraction. To assist in easing this burden, the faculty submitted his name for a special scholarship award. On April 11, 1911, Edwin Harleston received a letter from Alice Brooks, the school's business manager, stating that he had been awarded a full scholarship for the 1911–12 academic year.[11] Scholarships and prize money were awarded annually to students who had achieved excellence in drawing from a cast, drawing the nude figure, and oil portraiture. Female students were also given special recognition for their achievements and stipends were awarded to those students who wanted to study abroad. To be considered for one of these scholarships, however, students were required to submit an application and undergo scrutiny from a panel of instructors and trustees. But in Harleston's case, the award was given solely on the recommendation of his instructors, which made it a highly coveted honor.[12] Aside from the honorable mention he had received during his first year, this scholarship award was Harleston's first formal recognition of his artistic talent.

Now that his monetary worries had been eliminated, Harleston was able to take advanced painting classes in the fall of 1911 under Edmond Tarbell. This nationally recognized painter of tranquil interior domestic scenes and portraits taught only the advanced classes, which allowed him to concentrate on instilling in his students an appreciation for "technical superiority."[13] The evidence of this indoctrination can be seen in Harleston's *Standing Female Nude with Kimono*, one of the first works he produced under Tarbell's guidance. In this full-length nude study, the model stands in front of a loosely painted gray wall with her clasped hands resting on her posterior, allowing only the right half of her body to be seen. Her head tilts toward the left, away from the viewer, leaving her face veiled in heavy shadow. This type of pose was common not only because it protected the public's sense of propriety, but it also provided anonymity for the model.[14] A red Japanese kimono lies crumpled at her feet, creating an aura of exotic romanticism, which reflects the popularity of Oriental art during this period.

It is obvious that Harleston had been studying the works of other artists, for *Standing Female Nude with Kimono* represents a tremendous surge in his growth as a painter since completing *Nude Female Study*. The latter work constructed the figure with sharp contour lines, broad, flat strokes, and dramatic lighting. However, the full nude study has been rendered in a soft, delicate style akin to Tonalism.[15] He creates a sense of atmosphere by enveloping the figure in a soft, brown, gauze-filtered light that seems to dissolve at the edges of this figure into the shadows. Although this haze draws the eye toward some of the more subtly painted areas, this technique does not distort or obscure the viewer's ability to see the delicacy and sureness with which Harleston has applied his brush-strokes. This approach to painting can be traced to Tarbell's interest in fil-tered light and deep shadows as demonstrated in one of his better-known works, *Girl Reading*.

Tarbell's extraordinary ability to capture the essence of his subjects made his portrait painting course one of the school's largest and most popular classes. One reason for such high interest can be traced to the fact that American artists had always considered portrait painting a nec-essary survival skill; but by the end of the nineteenth century, it had taken on a new level of importance. Young artists returning to the United States from Europe, as well as those who had not been abroad, found it nearly impossible to sell their paintings because the public preferred to purchase pictures or reproductions of works by old masters.[16] The exception to this trend was in the area of portraiture, for Americans had a reputation for unceasingly commissioning portraits of themselves.[17] This obsession

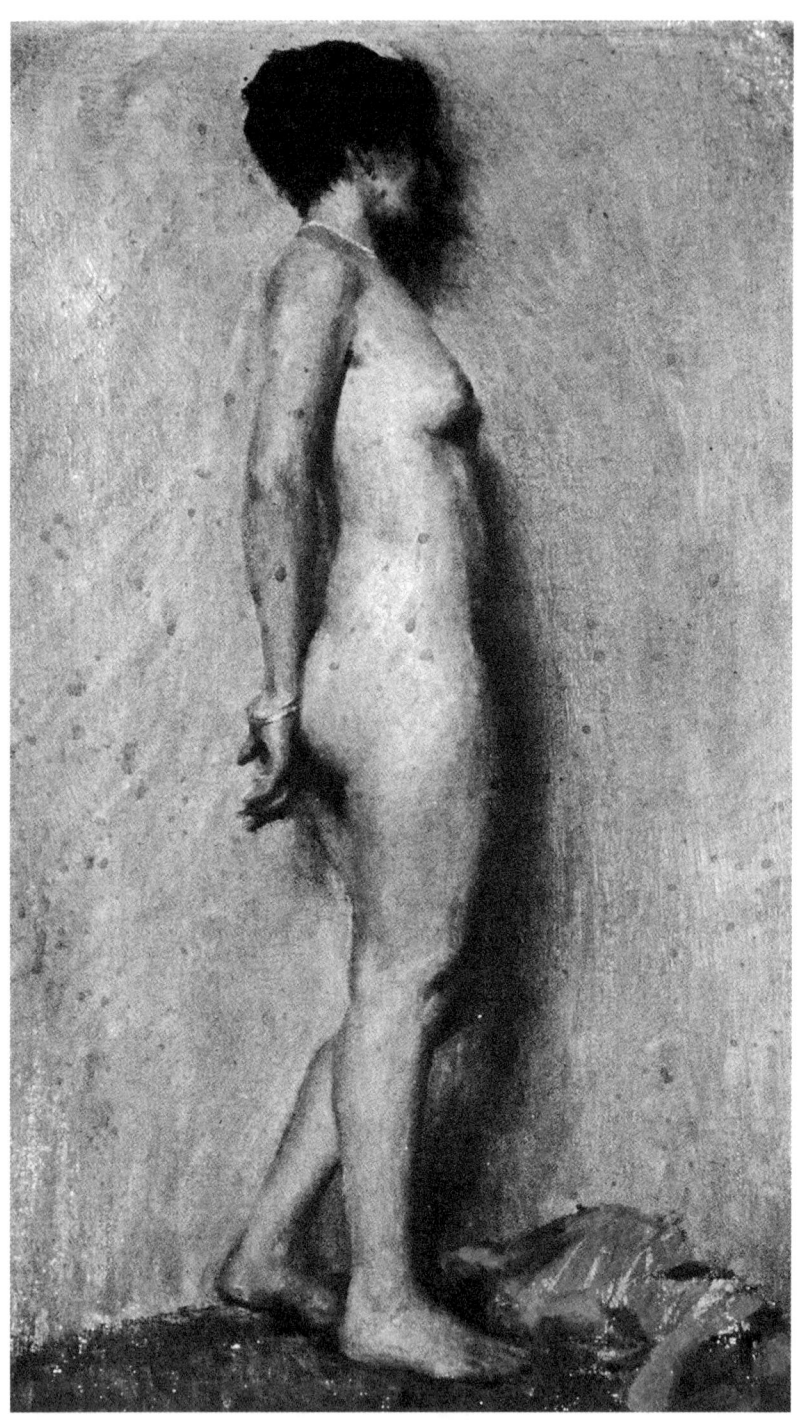

Edwin Augustus Harleston, *Standing Female Nude with Kimono,* oil on canvas, ca. 1911. Reproduced with permission of owner.

may have been caused, in part, by the need for Americans, particularly the wealthy, to create some semblance of permanence for themselves in a rapidly evolving world. Industrialization and urbanization had created a sense of urgency among the cultural elite to protect their way of life. Photographs, newspapers, and modern novels were considered dangerous, disseminating information that threatened their veracity as a group and challenged their taste as individuals.[18] To counter these cultural attacks America's genteel society used portraiture to provide a reassuring illusion that their traditions still mattered.

Only a few artists in the Boston area had both the practical and academic skills to give SMFA students insight into the portrait taste of the city's elite. Of all the teachers at the school, Tarbell was considered the best. Although he employed Impressionist techniques in many of his interior scenes, Tarbell's portrait style is characterized by dark backgrounds and filtered light. Those who have studied his paintings feel that his technique is more closely patterned after that of Titian, Rembrandt, and Degas, than of Hals and Sargent. This conclusion may have been reached because the aforementioned artists focus on the all-encompassing character and beauty of the subject rather than a few well-defined characteristics.[19] The influence of Tarbell on Harleston's portrait painting style can be seen in *Portrait Study: Woman in Black Hat*, completed in 1912. The subject is a young woman in profile whose melancholy, introspective gaze is brightened only by a dark red, loosely painted background. She wears a black dress with a high white collar accented at the neck by a large black bow. Her head is completely covered by a shapeless, black cloche with a narrow head-fitting brim, which directs the viewer's attention to her face. Harleston has successfully captured the physical characteristics of his subject but there are problems with his interpretation of shadows. As in *Nude Figure Study*, Harleston has applied his color in flat broad strokes with little regard for the subtle gradation of tone. The light that washes over the model's face is almost neutralized by the flat, harsh shaded areas found at the edge of her jawline and neck. As in the earlier works, this two-dimensional quality had been reinforced by the lack of any highlights in the subject's hat or clothing, causing these sections to appear as black silhouettes, void of mass or volume. The flat treatment of these low-keyed areas may have resulted from Harleston's literal interpretation of Tarbell's instruction to treat the shadows like patterns by following the "bedbug line," a line which separates light and shadow. By emphasizing the delineation of these areas, Tarbell probably felt that his students would be able to translate these shaded sections onto the canvas more easily.[20] However, for Harleston the result was a relatively two-dimensional figure.

Midway through the course, Edwin Harleston seems to have gained a clearer understanding of how subtle harmonies help to create a more naturalistic appearance in his subjects. *The Old Colonel*, ca. 1912, is an example of this realization. The model for this painting was a silver-haired Boston gentleman whose aristocratic air, thick mustache, butterfly collar, and tie reminded the artist more of an "idealized southern colonel" than a Boston Brahmin.[21] In this three-quarter view of the sitter, Harleston has placed the model's light profile against a charcoal gray background and used a palette similar to that employed in his earlier portraits. Placing a fully illuminated figure in dark clothing against a dark background had been a common compositional device since the mid-fifteenth century. Yet, some art historians feel that this approach received new interest when nineteenth-century French artist and teacher Thomas Couture revived the practice.[22]

Although he achieved great strides in his portrait paining technique in *The Old Colonel*, especially with his handling of light and shade, Harleston seems to have reached a high point with his portrait of the *Italian Woman with Kerchief.* The model for this painting is Josephine, an older, motherly woman who frequently modeled for SMFA classes.[23] Josephine's maternal appearance is enhanced by the white shawl collar that frames her face and the red kerchief partially covering her hair. In examining this painting, it is evident that Harleston has been able to capture the kind of artificial atmosphere created by a single beam of golden light that has been traditionally associated with Rembrandt.[24] The young artist has captured this light and the shadows it creates in a way that suggests that he has not only followed Tarbell's instruction but he also may have studied Rembrandt's *Portrait of the Wife of Dr. Nicolaes Tulp*, which hung in the Dutch and

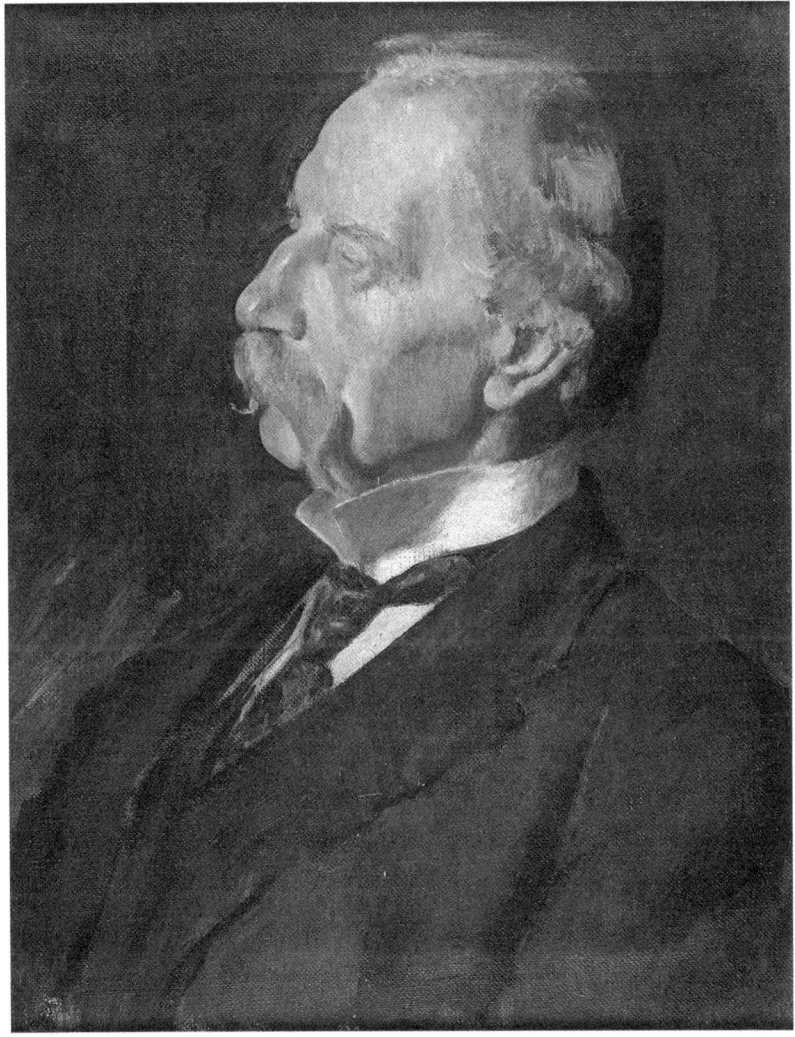

Edwin Augustus Harleston, *The Old Colonel*, oil on canvas, ca. 1912. Howard University Gallery of Art, Washington, DC, licensed by Art Resource, NY.

Flemish gallery in the Museum of Fine Arts.[25] The way in which Harleston has peered into the shadows and accurately captured the subtle changes in Josephine's face, especially the reflected light along the jawline, is comparable to that of the Dutch master. Harleston's sensitivity to tonal gradation in the shadows around the eye and along the bridge of the nose and cheek indicates that he was not interested in merely suggesting value changes but intent on reproducing each variation as it appeared (see Plate 1).

Edwin Harleston had completed most of the required courses by the end of the 1912 school term. The high quality of his technical skills had been achieved through nearly six years of hard work and study. During this time, he had grown from a naïve amateur into a fine artist whose technique was grounded in the French academic tradition and shaped by the Boston School of Painting. The school also experienced unanticipated growth during this period. From 1906 to 1912 the enrollment at the SMFA had nearly doubled. This rapid rise in the student population prompted the school's governing council to recommend that a director be appointed to manage the overall operation of the institution.[26] Up until now, the school had been run by a democratic, self-perpetuated body that seemed to have functioned efficiently. The fear of losing control to a newcomer forced the faculty to demand that the existing system remain intact, under threat of walking out if their demand was not honored.[27] Two weeks after their protest was lodged, Huger Elliot, architect, designer, and artist from the Rhode Island School of Design was hired as director of the Design Department and the SMFA. Clearly, the governing council had not taken the faculty's demand seriously.[28]

In response to this rebuff, Tarbell submitted his letter of resignation in December of 1912, citing only the "pressure of work" as the reason for leaving; there was no mention of dissatisfaction with the new director. However, a newspaper account of his departure stated that Tarbell's early leave was because of "resentment at the thought that the committee was seriously capable of proposing . . . a director of the school."[29] A few days after this account appeared in the newspaper, Frank Benson submitted his resignation; another by William Paxton soon followed. As word of these departures began to spread, supporters of the institution as well as local citizens agreed that the school council's decision had been ill advised. In a letter to the editor, Edmund Von Mach, editor of the *International Encyclopedia of Art*, stated that the loss of Benson and Tarbell was the result of the high-handed act of a board who had forgotten they were trustees and proprietors. He went on to say that the loss of these two men would seriously damage the SMFA's reputation as one of the nation's premiere art institutions.[30]

Students responded to the resignations by withholding their fee for the second term and threatening to withdraw from school if the matter of Tarbell and Benson's resignations was not satisfactorily resolved.[31] The fear of losing two of the school's most prominent teachers and many of its best students prompted the council to ask that the resignations be rescinded. However, both instructors refused. As a result, dozens of students changed their class schedules so that they could take the final portrait courses taught by Benson and Tarbell.[32] Since Harleston was among this group, he may have also been aligned with those who expressed concern over the quality of their art training and the future of the SMFA.

———

BACK HOME IN CHARLESTON, trouble was also brewing. The Harleston & Mickey Funeral Home was thriving under Captain Harleston's direction.[33] Even though the number of Black-owned funeral businesses had more than doubled since Teddy left home, his father had succeeded in providing services for some of the city's most prominent African American families. But in spite of this accomplishment, Edward C. Mickey, now a full-fledged undertaker and embalmer, resented Captain's heavy-handed control over the business and began making plans to reestablish the Mickey funeral enterprise with the help of his younger brother, Richard H. Mickey. Captain Harleston was also beginning to tire of the arguments with his nephew over money and funerary protocols but in order to establish his own business, he needed to find a new location and build a staff that would be loyal and accepting of his authority; a staff over which he would have full control.[34]

The most likely employee candidates for this enterprise were his children. As Captain evaluated their attributes, he knew it would be a difficult task, but he was determined to have at least one of his offsprings join him in his quest to build one of the most financially successful funeral businesses in the city. Katherine, Captain's firstborn, was an attractive, yet matronly looking woman who occasionally worked as a dressmaker. In 1908, she married Maithlun Fleming and left South Carolina after the wedding to live with her husband in St Augustine, Florida.[35] His oldest son, John Moultrie, was a tall, stern-looking man who has been described by a family member as obstreperous and uncompromising. Despite these shortcomings, his father concluded that if given the opportunity, his son could be an important contributor to the growth and expansion of the family business. After he graduated from Lincoln University, Captain Harleston sent John Moultrie to the University of Pennsylvania School of Veterinary Medicine to study large animals with the expectation that he would return to Charleston to manage the funeral home's horses and livery stables and assist him with daily affairs.[36] But after two years of study, John Moultrie announced he was no longer interested in veterinary medicine, left school, and moved to Brooklyn, New York, to live with a cousin while working as a bellman at a local hotel.[37]

Profoundly disappointed, Captain then turned to his youngest son, Robert Othello, who had followed in his brother Edwin's footsteps by attending Atlanta University. But Robert did not possess his brother's intellectual acumen nor his athletic ability so at the end of his second year he dropped out of school. Unwilling to allow his youngest son to drift aimlessly, Captain Harleston sent him to the prestigious Renouard Training School for Embalmers in New York City. The Renouard name was synonymous with undertaking in the United States for Dr. August Renouard had been a pioneer in the field of embalming since the late nineteenth century and wrote the first textbook on the subject. Although Robert conceded to his father's demand by completing the six-week course, he never showed any real interest in his obligatory vocation.[38]

Eloise, the youngest daughter, still lived at home and was fully employed as secretary/treasurer of the Jenkins Orphanage, established in 1891 by Reverend Daniel Joseph Jenkins, the man she would later marry. This was not the place Captain would have chosen for his daughter's employment because these orphaned boys were often associated with criminal activity, but she enjoyed her work and was treated well by Reverend Jenkins and the staff.[39] It seems that of all of his children, Teddy

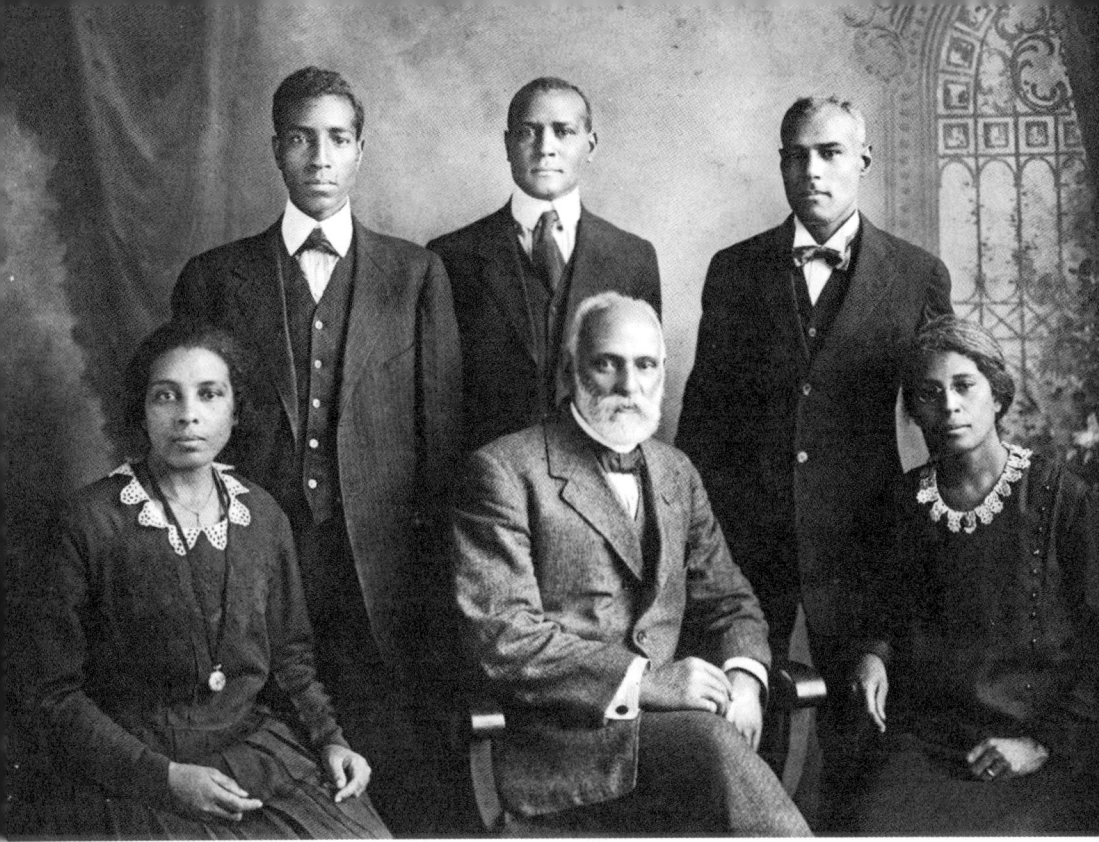

Edwin Gaillard Harleston family portrait, photograph, ca. 1914. Front row (*left* to *right*): Eloise Harleston Jenkins, Edwin Gaillard Harleston, Katherine Harleston Fleming; back row: Robert Othello Harleston, John Moultrie Harleston, Edwin A. Harleston. Collection of Mae Whitlock Gentry.

was the only one Captain Harleston felt he could rely upon because he was smart, purpose-driven, and dependable, but more importantly, he was the one who would follow his orders without much resistance. Therefore, under persistent pressure from his father, Edwin Harleston withdrew from school in December of 1912 with only one year left before finishing his degree, packed his bags, and reluctantly returned home to Charleston, South Carolina.

5

THE HOMECOMING

SOON AFTER EDWIN HARLESTON ARRIVED in Charleston, he strolled
the streets of his hometown to reacquaint himself with places he remem-
bered from childhood. But as he passed familiar houses and shops, he
could see and feel the changes that had taken place during his absence.
The vibrant charm of the city that had surrounded him in his youth was
now covered in a shroud of sadness. The stately antebellum mansions
near the Battery that had once been a symbol of the city's prosperity now
looked neglected and in desperate need of repair. Downtown streets that
had once been filled with vendors, shoppers, and horse-drawn carriages
now seemed strangely quiet when compared to the hustle and bustle of
Boston's dynamic commercial center.

At the root of this downward spiral was the hurricane of 1893, which
devastated mining and manufacturing in the area to the extent that it
caused the collapse of the region's phosphate industry.[1] With the decline
of this important segment of the city's economy, the South Carolina Railway Company fell into bankruptcy and was immediately purchased by a
northern syndicate. Locals had hoped the new owners would restore this
important regional link, but instead of revitalizing the railroad, the proprietors consolidated the southern district's lines, closed their Charleston headquarters, and rerouted train traffic through their new Norfolk,

Virginia, rail hub. Losing this crucial connection between northern and southern seaport cities had an immediate effect on Charleston's financial strength.

Wealthy residents who had made their fortunes from railroad shipping and associated businesses were now investing their money in other areas of the South. Those who had traditionally engaged in the transport of merchandise and perishable goods by cargo ship were also leaving Charleston's harbor for other ports. The final economic blow was delivered in 1911 when the city was battered by another ferocious hurricane that struck without warning. The storm hit with such force that it not only destroyed homes and businesses, but it also ravaged farmland. The result was a complete loss of crops that year and a permanent end to rice cultivation in the region.[2] Northern businessmen who had always enjoyed wintering in Charleston now thought of this once charming southern city as a "stinking, rotting, unhealthy, poverty-stricken, ill-governed town, better known for its vices than its culture."[3]

Although the negative economic condition of the city was considered temporary by most of its residents, the forced separation of South Carolina's African American citizens had become a way of life. These seeds of racial segregation had been planted in the late 1880s and watered by the new state constitution of 1895 legalizing all forms of discrimination involving people of color. Over the years, this new constitution had grown into a twisted vine, choking off African American access to the state's political, judicial, and educational systems. In matters of everyday life there was a general "understanding" as to where African Americans could go and what they could do in the white world.[4] But by the early 1900s, the vine had been fertilized by new Jim Crow laws causing its tendrils to become so thick that African Americans were almost completely closed off from mainstream life in South Carolina. Well-paying positions in the industrial and commercial markets were reserved for white people, while most of the lowest paying agricultural jobs went to Black citizens. In 1910, 60.2 percent of South Carolina's African American population over the age of ten worked in agriculture, forestry, and animal husbandry occupations, while only 17 percent held nonagricultural jobs.[5] To add insult to injury, Black citizens were prohibited from using the same public facilities as white citizens. Entrances, exits, and drinking fountains in public places bore signs which read "whites only." In those instances where Black and white workers occupied the same building, employees of different races were often prohibited from working in the same room or using the stairway at the same time.[6] Restaurants, schools, hotels, waiting rooms, and parks were also restricted. Even the Battery, which had traditionally been the culminating point for Charleston's annual Emancipation Proclamation Day celebration, was now off limits.[7]

As far as establishing a connection with the arts community was concerned, Harleston knew that among the city's wealthy residents, aesthetic interests focused on monuments memorializing Confederate war dead with portraiture coming in at a distant second.[8] But he also realized that despite his talent, he could never compete with white artists for commissions and there were only a few in the Black community who could afford the luxury of having a portrait painted. And even if there were enough paying clients, Edwin's father expected him to work full-time in the funeral business, which meant there would be little, if any, time for his art. This was the stifling environment to which Edwin Harleston had returned. Readjusting to life here would be difficult, for he now had to publicly conceal the air of confidence he had acquired in Boston, lower his hope of becoming a successful artist, and wear the mask of contentment befitting a dutiful son who had been summoned home to serve as his father's right hand.

Edwin Harleston's homecoming had not been the triumphant return he had envisioned, and yet, there was a bright spot. His brother Robert had been courting Marie Isabelle Forrest, the daughter of a local bookkeeper, Augustus H. Forrest and his wife, Elvira. The couple, along with their seven children, lived at 97 Morris Street in a large two-story house with Victorian-style furnishings. Like the Harlestons, their children had attended Avery Normal Institute, beginning with their oldest daughter, Elise Beatrice Forrest, who was twenty-two years old. She was an attractive, effervescent woman who stood five feet tall with large dark glistening eyes and a flawless complexion. On one occasion, Robert asked Edwin to deliver a gift to Marie. When Elise answered the front door, she was immediately enamored of the handsome man standing on her porch. He was polite but seemed distant and aloof. Even though he gave little thought to their first encounter, she had decided at that very moment that Edwin Augustus Harleston was going to be her husband. A few months after they met, she sent him a note inviting him to a party as her guest. From then on, family and friends thought of them as a couple.[9]

Even though Edwin enjoyed Elise's company, there was little time for socializing because his father immediately put him to work as an undertaker's assistant. With a new employee in the office to greet callers and make funeral arrangements, Captain could now focus his full attention on plans for a new, state-of-the-art undertaking facility. The business agreement he had with his nephew and sister for nearly a decade had finally collapsed, leaving him with little to show financially for his years of arduous work once the company's assets had been divided. However, the dissolution of this partnership made him even more determined to build the largest, finest "Negro firm" in Charleston.[10] To make this dream a reality, he acquired property at 121 Calhoun Street, which was only a few doors away from the Mickey's establishment.

The location for this new building was extremely important because it was situated in the heart of the African American business district on a street that served as the dividing line between Black and white communities. It was also across the street and only a few doors away from one of the oldest and most prominent Black churches in the South, Emanuel African Methodist Episcopal Church (aka Mother Emanuel AME Church), cofounded by Reverend Morris Brown and Denmark Vesey in 1816.[11] Captain Harleston's plans for this three-story facility were being carried out by Thomas Mayhem Pinkney, a master craftsman who was the most sought-after African American contractor of his day.[12] The plans called for a building that was 35 × 80 feet with a stylish showroom, a chapel with seating for 150 people, trimming room, embalming room, and a morgue on the first floor. The second floor would have a spacious hall, large enough for formal dances, recitals, receptions, and theatrical performances with sufficient stage space, two dressing rooms, a cloak room, and hat room. The space on the third floor would contain two large apartments with each having five rooms and a bath along with the offices of the State Grand Lodge of Good Samaritans.[13] When the new Harleston Funeral Establishment officially opened for business on December 21, 1914, it was described in the local newspaper as "the largest building constructed by a colored resident" in the city's history.[14]

While his father was overseeing final changes to the interior of the new building, Edwin was moving into one of the upstairs apartments, the other residential space was going to be occupied by paying tenants. As he began settling into his new residence, he discovered he had been saddled with a roommate, his older brother, John Moultrie who had returned from New York. Captain Harleston knew the two were constantly at odds with each other, but he wanted John Moultrie out of his house and the most logical place for him to live rent-free was in the Calhoun Street apartment. Since Edwin had no say in the matter, his father tried to compensate for this unwelcomed pairing by feigning interest in his son's art career while

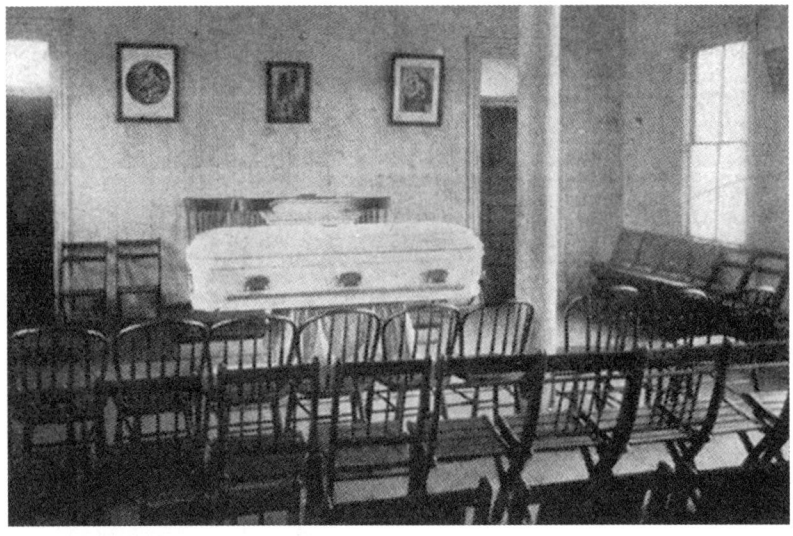

Harleston Funeral Establishment: chapel, photograph, ca. 1922, brochure. Edwin A. Harleston and Edwina Harleston Whitlock Family Papers, Stuart A. Rose Manuscript, Archives, and Rare Book Library, Emory University.

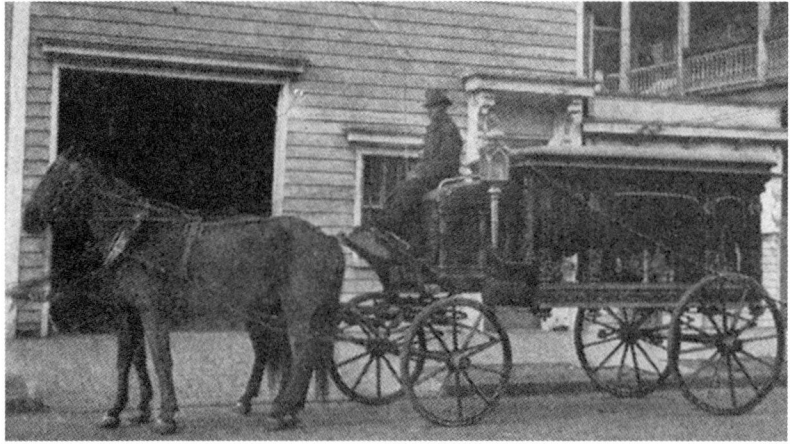

Harleston Funeral Establishment: horsedrawn hearse, photograph, ca. 1906, brochure. Edwin A. Harleston and Edwina Harleston Whitlock Family Papers, Stuart A. Rose Manuscript, Archives, and Rare Book Library, Emory University.

furtively hoping his obsession with painting would eventually fade away; however, this brief hiatus only strengthened Edwin's creative desire. In 1915, he picked up a brush again but seems to have been apprehensive about his skills after being away from his artwork for more than a year. In a thank-you letter from his friend, H. C. Dugas Sr., agency director of Standard Life Insurance Company in Augusta, Georgia, he commends Harleston for a painting he has received and praises the artist on the selection of the subject, manner of treatment, and expresses satisfaction with every detail of the artwork. Yet, the tone of this correspondence suggests that the artist may have solicited not only Dugas's critical opinion of his work but also reassurance that his artistic skills had not diminished. In an effort to boost his friend's confidence, Dugas tells the artist that while he had been privileged to see some of the masterpieces of the world, he prized and admired Harleston's work above all others.[15] The fact that Harleston kept this letter gives credence to the idea that he appreciated Dugas's affirmative criticism. This correspondence further supports the idea that his artistic aspirations were still not fully supported by his father and other family members, thereby creating a need for external confirmation.

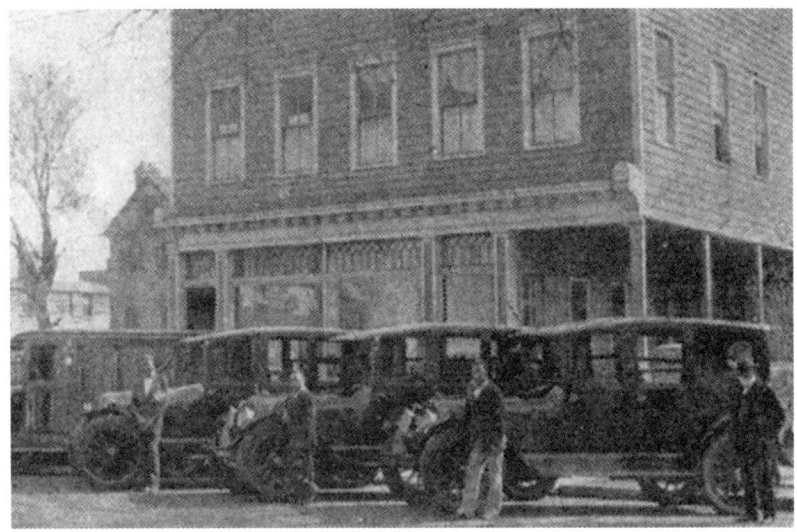

Harleston Funeral Establishment: Cunningham limousine fleet, photograph, ca. 1925, brochure. Edwin A. Harleston and Edwina Harleston Whitlock Family Papers, Stuart A. Rose Manuscript, Archives, and Rare Book Library, Emory University.

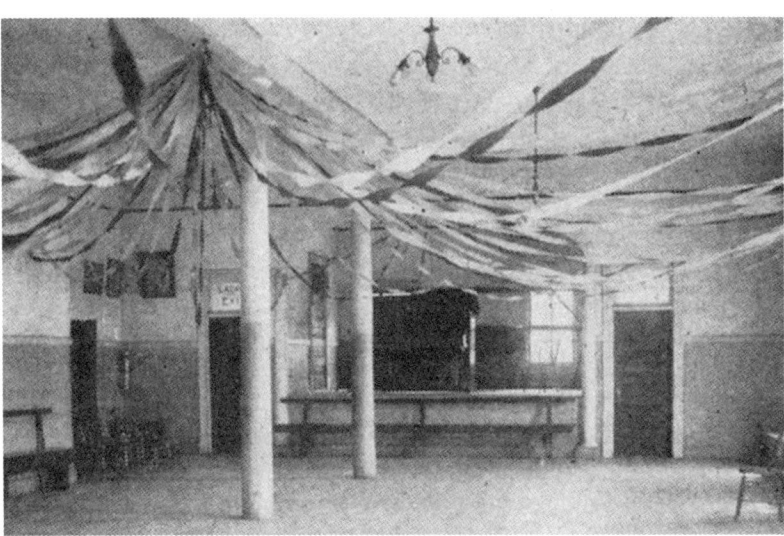

Harleston Funeral Establishment: Harleston Hall, photograph, ca. 1922, brochure. Edwin A. Harleston and Edwina Harleston Whitlock Family Papers, Stuart A. Rose Manuscript, Archives, and Rare Book Library, Emory University.

To keep his recaptured aesthetic momentum going, Harleston painted a portrait of himself, but this was not his first attempt. While attending the SMFA, he completed his initial self-portrait circa 1911 from a photograph he probably had taken while living in Boston.[16] This self-study may have been a class assignment for it lacks the type of detail seen in later works from this period. In this portrait, Harleston presents himself in profile wearing a black suit jacket and a white butterfly-collared shirt. Normally, the subject's face would be the focal point but, in this case, the viewer's attention is drawn to the high tonal value of the shirt collar because of its placement near the center of the picture plane and the dramatic contrast with the black jacket. The artist has placed subtle highlights along the bridge of the nose and cheek of his smooth brown face, but his use of dull shades of brown gives the impression he had never been taught how to successfully depict melanated skin. Harleston has accurately captured his features in his profile, which appear to melt into the dark gray background, but he struggled to treat his ear with the same accuracy (see Plate 2).

Looking at the subject's somber expression and the lack of reflective light in the eye, a psychologists would probably suggest that the dark, somber nature of this painting may have been reflective of Harleston's feelings of loneliness and isolation as the only Black student at the school. But in his informal, three-quarter *Self-Portrait*, completed in 1916, Harleston presents himself in a manner that is quite different from his earlier effort. In this version, the artist is depicted as a serious, yet thoughtful individual who engages the viewer by making direct eye contact. This feeling of compassion has been enhanced by using a warm, neutral color pallet of light brown, tan, and cream colors that have been applied with dynamic brush strokes to define the subject's face and clothing. The primary elements used to structure the face are light and shade. In highlighted areas of the forehead, nose, and cheeks, Harleston has used golden brown tones that are similar in value to the warm colors of the background. In contrast, the shaded sections of his face, which include the mouth, jaw, and neck, have been rendered in darker brown hues that are muddy and void of vibrancy, indicating that Harleston is unsure how to achieve the proper blend of colors in these areas. The failure to imbue the lower section of his face with the same lifelike skin quality seen in the upper area may have been the result of an earlier tendency to simplify and unite areas with shadow. However, it is possible that this variation in facial treatment may also be attributed to the fact that he is still struggling on his own to discover the formula for melanated skin through trial and error.

Edwin continued to develop his painting skills in between work assignments, but his father was becoming impatient with the lack of time and attention he and his brother were giving to the new funeral home. Robert had never shown a great deal of interest in being an undertaker, but since his marriage to Marie Forrest in June of 1915, he had become increasingly unreliable and with the birth of their first child, Gussie Louise Harleston (aka Edwina Augusta Harleston Whitlock) in September of 1916, his attention to the family business had decreased even further. To meet the growing demand for services, Captain Harleston insisted that Edwin put his artwork aside and enroll in the Renouard Training School for Embalmers in New York City to acquire his professional license. On January 2, 1917, Edwin A. Harleston found himself sitting in a lecture hall taking notes for the first of several courses needed for his certification.[17] At the end of six weeks, he had done exceptionally well in all his classes, including the required anatomy, physiology, and chemistry classes. His curriculum at the School of the Museum of Fine Arts and time spent in the science labs at Atlanta University had given him a tremendous advantage over his peers in these areas. As proof of his outstanding performance, Harleston was commended for making the second highest score in the history of the school on the final exam.[18]

The weeks Harleston spent in New York City during the winter of 1917 had been grueling. A late December storm left nearly ten inches of snow on the ground and in the weeks that followed, the temperature only reached a high of twenty-eight degrees.[19] In spite of the wintry weather and long nights studying, Harleston's spirits were buoyed by thoughts of Elise. She had hoped to follow quickly in her sister's footsteps down the aisle, but unlike his brother, Robert, Edwin was in no hurry to marry. In an effort to make his heart grow fonder, Elise moved to Long Island, New York, in 1916, to serve as a matron at the Howard Orphanage and

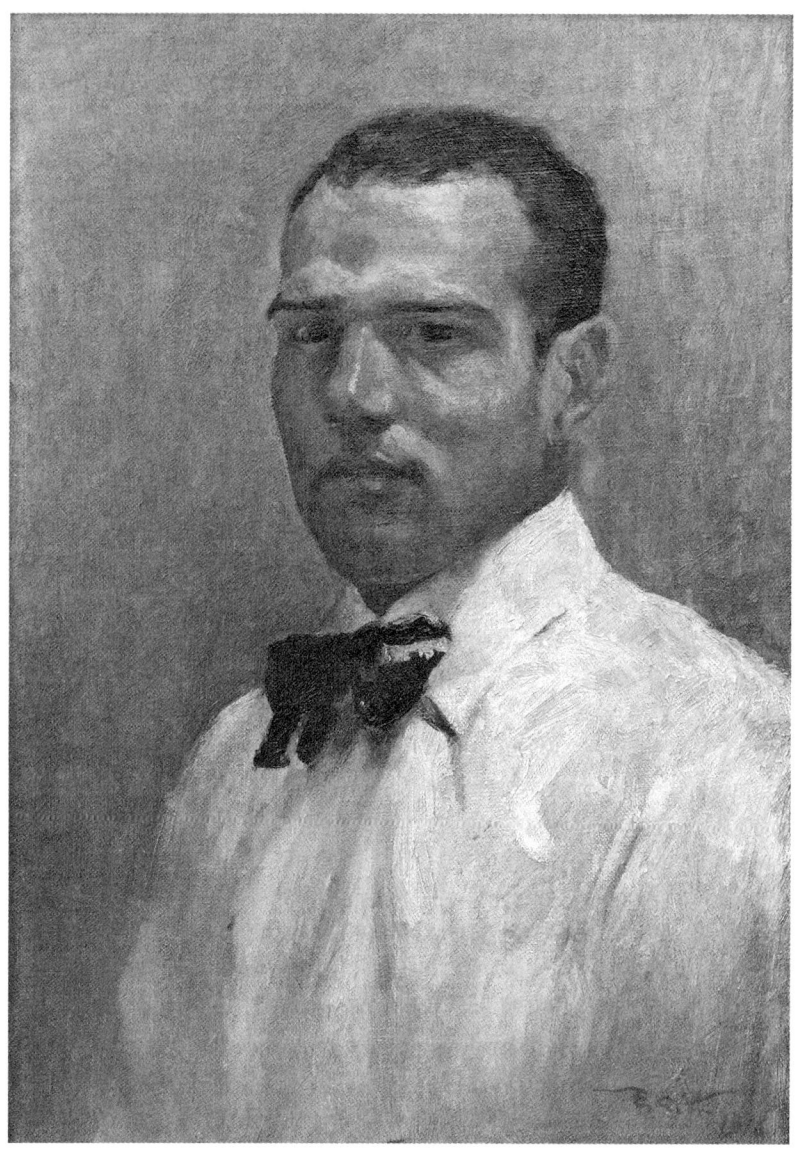

Edwin Augustus Harleston, *Self-Portrait*, *Charleston*, oil on canvas, 1916.
Collection of Mae Whitlock Gentry.

Industrial School.[20] Unwilling to abandon her hope for marriage, Elise spent every weekend she could commuting to the city to be with Edwin while he was in New York. As time passed, Elise became increasingly impatient with Harleston's lack of interest in marriage. In one of her letters she laments, "I had reason to believe that we would by this time be Next door to heaven . . . Christmas coming makes two years we have surely lost." The notes that followed usually included references to marriage, and at one point she tried to use jealousy as a lure by hinting that there were other gentlemen in New York who had expressed a desire to come calling.[21] But nothing seemed to motivate him.

When he returned to Charleston, Harleston's responsibilities at the firm increased exponentially now that he was a certified embalmer, but even with a heavier workload, he refused to give up hope that he would one day become a full-time artist. His ambitions were kept alive by the occasional offers for portrait commissions and illustration work. One such inquiry came from the Western Book Supply Company in Lincoln, Nebraska, shortly after he returned from New York. The publishing company was looking for an artist who could do a series of ink wash drawings for *The Homesteaders*, a new novel by African American writer Oscar D. Micheaux. It seems that another artist had been contracted to do the work, but the publisher was not satisfied with the results and was desperately searching for an immediate replacement. Despite their urgent need, there is no evidence that Harleston responded to their request.[22] He may have ignored the company's solicitation because he was their second choice, but more than likely, his work schedule would not have provided the time needed to meet the one-week deadline set by the book company.[23]

This missed opportunity prompted Harleston to become even more aggressive about moving his art career forward. Although he had received only a few portrait requests since his return, the artist wanted to maintain and improve upon the skills he had acquired at the SMFA, while exploring ways in which he could successfully paint a dignified African American image by mastering the intricacies of melanated skin. The artist's attempt to unlock this mystery is seen in his *Self-Portrait* of 1916 and he continues to grapple with this challenge in *The Little Seamstress* completed in 1918.

In this lovely painting, Edwin Harleston has captured the image of Elise's niece, eleven-year-old Mae Richards, who had recently traveled from Asheville, North Carolina, to visit her Charleston relatives.[24] She is sitting on the arm of a chair, wearing a white dress, white knee socks, and black shoes with her legs crossed at the ankle, cutting a piece of white fabric with a pair of scissors. He has placed his subject against a light brown background that is reminiscent of a Japanese screen, for it is adorned with thin branches bearing tiny white blossoms. The quiet atmosphere he has created, however, is not new, but follows the style of his teacher, Edmund Tarbell, who was known for his Vermeer-influenced portraits of solitary female figures in domestic settings. Harleston has also applied techniques he learned in the classroom for he has constructed his subject's white dress and light brown background with dynamic brushstrokes, reflecting the Impressionistic style of his SMFA painting instructors. Although the skin coloring of his brown girl is still lacking in the tonal vibrancy seen in his earlier student portraits, the artist has been successful in creating a moment of tranquility rarely seen in African American portraits of this period.

In *The Nurse*, a painting he started around 1917, Harleston is still searching for the right paint formula to successfully reproduce African American skin tones. In this painting, the artist has captured a young woman, dressed in a gray and white nurse's uniform carrying a breakfast tray, which holds a silver tea service, cup and saucer, and a large orange. He has replaced the traditional dark atmosphere associated with Boston School portraiture with a bright, textured, yellow ochre background, which gives the painting a light, airy feel. But instead of presenting his subject in the traditional three-quarter pose, accompanied by an introspective gaze, the artist has chosen to present the nurse with a wide-eyed, unflinching stare directed toward the viewer. Although her eyes are captivating, Harleston's flat treatment of her face and limited pallet indicate that he has not yet found the correct color combinations necessary to produce radiant, nuanced skin tones. The artist does, however, show the depth of his skills with the breakfast tray because he has taken great care to render these items with precision, especially the silver sugar bowl, demonstrating his ability to depict dramatic lighting as well as a variety of textures. In so

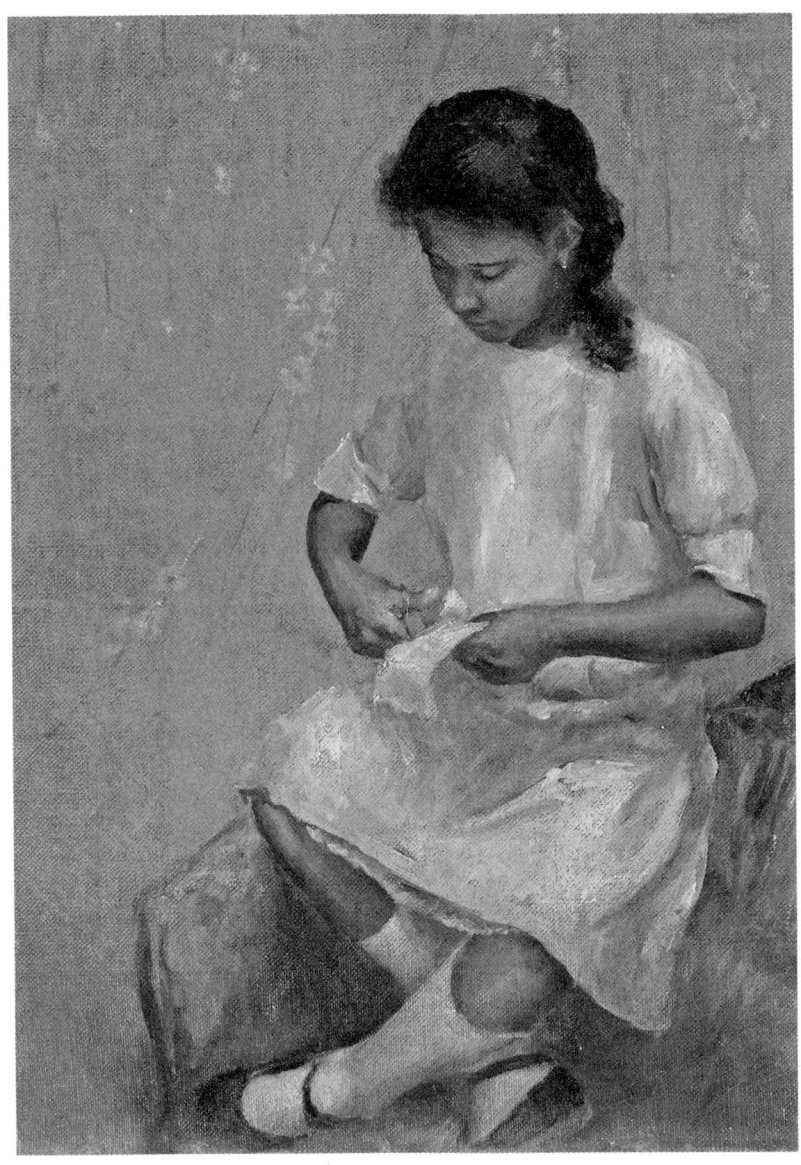

Edwin Augustus Harleston, *The Little Seamstress*, oil on canvas, 1918. Courtesy of the South Carolina State Museum.

doing, Harleston made the tray the main focus of this painting. However, the attention to detail and the accuracy with which he has rendered the tray items compared to the heavy-handed treatment of the face suggests that the artist may have started this painting around 1919 and continued to struggle with the face until the late 1920s.[25]

Although he enjoyed working from pictures he found in books and magazines, what Edwin Harleston needed were live subjects to move his career forward. One of the first steps he took in this effort was to contact his Atlanta University former classmate and friend, Truman K. Gibson, who was the vice president and secretary of Atlanta Mutual Insurance Association (now known as Atlanta Life Insurance Company). Gibson's position with the company placed him in close association with many of Atlanta's most prominent citizens. Therefore, Harleston was convinced that Gibson could introduce him to clients who might be interested in purchasing artwork or having their portraits painted. To augment this strategy, Harleston took the added step of sending a small portrait he had painted of *Sophenie*, the mother of Alonzo Herndon, founder and president of Atlanta Mutual, in an effort to showcase his artistic skills to a potential client. In a letter dated October 16, 1917, Gibson informed Edwin that at first Mr. Herndon had shown little interest in the portrait of his mother, but as the days passed, he grew to deeply admire the painting. As a result, he was now a supporter who stood ready to vouch for Harleston's artistic abilities to any prospective patrons.[26] Even though the insurance company mogul was still not interested in having his own picture painted, Gibson proudly informed his friend that he had secured a commission for a portrait of the Honorable Benjamin Jefferson Davis, district grand secretary and head of the Grand United Order of Odd Fellows, an African American mutual aid and fraternal organization in Georgia. Davis was also a leading Black Republican in Georgia and the editor of the *Atlanta Independent*, which was considered by some to be the most radical newspaper in the South.[27] The portrait recommendation had been introduced at the local lodge meeting, and a price range of fifty to one hundred dollars had been agreed upon. At the end of the correspondence, Gibson implored his friend to respond to their offer immediately and

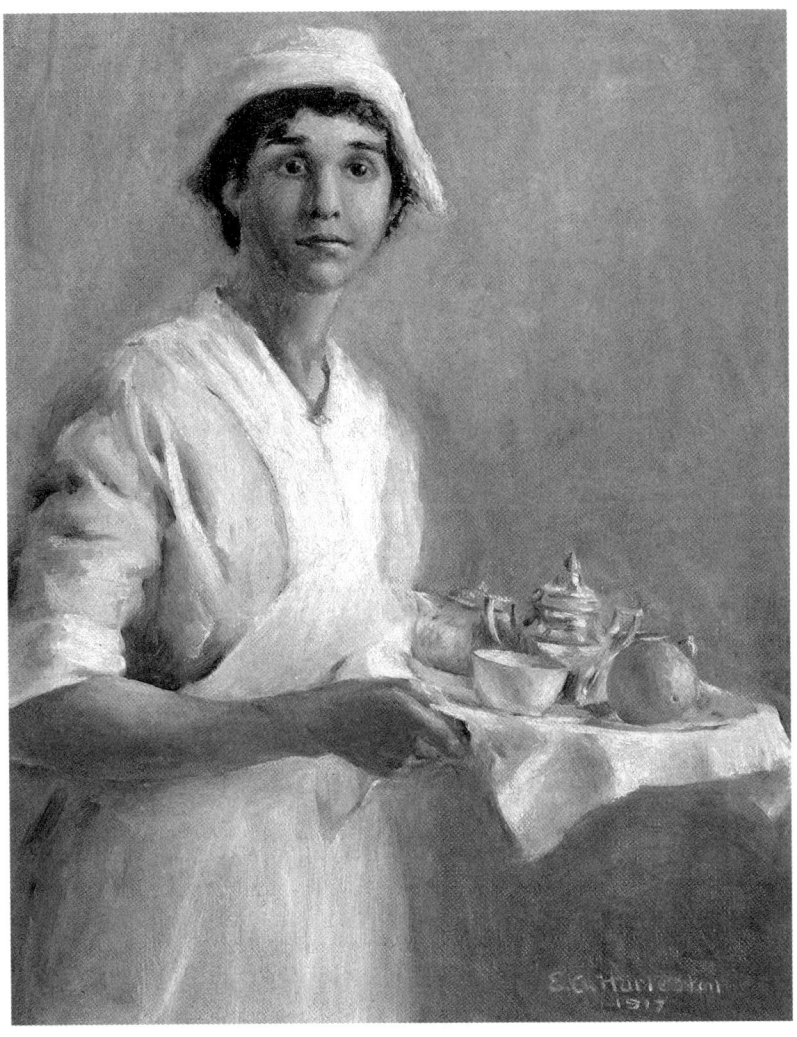

Edwin Augustus Harleston, *The Nurse*, oil on canvas, ca. 1917. Gibbes Museum of Art, Charleston, South Carolina.

advised him not to procrastinate for the Davis portrait was a guaranteed commission.[28]

Edwin Harleston was delighted by this news. The opportunity to create a portrait of Benjamin J. Davis, a man whom many described as "Atlanta's leading colored citizen," was just the kind of commission he needed to launch his career.[29] Because of the importance of this once-in-a-lifetime opportunity, most artists would have responded without hesitation, but Harleston had a penchant for procrastination and perhaps a deep-seated fear of failure that prevented him from acknowledging Gibson's letter immediately.[30] When more than two weeks had passed, Gibson sent the artist an angry note informing him that an announcement of the commission had already appeared in the newspapers. Lodges across the state had also been notified that a life-size portrait would be given as a grand prize in the statewide Odd Fellows membership campaign. At the end of the correspondence, Gibson demanded to know immediately whether Harleston was planning to honor his commitment.[31] Harleston finally responded and made good on his promise by completing the *Portrait of Benjamin J. Davis* (whereabouts unknown) in time for the presentation in February of 1918. The prize was awarded to Century Lodge No. 3435 in Atlanta, the lodge to which Davis held membership.[32] But Harleston's delayed response may have been caused by more than a heavy workload at the funeral home or his fear of failure for there were local, national, and international events whirling around him that would also demand his attention.

———

As RACIAL TENSION BEGAN TO RISE in South Carolina and across the South, lynching became the primary method of terror used to keep African Americans from striving for a better life. With no organizations in position to provide leadership or support when important matters affecting the Black community presented themselves, Harleston felt it was time to establish a local chapter of the National Association for the Advancement of Colored People (NAACP) in Charleston. His continued association with this teacher and friend, Dr. W. E. B. Du Bois, who was now the director of publications and research for the organization, and his affilia-tion with leaders of the Boston branch of the NAACP during his student days gave him the advice and support he needed to form a Charleston chapter. These connections, along with his long-standing reputation as an outgoing civic-minded individual, an eloquent speaker, an enthusiastic civil rights advocate, and a willing community leader, facilitated his elec-tion as the chapter's first president in March of 1917.[33]

The formation of this new branch was not a coincidence. In the eight years since its founding, the NAACP had concentrated its efforts primar-ily in northern cities, but in January of 1917, the national office decided to broaden its base of support into areas where it was needed most, the South.[34] There had been past attempts to form groups in South Carolina and other southern states to address the issue of white supremacy but none had been successful.[35] To remedy the situation, the NAACP decided to develop a new southern district as the association's first line of defense against racial discrimination in Virginia, North Carolina, South Carolina, Georgia, and Florida.[36] This effort was coordinated by James Weldon John-son, the organization's new field secretary. Although Johnson was known as a poet and writer for *The New York Age*, an African American news-paper, he brought much needed insight to this position because he had grown up in Jacksonville, Florida, and spent his college years at Atlanta University, which made him familiar with cultural norms and problems in the South.[37] Johnson felt that in order to win the battle against white supremacy, the southern branches of the NAACP needed to select strong, courageous leaders who were capable of recruiting and leading these fledg-ling chapters. In a letter to Harleston that spring, Johnson implored him to enroll as many new members into the organization as possible for it would be only through strength in numbers that the challenges ahead could be won.[38] Harleston and the other founders of the Charleston Branch had already taken steps to meet this task by enrolling an impressive list of the city's most prominent African American citizens. The twenty-nine names that accompanied their application for charter, dated February 27, 1917, also included the occupations of these new members. The medi-cal professionals represented the largest group, followed by undertakers, businessmen, dressmakers, milliners, tradesmen, as well as school and government employees.[39] In March of that year, the chapter's efforts to recruit members were boosted by a visit and speech from Du Bois, himself, which garnered the chapter twenty additional members.[40]

During Du Bois's visit, members of the Charleston Branch discussed one of the most pressing issues facing their community: allowing "Negro teachers [to] teach Negro children."[41] Unlike other southern cities, Charleston had the distinction of being the only city among all the thirteen former slaveholding states that permitted only white people to teach in African American schools.[42] This was an issue of special significance not only for Harleston and other members of the new NAACP branch but for the entire Black community for it had been made clear through word and deed that these teachers "believed in the inferiority of all Negroes, in the 'supremacy' of the White race, in the absence of all social contact between teacher and taught, in discrimination against Negroes and in limited Negro education."[43] In recent months, the subject had apparently been broached in white circles as well. The 1916 January issue of *The Charleston American* carried an editorial supporting the African American appeal for "colored teachers in the colored schools." The article stated that over the years, white teachers had successfully filled the teacher void created by the lack of professionally trained Black teachers. Now that the shortage had been eliminated, white teachers were no longer needed in "colored" schools. The editorial also debunked the myth that African American children were being educated by white tax dollars which, for many, justified the white-only status of teaching positions in the city by proclaiming that "whoever produces by labor or otherwise the wealth of a community, is of course the REAL TAXPAYER, because it is out of production that taxes must come, and nowhere else." The author closed by stating that while equality between the races can never be achieved, fairness should be the city's goal.[44]

The delicate tone with which this dilemma had been addressed in *The Charleston American* was absent from the editorial that appeared in the April 1917 issue of the NAACP's magazine, *The Crisis.* The article by Du Bois, written less than a month after his visit, accused the city's school system of subjecting Black children to cruel and inhumane treatment by allowing white teachers, who despised their students, to remain in the classroom. The editorialist stated that the school board had given "two and only two reasons for keeping up this farce: first, that they want to teach Black folk their place: and, secondly, that they want to supply certain White people with employment." Because African Americans outnumbered white people in Charleston, Du Bois urged Black citizens to "register, petition, vote and then, if need be, strike and let every child stay at home until teachers were installed who believed them human beings."[45] This call for action did not go unheeded by the Charleston NAACP branch. In December of 1917, Edwin Harleston's cousin, Richard Mickey, who served as chapter secretary, sent a letter to the board of directors of the NAACP requesting support and counsel on the local branch's decision to file a formal grievance against the Charleston Board of Education.[46] A few days later, Mickey received a response from the board stating that the NAACP's national office stood ready to give them "all of the suggestions and advice possible."[47] The fight was on!

———

WHILE PREPARATIONS WERE BEING MADE to confront the school board over the issue of hiring Black teachers, Harleston was also concerned about newspaper articles chronicling the Great War unfolding in Europe. Initially, this event generated little interest among most American citizens, especially those in the Black community. But with the sinking of the ocean liner *Lusitania* by German U-boat, killing 128 Americans, and the destruction of four US cargo ships a month later, President Woodrow Wilson asked Congress to officially declare war with Germany on April 6, 1917. In his appeal to Congress, Wilson stated that the country must enter the war not for territorial gain or national empowerment but for the singular purpose of "making the world safe for democracy."[48]

The majority of Americans supported his assertion, but Wilson's cry for democracy rang hollow among African Americans. Their experience with post-Reconstruction era politics made them wary of this new appeal for global fairness and equality, for Wilson had shown little interest in accommodating the urgent needs of Black citizens. In fact, as soon as he was sworn into office, he placed southern white supremacists in important cabinet positions, implemented racial segregation policies in government agencies such as the post office, which had a large number of African American employees; oversaw the 1915 invasion of Haiti by US Marines, and had a screening of D. W. Griffith's inflammatory film, *Birth of a Nation*, at the White House. The film was adapted, directed, and produced by Griffith and purported to show the "true" history of the Reconstruction era. In fact, the movie was a twisted interpretation of the past that glorified lynching, encouraged prejudice, and falsely represented the character of African Americans, even espousing the undemocratic and unlawful doctrine that all "colored people should be removed from the United States."[49] Its extraordinary combination of visual images and moving picture technology became a dangerous propaganda tool, perpetuating stereotypes in popular entertainment even more powerfully than minstrel shows. But it was not just Griffith's distortion of history itself that made this film so destructive. It was his use of "monstrous caricatures of colored politicians, officials, army officers, soldiers, and servants" as marketing devices that made it so malevolent.[50] Unfortunately, this advertising strategy proved highly effective in drawing larger audiences to the theater than had attended previous films. The NAACP and other Black organizations coordinated protests across the country at theaters showing this provocative, racially divisive movie, but Wilson ignored the criticism and gave the movie his full-throated endorsement.[51]

President Wilson's actions made it clear to many in the Black community that his definition of "democracy" was antithetical to their own characterization of liberty and freedom. As a result, anti-war groups concluded there were battles to be waged against segregation, job discrimination, disfranchisement, and racial violence at home, not in Europe; therefore, Black men were encouraged to refuse the call to foreign military service. In an editorial published in *The Baltimore Afro-American* newspaper, the author recommended the following: "Let us have a real democracy for the United States and then we can advise a house cleaning over on the other side of the water." A New York-based African American magazine, *The Messenger*, published by A. Philip Randolph and Chandler Owens, declared that instead of sending troops abroad to fight in a foreign land, "we would rather make Georgia safe for the Negro."[52] Fearing the impact of these dissenting voices, Congress passed the Espionage Act of 1917 making it a crime punishable by a fine or imprisonment for anyone who interfered with recruitment or refused to participate in military service. The following year, the Sedition Act was passed, which criminalized anyone who spoke out against or published information criticizing the government. In the November 1917 issue of the *Messenger*, the editor sarcastically stated, "Suppression of free-speech and free-press in the United States is making the world safe for democracy."[53]

On the other side of this debate were African American civic leaders who strongly supported the war. Some of the main advocates were W. E. B. Du Bois and members of the NAACP, which now included Edwin Harleston's newly formed chapter. The organization's literary arm, *The Crisis*, with more than thirty thousand subscribers, became the primary tool with which Du Bois spread his message of support for the Great War. In the November 1914 issue, Du Bois boldly stated in his editorial, "World War and the Color Line," that the root cause of the war was not militarism or nationalism as others had claimed, but imperialism. "The triumph of Germany means the triumph of every force calculated to subordinate darker peoples."[54] Three years later, in a 1917 editorial, he clarifies his position by stating that "despite the unfortunate record of England, of Belgium, and of our own land in dealing with colored peoples, we earnestly believe that the greatest hope for ultimate democracy, with no advantageous barriers of race and color, lies on the side of the Allies, with whom our country had become companion in arms." To support this idea, Du Bois asks his readers to examine "...the wretched record of Germany in Africa and her preachment of autocracy and race superiority. The colonization of Africa by England, Belgium, France, and Germany shows a belief in the inferiority of the African people and their contempt for their rights and aspirations."[55]

To illustrate this point, Augustus G. Dill, business manager of *The Crisis* and Atlanta University former classmate, asked Harleston to create a political cartoon for the 1917 March edition of the magazine to remind readers of the atrocities Africans had suffered under European rule.[56] The drawing he submitted, *Voice of Congo*, shows a Congolese man in tattered clothes walking toward a seated European male dressed in a military uniform. The forearms of the African man are extended in an attempt to gain the soldier's attention; however, both of his hands are missing. The seated figure appears to be deep in thought, unaware of the mutilated man's presence. Behind the soldier's head hangs a picture of an older bearded man who is also in uniform. The cartoon's caption reads, *"If your Uncle had left us our hands, Albert, we could be of more use to you now!"* In this drawing, Harleston has skillfully conveyed his opinion regarding one of the most barbaric chapters in the history of European imperialism.

The man in the framed picture is King Leopold II of Belgium, who proclaimed himself the sole owner of what he called "Congo Free State" (now known as the Democratic Republic of Congo) in 1885. He was able to amass a personal fortune by exploiting the natural resources of the country, especially rubber. When the worldwide demand for this natural resource soared, King Leopold used forced indigenous labor to harvest the sap from rubber plants. Workers who did not meet their quota were routinely beaten or killed. However, the cruelest practice was the severing of hands, a tactic used to terrorize laborers in an effort to increase production. After the death of Leopold II, his nephew, Albert I of Belgium, began his rule a few years before the outbreak of World War I. During this conflict, Belgium's army was forced to retreat as German troops advanced and occupied the country.

Du Bois optimistically theorized that despite the mistreatment of African peoples, the victory of our European allies, coupled with Wilson's desire for democratic fairness would also apply to Black people in the United States and "would eventually create new meaning for democracy in the American South."[57] He also described the war as an opportunity to improve the status of all African Americans, believing that as a result of their support they would acquire the rights to full citizenship.[58] But he was not naïve enough to embrace war advocacy without a demand. In *The Crisis* editorial, Du Bois insisted that if Black men were going to be eligible for military draft, then there must be "Negro officers for Negro

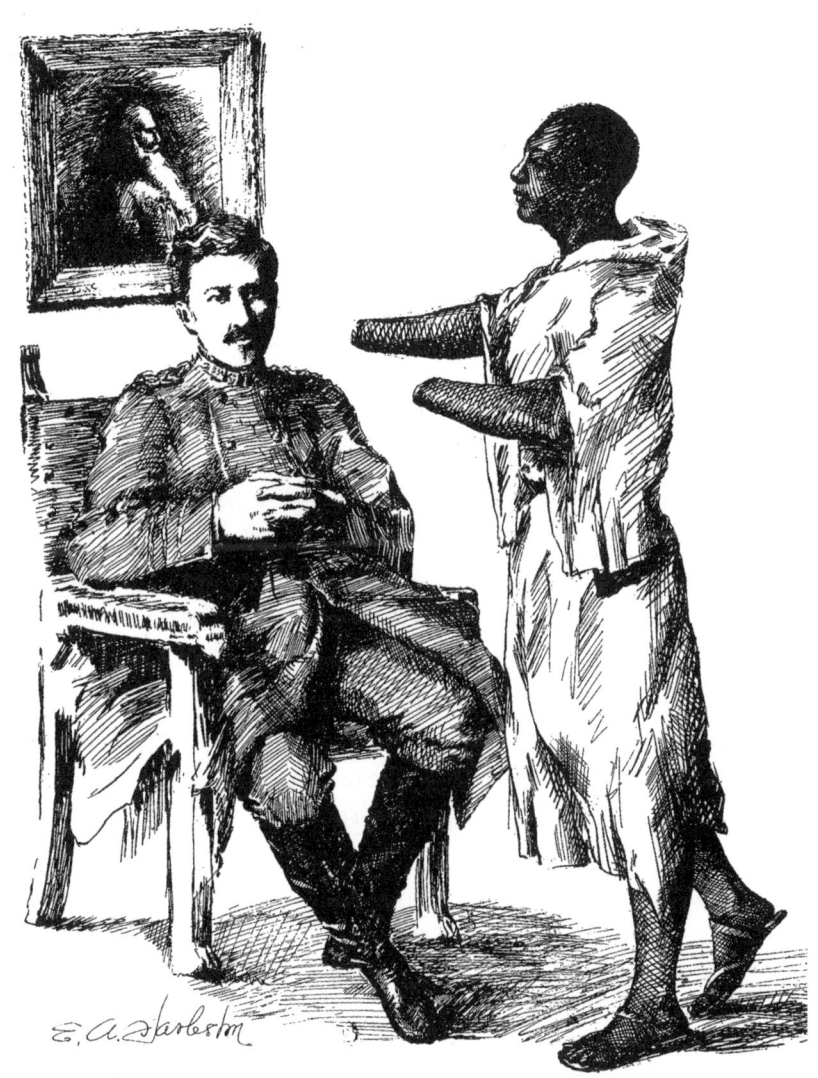

Edwin Augustus Harleston, *Voice of Congo*, political cartoon, March 1917,
The Crisis: A Record of the Darker Race.

troops." He went on to say that if our best and brightest men are going to lead troops of their own race on the battlefield, they must receive officer training in preparation for leadership. But, if the War Department is unwilling to send Black soldiers to white training camps, then they must have a camp of their own.[59]

The idea of a segregated officers' training camp was a source of contention in the Black community as well as the War Department, but for varied reasons. Those who were opposed to a segregated camp felt that it would reenforce Jim Crow laws already in place and guarantee substandard training for Black soldiers. However, decision-makers in Washington, DC, were convinced that these men were intellectually and psychologically incapable of military leadership; therefore, it would be a waste of time and money to establish a "Negro" officer training facility.[60] Senator James K. Vardaman of Mississippi declared that he was against African Americans serving in the military at any level, for it meant that they would be armed and he knew "of no greater menace to the South than this."[61]

Even though the idea of a segregated officers' training camp received strong opposition from both Black and white critics, the project was approved by the War Department and pushed forward by Joel Elias Spingarn, a white intellectual who was one of the incorporators and first president of the NAACP. Spingarn considered segregation an unacceptable social condition, but he felt that a separate camp was only the first step toward a more open racial policy in the US armed forces.[62] A location for the camp was the next hurdle. The campuses of Howard University, Morgan College, Tuskegee and Hampton Institutes were offered as suggested sites, but Brigadier General Joseph E. Kahn, chief of the War College Division, objected to these locations because there were too many possible distractions.[63] To avoid scrutiny from the press and public embarrassment if the experiment failed, Fort Des Moines in Iowa was chosen as the campsite.[64] In February of 1917, Spingarn assisted in the campaign to recruit the best candidates by sending an open letter to "Educated Colored Men of the United States" requesting that they enroll in the officers' training camp or assist with identifying eligible men.[65] Edwin Harleston must have submitted a list of names, for in early May, he received a letter from

First Lieutenant E. B. Garney, the acting officer in charge of the training camp, thanking him for compiling information on possible recruits for the new Des Moines, Iowa, installation. Garney's correspondence describes Harleston as a "double A man" who is "morally and mentally equipped" to become an officer.[66] Shortly after the recruitment letter was circulated, it was announced that the three-month Fort Des Moines Provisional Army Officer Training School would be opening in Des Moines, Iowa, on May 19, 1917, with approximately 1,250 candidates in attendance.

Apparently, Harleston's business and civic responsibilities, along with his father's political connections, kept him from being inducted in the early rounds of the draft. But on September 12, 1917, his brother, Robert O. Harleston and his cousin, Edward C. Mickey, registered for military duty and were sent to Fort Des Moines.[67] They were joined by an exceptional group of men comprised of college professors, physicians, lawyers, business leaders, undertakers, star athletes, and students from Ivy League and historically Black colleges. These new recruits were described in a camp report as "remarkably strong, earnest and well-educated."[68] Unfortunately, living quarters at the camp were less than desirable, but most of the men were proud to be there.[69] Lieutenant Colonel Charles Young, a West Point graduate and the highest ranking Black army officer at the time, was originally appointed to train this inaugural class of potential officers, but he was deemed physically unfit to serve and was forced to retire. Young's replacement, Colonel Charles Ballou, had previous experience training Black soldiers and respected their ability as fighters but questioned their ability to lead. As a result of Ballou's recommendation, the African American officers training program was abbreviated to include combat strategies only; a curriculum that was vastly different from their white counterparts.[70] Black newspapers were filled with articles detailing how soldiers were given substandard training, routinely harassed by white army officers while on duty and by civilians on the street.[71] Hostility over issues of African American leadership in the military, poor living condition and widespread mistreatment grew to such levels that the United States War Department decided to close the officers' training camp on October 14, 1917, after less than five months of operation.[72]

Despite this setback, the support of African American soldiers by their community remained strong, for these men had become "symbols of patriotism, racial pride, manhood, and citizenship."[73] As a demonstration of loyalty to the troops, churches, clubs, and other institutions throughout South Carolina made donations to statewide Liberty bond drives and war savings stamp purchases. Civic organizations showed their support by collecting supplies for the Red Cross and launching programs to boost the morale of Black soldiers whenever possible.[74] These widespread efforts to encourage those serving in the military may have inspired Edwin Harleston to write and produce his first two-act play entitled *The War Cross*. This patriotic drama, which Harleston also directed, focuses on a young soldier, Phillip Harris, who has just returned home to Beaufort, South Carolina, after being seriously wounded in France. Prior to his homecoming, word had spread throughout his community that he had been given the French War Cross for his valor, but there is some confusion as to which Phillip Harris had been awarded the medal of honor for there are several soldiers on the list of recipients with the same name. Because the honor came with additional financial benefits, Harris's fiancée, Carrie, is unwilling to commit to marriage until he can prove that he has received the medal. When he refuses, Carrie rejects his proposal of marriage, but after her departure, Phillip reveals that he had, in fact, receive the coveted Croix de Guerre.[75] *The War Cross* would be considered melodramatic by today's standards; however, the production succeeded in recognizing the racial, physical, and emotional "cross" Black soldiers bore during the war for the sake of an elusive democracy. The play opened in Harleston Hall to a capacity crowd in August of 1918. When the final curtain closed, the audience, as well as the Atlanta University Club of Charleston, which sponsored the production as a fundraiser, declared Harleston's play an undeniable success.[76]

As the European conflict wore on, more young men from the Charleston area were called upon to serve. On September 12, 1918, Edwin Augustus Harleston also joined this group by registering for the military. He was now thirty-six years of age and described on his draft card as medium height and "stout."[77] During the previous two years, he had been actively involved in supporting the officers' training camp, participating in local fundraisers, building Charleston's local NAACP chapter while working full-time at the funeral home. Harleston's brother, Robert, had described his experience at Fort Des Moines as miserable and some family members believe he may have contracted tuberculosis at the camp.[78]

With this knowledge, why would Harleston willingly join the military at this stage of his life? More than likely, he was called to register for the draft, but the war ended less than two months later, vacating his mandate to serve; however, this did not keep him from trying to help his country. Shortly before the war ended, Harleston was asked by the Young Men's Christian Association's (YMCA) National War Work Council to assist with an educational program designed to help African American soldiers in France. The US Army allowed their men a one-week leave every four months for rest and recreation. During this time, they could participate in a wide range of leisure activities or take education courses in basic English as well as college-level classes, but Black soldiers did not have access to the majority of these programs. The War Department became concerned that their military service record might become tarnished because of misconduct on the part of African American troops, especially when it came to unsupervised fraternization with women. In an effort to make sure these men stayed out of trouble, a plan was devised to occupy their time with education programs and rigorous drills, in spite of the fact that several Black regiments had received citations from the French High Command for bravery.[79]

The content of the instruction Harleston was expected to provide is not known, but he enthusiastically embraced the opportunity to travel to France with the hope he would find enough time during his assignment to visit the Louvre and other great museums while in Europe. The thought of going to Paris, if only for a few days, to walk in the footsteps of his teachers and other American artists who had preceded him, along with the hope of visiting the famous African American expatriate artist Henry Ossawa Tanner filled Edwin Harleston with excitement. In preparation for the trip, he sent out requests for the required letters of recommendation and had his passport picture taken, but before all of the necessary paperwork had been gathered, the program ended along with his dream of going to France.[80]

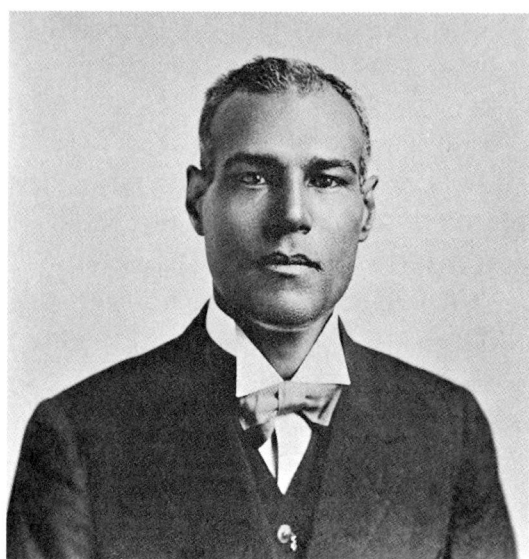

Passport photograph of Edwin Augustus Harleston, 1918.
Collection of M. Akua McDaniel.

To ease his disappointment, Harleston redirected his attention toward his artwork and continued developing the theme of sacrifice for cause and country in a series of paintings depicting aspects of the Great War. One such work, *The Gas Attack*, completed in 1919, was probably based on a photograph from a magazine or newspaper. In this painting, Harleston shows three Black soldiers dressed in full battle gear coming over the crest of a hill during a chlorine gas attack. The man in the middle of this triangular composition and the ones to the right are wearing helmets, gas masks, and carrying rifles with fixed bayonets. However, the figure to the left has lost his protective gear and is being overcome by gas fumes. Just behind these three men is a group of soldiers similarly attired but crouching close to the ground as they struggle through the barbed-wire barricades to reach the top of the hill. These troops are partially obscured by the thick gas haze surrounding them and filling the sky overhead. Harleston has made the stricken soldier the focal point of this painting by using strong tonal values to model the figure and reinforcing this contrast with

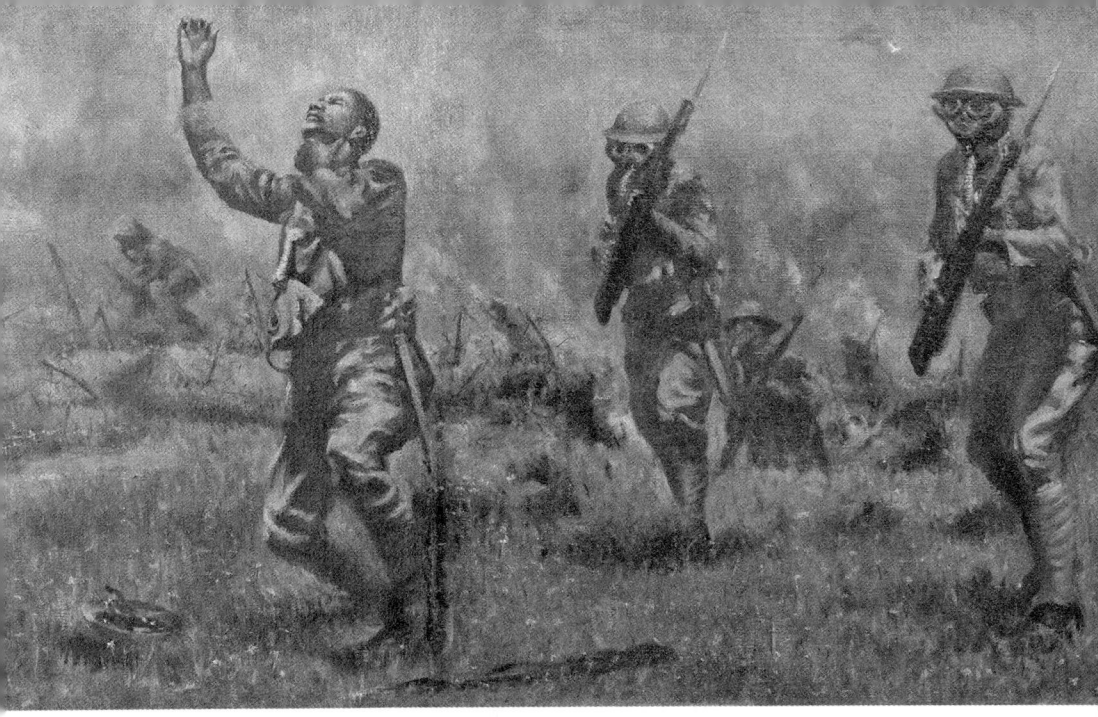

Edwin Augustus Harleston, *The Gas Attack*, oil on canvas, 1919.
Collection of Mae Whitlock Gentry.

a cloud of light smoke rising behind the subject. The drifting gas clouds, and the background soldiers also create diagonal lines that guide the viewer toward the stricken figure, further strengthening his position as the central focus. It is interesting to note that although Harleston employs a somber color scheme of soft blues and browns in a manner associated with Tonalism, he applies the paint to the field in the foreground using an Impressionistic technique. The landscape is structured through a series of short, broken strokes of dark green juxtaposed by flecks of brown or blue with dabs of white scattered throughout; an Impressionist's technique influenced by his teachers Benson and Tarbell.

When *The Gas Attack* was put on display in Harleston Hall, this painting, which dramatically captured the horrors of war, generated a sad and often tearful response from viewers. While Harleston's life-size portrait of a Charleston army officer, whose last name was Grant, evoked a sense of reassurance and pride in all who saw it. This painting, entitled *The Soldier*, may have been inspired by the words written in an opinion piece by Du Bois in *The Crisis* (May 1919), which read:

> We return.
>
> We return from fighting.
>
> We return fighting.
>
> Make way for Democracy! We saved it in France, and by the
>   Great Jehovah, we will save it in the United States of
>   America or know the reason why.[81]

Grant was a decorated Army sergeant who served in the Ninety-third Infantry Division, a segregated "colored" unit of the United States Army that assisted the French military during the war. Harleston has taken great care to communicate Grant's history of exemplary service to viewers by including his medals, the Croix de Guere and the Médaille militaire, decorations awarded by the French for heroism during combat. On the left sleeve of his jacket, Grant displays his Army stripes which indicate his rank along with two gold chevrons symbolizing his twelve months of active duty abroad. The artist completes his subject's military profile with the round Blue Helmet shoulder insignia conclusively identifying him as a member of the celebrated Ninety-third Division.[82] But more important, Edwin Harleston has presented his subject as an archetype of the African American military recruit who is prepared to win respect abroad and at home, no matter the cost. With folded arms resting at his waist and his steady gaze directed at the viewer, this soldier presents the image of a proud, determined man who is resolute in his quest to have his rights as an American citizen acknowledged and affirmed.[83]

———

WHEN WORLD WAR I OFFICIALLY ENDED on November 11, 1918, winds of change were already blowing across the state and the nation. Seventy-eight Black people had been lynched that year during a continuing reign of terror, including men in uniform returning from the war. But there was also a new sense of self-determination spurring those who had traditionally existed on the margins of poverty and despair to seek new lives in the North. For African Americans who chose not to join the Great Migration, the local branch of the NAACP provided the opportunity to make their

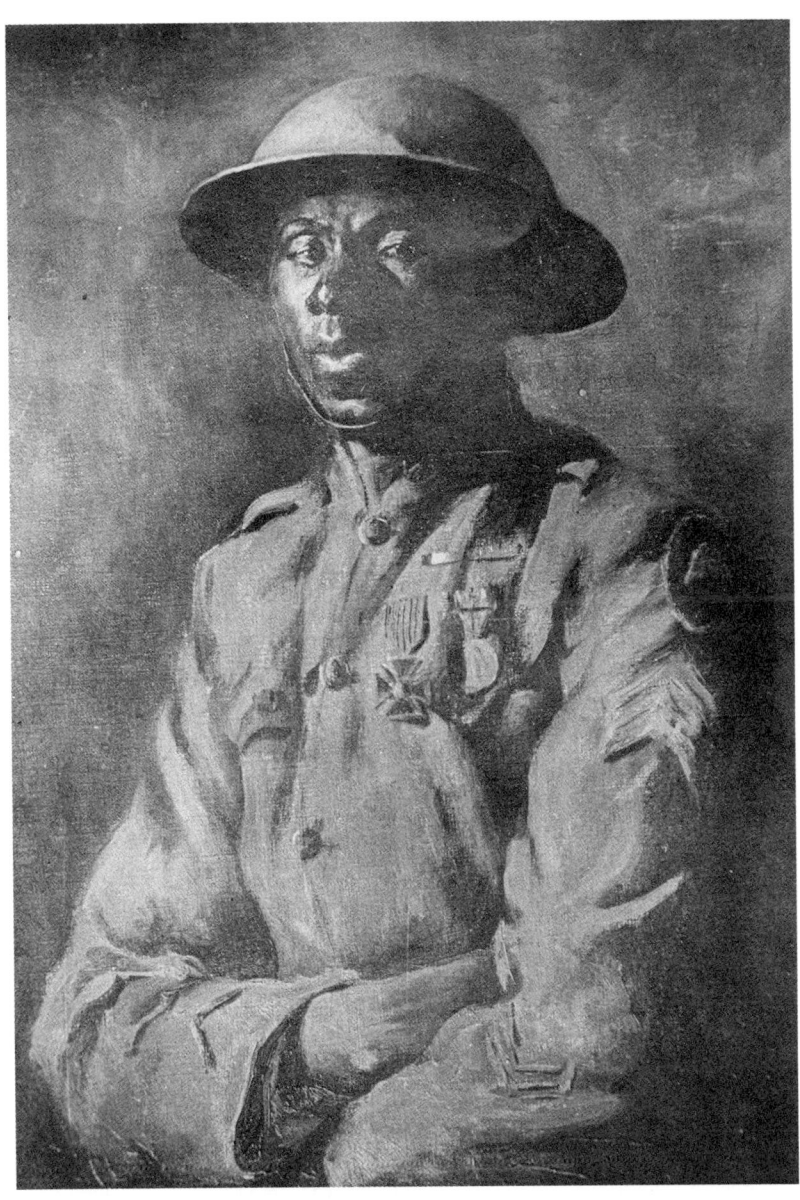

Edwin Augustus Harleston, *The Soldier*, oil on canvas, 1919. Courtesy National Archives photo no. H-HN-HARL-7. The whereabouts of the original painting are unknown.

sacrifices meaningful by standing their ground and fighting for justice on home soil. The integration of Black teachers into the Charleston public school system was still at the top of their list of priorities, and yet, this effort was sidetracked once again by innumerable requests for assistance with problems ranging from identifying war dead to helping with the prosecution of a white man who murdered a Black mechanic.[84] The chapter had also taken the lead in a labor dispute involving six hundred new jobs being advertised by the Charleston naval base clothing factory with the restriction that "only white women . . . need apply." This conflict was finally resolved when the Navy agreed to employ 250 African American women in their factory.[85] With the settlement of these issues, the branch redirected their efforts toward the school problem.

On January 14, 1919, a petition with ten thousand signatures was submitted to the Board of School Commissioners of the City of Charleston requesting the inclusion of "negro teachers in the free public schools."[86] The document also carried the signatures of Thomas E. Miller, who chaired the petition drive, followed by branch members William H. Johnson, John M. Thompson, Charles C. Jacobs, secretary; and Edwin A. Harleston, president. Miller was selected to spearhead the petition effort because of his skill as an attorney, his leadership in the state Republican Party, his close association with the state House of Representatives and the Senate, and his reputation as a respected educator.[87] Despite Miller's political power, the board adopted the following position effectively protecting the immediate future of city school funding:

> On motion, it ordered that as the enlargement of the Charleston public
> school facilities, both for white and for colored children is dependent
> on a bond issue now pending, the board at present is not in a position
> to change the personnel of the teaching staff in the colored schools, but
> that when the enlargement of the school system contemplated has taken
> place . . . the board hopes . . . to be able to give favorable consideration to
> this petition.[88]

In anticipation of rejection from the Charleston school board, members of the NAACP held sixteen mass meetings across the city to inform the community that a second petition was being written for presentation to the governor, the state superintendent of education, and members of the state legislature at a meeting of the South Carolina General Assembly on January 18, 1919, and volunteers were needed to gather signatures. On the morning the committee left for Columbia, they were greeted at the train station by throngs of volunteers with signed petitions, which stated that "we, the citizens of the Negro race and parents of pupils of the aforesaid race in attendance as pupils of the public schools of Charleston, do, through our committee . . . most respectfully petition for assistance and relief from the uncalled for, unnecessary, unusual, abnormal conditions that surround and control the management, instruction and teaching of the children of the aforesaid race in the public schools of the city of Charleston."[89] Those who had signed the document asked that "the civil code of 1912 be so amended that negroes be allowed to teach in the negro schools."[90] The closing paragraph of the petition states that the committee was not a self-constituted committee of "a few highbrows and mulattoes trying to do what the real Negro of Charleston did not want done," as claimed by Charleston Senator A. R. Young and other members of the legislative body, but authentic representatives of 22,755 African American citizens (equaling nearly two-thirds of the population) from the City of Charleston who simply wanted the General Assembly to apply "the golden rule" in reaching their decision.[91] But Senator Young refused to support the NAACP's effort. Fortunately, Miller had maintained a good relationship with several members of the General Assembly, including House Representative R. A. Meares of Fairfield County, who agreed to draft a letter to Senator Young requesting his support for a one-year transition period.[92] After September 1, 1920, it would be "unlawful for a person of the white race to teach in the free public schools in the State of South Carolina that have been designated and set aside for children of the negro race."[93] Young finally agreed, and the measure passed, giving the Charleston Branch of the NAACP its first major triumph!

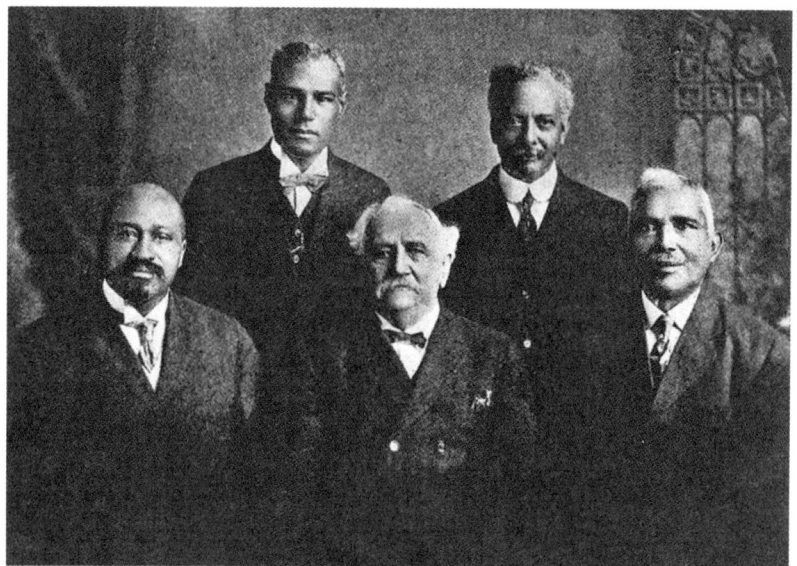

The Charleston Committee, photograph, June 1921. Front row (*left* to *right*): Dr. W. H. Johnson, Hon. Thomas E. Miller, Dr. J. M. Thompson; back row: E. A. Harleston, Rev. C. C. Jacobs. *The Crisis: A Record of the Darker Race.*

News of this victory and Harleston's role in its success spread quickly. Atlanta University President Edward T. Ware wrote Harleston congratulating him on overturning teacher segregation in the Charleston public schools and promised to inform any Atlanta University graduates who might be interested in applying for a teaching position that the public schools in Charleston were hiring.[94] Mary White Ovington, NAACP board chairman, invited Harleston to speak about the success of the Charleston school campaign at the organization's Tenth Anniversary Conference in Cleveland, Ohio.[95] This correspondence was followed by a letter of recognition from Du Bois asking Harleston to submit an article on the teachers' fight for *The Crisis* magazine.[96]

Although Harleston's achievement as leader of the Charleston Branch of the NAACP had brought him national recognition, he felt he could best memorialize the committee's success by painting a *Portrait of Thomas E. Miller*, the architect of this transformational achievement.

February 10, 1920.

Mr. E. A. Harleston,
121 Calhoun Street,
Charleston, S. C.

My dear Mr. Harleston:

I want very much to have
for THE CRISIS the full story of
your fight for colored teachers
and its final outcome. Will you
write it and send it to me at
your earliest convenience?

My best regards to all
my friends.

Very sincerely yours,

WEBD/PF

W. E. B. Du Bois

*Could you send us some
photos of schools & teachers?*

Typewritten letter signed by W. E. B. Du Bois. Edwin A. Harleston and Edwina Harleston
Whitlock Family Papers, Stuart A. Rose Manuscript, Archives, and Rare Book Library,
Emory University.

This formal portrait of Miller is executed in a manner closely associated with the Boston school of portraiture, for Harleston has placed his subject against a dark background using dramatic value contrasts and a limited palette to construct the figure. The artist focuses the viewer's attention on Miller's light brown face and hands by placing them in stark contrast to the dark background and the subject's black suit. When this portrait was painted, Miller had served in the South Carolina House of Representatives, the state senate, chaired the state Republican Party and he had served in the United States Congress from South Carolina. Following his illustrious political career, he was appointed the first president of the Colored Normal, Industrial, Agricultural, and Mechanical College (now South Carolina State University).[97] Edwin Harleston is able to present Miller as a regal statesman by meeting the viewer's gaze with dignity and authority. The artist did not think it necessary to include any of the traditional props used to symbolize his subject's political status or intellectual prowess but relied instead on Miller's self-assured facial expression and formal body language to convey his influence and power (see Plate 3).

After completing the painting of Miller, Harleston received numerous requests for portraits, but his involvement with civil rights, the war effort, and the family business kept him from accepting most of the commissions. He did, however, honor a request made by the alumni of his alma mater to paint a *Portrait of Dr. Myron Winslow Adams*, dean of faculty at Atlanta University, in recognition of his thirty years of service to the institution.[98] Adams is shown wearing a black suit, white shirt, and gray tie and is placed against a dark, grayish-green background. Although the color scheme in this portrait is primarily neutral, Harleston structures the face with flesh tones laced with delicate strokes of pink and yellow in the highlighted areas and pale blue and violet in the shadows. His technique of infusing Adams's pale complexion with pastel hues helps to give it a measure of vitality and interest, but this is not enough to prevent the portrait from appearing bland and spiritless. The dry personality that emanates from this image of Adams may have reflected his true character, judging by the favorable public responses when the portrait was officially unveiled during a special ceremony held in Atlanta University's chapel on November 29, 1919. Members of the school newspaper, *The Crimson and Gray*, reported that "Mr. Harleston had caught that something from Dr. Adams' personality and put it into the portrait." While other visitors marveled at the "life-like" quality of the work, everyone who saw the painting agreed that it was "a very good portrait indeed."[99]

After the Adams commission, Harleston continued developing his portrait-painting skills by using his siblings as subjects. Evidence of his continued growth can be seen in the impressive portraits of his older sister, *Katherine Isabelle Harleston Fleming*, and older brother, *John Moultrie Harleston*, which were also completed in 1919. The painting of Katherine Harleston Fleming is similar to Harleston's earlier *Self-Portrait*, for he has placed her in a three-quarter pose against a gray background infused with the same rose-colored accents. The artist has also repeated the loose brushwork used in his earlier work to structure his sister's elegant black dress and its white, V-shaped collar with scalloped edges. But instead of revealing some aspects of Katherine Fleming's inner spirit, Harleston has kept the viewer at a distance by presenting her at an introspective moment with her gaze averted from the observer. The artist does not use as much color in the background of his portrait of *Katherine Isabelle Harleston Fleming* or *John Moultrie Harleston* as he did in his own self-study. Harleston chose instead to return to a darker background and the simplified treatment of form. This point is substantiated by the *Preliminary Sketch for the John Moultrie Harleston* painting in which he clearly maps out the highlights, middle, and darker values of the figure. Although the use of color is subordinate to his interest in light and shadow, Harleston has finally mastered the tonal subtlety of African American skin color, for both subjects possess the glowing, golden brown complexion that he seemed to have been striving for in his *Self-Portrait*.

Painting portraits of family members and friends seemed to have occupied much of Harleston's studio time. But in the fall of 1919, the opportunity for which he had been waiting finally arrived. A group of employees at Atlanta Mutual Insurance Company wanted to express their appreciation for the arduous work Alonzo Herndon had done for the company and the community. After much discussion, the employees decided

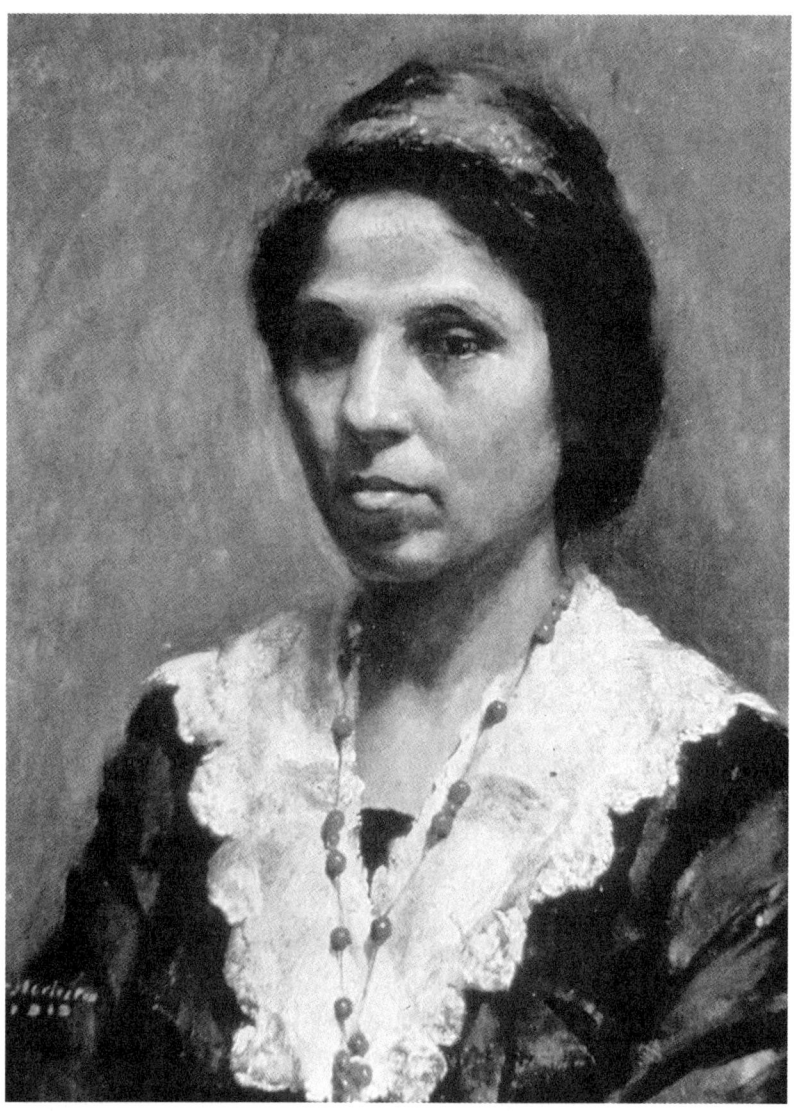

Edwin Augustus Harleston, *Katherine Isabelle Harleston Fleming*, oil on canvas, 1919.
Collection of Mr. Martin Fleming.

that a life-size portrait of their company's president and founder would be a fitting tribute. The artist they selected for this important commission was Edwin A. Harleston. Their choice was probably based on the fact that most of the committee members were familiar with his work since several of Harleston's portraits hung in the homes of prominent Atlanta citizens and on the Atlanta University campus. A local newspaper enthusiastically praised Harleston's selection describing him as "one of the greatest portrait painters in the country" and declaring that Herndon was to be "honored in a remarkable way."[100]

Harleston began preparing for the commission immediately because he knew it might be an important turning point in his career. His portfolio contained several unidentified sketches of portraits by other American artists, but his sketch of the George Hearn portrait appears to have been the prototype for this commission. The original *Portrait of George Arnold Hearn*, an American art collector and industrialist, was painted by Irving Ramsey Wiles (1862–1948) and hangs in the Metropolitan Museum in New York.[101] There is a distinct possibility that Harleston was familiar with Wiles's work for he was modestly successful during the time Harleston was attending the SMFA and was considered a master Tonalist painter.[102] Furthermore, Wiles's painting style was often compared with that of his teacher, Frank Benson, making Harleston's knowledge of the artist even more probable.[103] In any case, Harleston's notation of the name of the work, the artist, the location, and size of the painting at the top of his sketch and notes on how Wiles treated the light in the lower half of the drawing indicates that he had more than just a passing interest in the painting.[104] It is difficult to determine whether or not Harleston did this preliminary sketch from the actual portrait or from a photograph, since he often asked his friends in New York to send pictures of well-known paintings.[105] But the hasty manner in which his drawing was rendered strongly suggests that Harleston may have been working from the original painting, for he was very familiar with the Metropolitan Museum as well as the New York City Public Library and its collection of prints and photographs of important works of art.[106]

Under normal circumstances, the next step in determining the source of Harleston's compositional model would be to examine the two paintings to see how closely they compare, but unfortunately, the *Portrait of Alonzo F. Herndon* has been cropped to bust size. Although only half of the painting remains, evidence supports the probability that Harleston used the Hearn portrait as his prototype. In a letter written in December of 1919 to Elise, Harleston included a small sketch of the Hearn portrait and described the painting as being nearly full length and 4 × 6 feet in size.[107] The pen-and-ink sketch in the body of this letter is compositionally identical to the Wiles portrait.[108] Although only the upper third of the Herndon portrait remains, it is clear that Harleston employed the same tonal approach in the *Portrait of Alonzo F. Herndon* that he used in the Adams painting.

When the portrait was unveiled at a special ceremony held in Atlanta's First Congregational Church, public response was overwhelmingly favorable.[109] His duties at the funeral home in Charleston kept Harleston from attending the celebration; however, friends who were present wasted little time in writing to inform the artist of his success. One of the letters proclaimed Harleston's portrait of Herndon a triumph and informed the artist that there were several patrons who would be anxiously awaiting his return to Atlanta in the spring. Harleston was pleased with the public's response to his work but in a letter to Elise he expressed disappointment at not being offered more commissions. At the close of this correspondence, Harleston voiced his hope that the state of his artistic career would soon be improving.[110]

———

NOT ONLY WOULD HARLESTON'S ART CAREER improve during the coming decade, but his personal life would also change. In the midst of managing a business, community initiatives, and an art career, Edwin and Elise were also growing closer. Although she was still living in New York, Harleston visited her whenever he could, but their letters helped to erase the miles that separated them. During one of his visits, Harleston gave Elise a box Brownie camera and encouraged her to practice taking pictures. To demonstrate her budding interest in photography, Elise would often enclose photos of interesting subjects or pictures of herself in her letters along with playful hints about marriage: "May I get ready for 'a trip to the moon' in September?" she asked, but his responses were usually ambiguous.[111]

In an effort to hasten their wedding plans, Elise made the decision to become actively involved in Harleston's art career. When talking about his portrait commissions, he would often mention the importance of photographs as a painting aid for portrait and genre painters. She knew Harleston held the art of photography in high esteem; so, to make herself indispensable to him, she decided to enter photography school. On September 15, 1919, Elise Forrest officially became a student at the Emile Brunel Training School of Photography in New York (now the New York Institute of Photography).[112] Brunel, a French immigrant artist and photographer who had been trained in Paris, opened a photography store at 1269 Broadway, near Penn Station, in 1910 to demonstrate and sell photography equipment, but the growing demand for formal instruction in the use of the camera convinced him to open a school. In an ad that appeared in *The American Magazine* the same year Elise applied, the school claimed it would teach students the art of photography in a few months with special emphasis in the techniques of photoetching and photoengraving.[113] Harleston was elated with her decision to study photography, and to show his support he sent Elise one hundred dollars to pay for her tuition and five dollars spending money along with "wishes for success."[114]

When Elise arrived for her first day of classes, she was surprised by the institution's diverse student body, which included German, Irish, and Japanese photographers who were anxious to learn new picture-taking techniques; however, she was one of two African Americans and the only woman studying at the school. Considering these facts, the atmosphere at Brunel was unexpectedly open, cordial, and supportive. Her classmates were always willing to help her, and the instructor encouraged Elise by giving her negatives to retouch in order to assess her artistic aptitude. Even though she was doing well in her classes and making a little money with small side jobs, Elise was growing homesick with each passing day. Harleston, however, dismissed her longing as a temporary case of melancholy, admonishing her not to "court the blues."[115] To buoy her spirits, he lavished her with praise in his letters and urged her to learn everything she possibly could about portrait photography and methods of photographing drawings and paintings.[116]

With a heavy heart, twenty-eight-year-old Elise Forrest continued with her studies. But it was more than just homesickness that was causing her to lose interest in photography, for it had become evident that success in her courses had still not been enough to convince Harleston to propose marriage.[117] In a final attempt to win him over, Elise sent Harleston a letter telling him she would not be returning to Charleston at the end of her studies because she had been offered a job in Washington, DC, in the Census Bureau. She was accepting this position not only for the income, but also for the opportunity to work part-time at the photography studio of Addison N. Scurlock, a nationally recognized African American photographer whose excellence in the field had been acknowledged with a gold medal at the Jamestown Exposition in 1907.[118] When Harleston received this news, he did not respond immediately. But in an undated letter to Elise he shares his feelings about the evolution of their relationship by telling her

> Today I had occasion to look through a batch of my mother's old papers and letters and found documents which I had read often . . . But two in particular are of general interest. Of these, one is the Bill of Sale delivered to my Great-great grandmother in 1804 when she bought herself and Flora her little daughter from slavery—brave woman. The other is the deed of emancipation and manumission which she presented to her daughter Flora in 1820 so that this daughter might marry there as a free woman of color . . . That was a hundred years ago. Nineteen hundred and twenty must be our year. It may seem like more than a hundred years since first we met, and it has been a fairly long time but then you know we have not been in love that long—I didn't know you and you surely didn't know me, but love did come—it grew with me which is safer than

a flashing spirit. You must know that I regard it (love) as a holy thing . . .
of course I love you, of course I want you, of course we will marry, and of
course it will be this year.[119]

On July 12, 1920, he wrote to Elise's mother, Elvira Forrest, asking for
her daughter's hand in marriage.[120] Now that he was thirty-eight years of
age, the accumulating years of loneliness were beginning to weigh heavily
on him. After seven years of delay, Harleston realized that he loved Elise
and needed her by his side to provide the kind of support only a loving
spouse could give.[121]

Perhaps as a tribute to his bride-to-be, Harleston painted a *Portrait
of Elise* from a photograph she had given him. The painting is comparable
in style and technique to the earlier paintings of his siblings; however, the
expression on Elise's face is quite different. In previous works, Harleston
surrounded his subjects with an introspective aura that places an invisi-
ble barrier between the subject and the viewer. But in this painting, Elise
looks directly at the viewer with a steady, determined gaze. By presenting her in this manner, Harleston felt that he had so successfully captured
Elise's essence that he often had "little chats" with the painting in the days
before their marriage (see Plate 4).[122]

On September 15, 1920, at one o'clock in the afternoon, Edwin
Harleston and Elise Forrest were united in holy matrimony by the Reverend Henry H. Proctor in a private ceremony held in the parsonage of the
Nazarene Congregational Church in Brooklyn, New York.[123] There was no
white satin gown, flowing veil, or flowers—just the two of them along with
Harleston's cousin, Rosalie Mickey, and a few close friends who served as
witnesses. After they exchanged vows, the couple boarded the *Metropolitan SS Calvin Austin* for a cruise to Boston where they spent their honeymoon with friends.[124] As a testimony to the perfection of their new union,
Elise wrote the following passage in her diary on September 20, 1920:

> Shall I ever forget the sensations experienced when I realized that I was
> in the arms of the one and only man on earth? Shall I never forget how,
> before he came to bed, he knelt beside the bed, gathered me in his arms

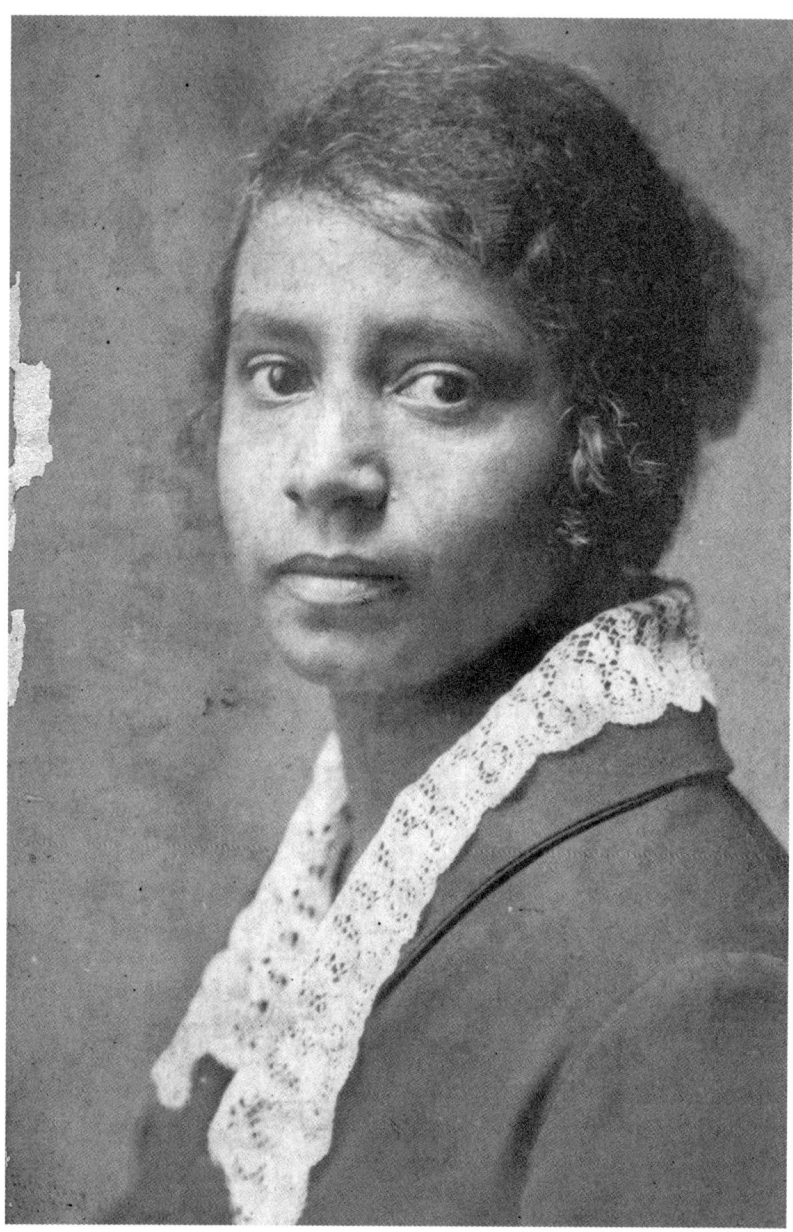

Photograph of Elise Forrest (Harleston), which Edwin Harleston may have used as reference for his portrait of Elise. 1924 pocket calendar, Edwin A. Harleston and Edwina Harleston Whitlock family papers, Stuart A. Rose Manuscript, Archives, and Rare Book Library, Emory University.

and prayed God's blessing on our union? Shall I forget the peace which stole over me when he finished his prayer and laid down beside me, all the while speaking in terms of endearment to allay my fears and help make a difficult situation easy.

He is wonderful! He is worth all I've gone through in waiting for him. He is the soul of honor, and he is my husband!

Five days of married life

Five days of Bliss

Five days of Love

Five days of Extreme Pleasure

Five days of living and loving

Five days stolen from Eternity.

I was not prepared for the abundance of joy. I was not prepared for the manifestations, the protestations, the adoration, for the one thing I am sure, my husband adores me. He loves me as I do him, for himself, regardless. It is up to me now to keep him so loving, adoring and God being my helper, I will.[125]

At the end of their honeymoon, they returned to Charleston to begin their new life together, not only as husband and wife, but as artists.

6

THE EMERGENCE
OF THE NEW NEGRO

ON THE EVENING OF OCTOBER 1, 1920, Mr. and Mrs. Edwin Augustus Harleston were greeted with congratulatory handshakes, hugs, and well-wishes from family and friends at their Charleston wedding reception held in Harleston Hall. Those who knew them best were certain theirs was a match made in heaven and had no doubt that a bright future was in store for this handsome couple.[1] After the celebration, Harleston and his bride settled into the third-floor apartment above the funeral home that he and his brother, Moultrie, had once shared. Because money was scarce, the couple spent their days working downstairs alongside Captain, while simultaneously pursuing their artistic careers; but what they had not anticipated was the suddenness of their transition from newlyweds to parents.

Edwin's youngest brother, Robert, had been infected with tuberculosis at the Fort Des Moines Officers' Training Camp and had unknowingly infected his wife, Marie, after returning home from Iowa. Although he had developed a cough and was experiencing some fatigue, Robert seemed to be managing his illness, but Marie's infection quickly entered the secondary phase, leaving her critically ill.[2] Medical cures to eradicate this disease, known as "consumption," had not yet been developed; consequently, treatment consisted only of quarantined bed rest, nutritious food, and fresh air. Sanitoriums were built for those who could afford private care, but very few of these facilities were open to African American patients, and qualified Black doctors who had been trained to treat those who had become infected were almost nonexistent in South Carolina. The mortality rate for Black tuberculosis patients was three times that of white patients; therefore, it was recommended that Robert and Marie move to Summerville, South Carolina, an international destination for those suffering from throat and lung ailments.[3] Located approximately twenty-five miles northwest of Charleston, the town of Summerville was known for its dry air, sandy soil, and abundance of pine trees whose turpentine-like scent was thought to have curative powers.[4] To sustain the couple in this new community, Captain Harleston established a branch of the Harleston Funeral Home on Blackjack Street in Summerville, with Robert O. Harleston serving as the resident undertaker.[5] Unfortunately, the hope of recovering from this dreadful disease would not be realized, especially for Marie. As her condition deteriorated, doctors urged the couple to send their two daughters to family members so that the fragile health of their children would be protected. Four-year-old Gussie was sent to live with Edwin and Elise (aka Tantie), while her fourteen-month-old sister, Sylvia, was sent to live with Harleston's youngest sister, Eloise, and her husband, the Reverend Daniel J. Jenkins.[6] Their parental roles became permanent, however, when Marie Forrest Harleston died four months later on January 14, 1921. This tragic loss, coupled with the realization that he now had a wife and child to support, made Edwin painfully aware of the fact that he had to do whatever he could to provide for his new family, and to accomplish that, he had to sell more artwork.

In Boston, Harleston participated in exhibitions while studying at the SMFA, but public showings of his paintings and drawings had been nearly nonexistent since returning to Charleston. This circumstance was not caused by a lack of desire but rather by a lack of opportunity. Works by African American artists were rarely, if ever, shown in established art galleries or museums. To compensate for this absence of professional exhibition spaces, Harleston and his peers usually displayed their pictures at events such as fairs, club meetings, or conventions held in libraries, churches, lodge halls, and other facilities open to the Black community.[7] But Harleston typically bypassed even these meager opportunities because of the heavy demands placed on him by his father's funeral business. However, in May of 1921, Harleston received an unexpected chance to show his work at the National Negro Business League conference in Atlanta. His college classmate and supporter T. K. Gibson, who had recently left Atlanta to join the Supreme Life and Casualty Insurance Company in Chicago, sent him information concerning the upcoming exhibition. Gibson thought this might be the perfect chance for Harleston to show his work and perhaps receive a few portrait commissions, since many of the most important African American businessmen in the country would be in attendance; therefore, he urged his friend not to miss this opportunity.[8]

Harleston took Gibson's advice and applied for booth space at the league conference held at the Butler Street YMCA. As in many of the other places the artist had exhibited, there was no formal area set aside for showing pictures. Consequently, Harleston had to make do with hanging his paintings between booths featuring an array of toiletries on one side, while peanut and sweet potato products developed by Professor George Washington Carver of Tuskegee Institute (now Tuskegee University) were prominently displayed on the other.[9] At the beginning of the exhibition, Harleston was excited by the number of people who gathered to marvel at his paintings and drawings as they were being hung. Their enthusiastic response to his work convinced him that he would be receiving requests for portraits during the conference. In a letter to his wife, Harleston described the exhibition experience as "very gratifying to have so many folks come in and gaze around at the pictures and say 'wonderful,' 'fine,' 'beautiful' and so forth. As of yet, I have had no positive engagements, but many took my cards for future reference."[10] He remained hopeful until the end of the show, but by the time his works had been crated for the return trip home, he had not received a single portrait commission.

Edwin Harleston was not only disappointed in the lackluster state of his own art career, he was also frustrated with Elise's waning interest in mastering the fine points of photography, especially in the area of pictorialism, a popular photography style that emphasized soft focus and a painterly manipulation of the image that gave the subject an air of sophistication.[11] The couple had been making plans to open a painting and photographic studio in the new residence Captain Harleston had agreed to build as a wedding gift. Located across the street from the funeral home, at 118 Calhoun Street, the lot had previously housed the livery stable and carriages for the business, but now it would become the home of the Harleston Studios. But if the new enterprise was to be a success, Elise had to do her part by sharpening her photography skills.

Harleston knew he could not afford to send Elise back to New York for additional training, so he decided to do the next best thing by seeking the services of a well-known master photographer who lived and worked in Tuskegee, Alabama. Cornelius Marion Battey, an African American photographer who had been trained in Cleveland, Ohio, and New York City, gained national recognition for his 1914 series of portraits he called "Our Heroes of Destiny," which included leaders such as Frederick Douglass, John Mercer Langston, Booker T. Washington, and W. E. B. Du Bois. After seeing his photographs, Washington was so impressed with Battey's work that he invited him to come to Tuskegee Institute to establish a photography department and serve as its chief instructor.[12] Battey enjoyed teaching but he rarely gave instruction to independent students; however, Harleston was convinced that if he met with the photographer, he could persuade him to take Elise under his wing.[13] During his visit, Harleston toured Battey's studio and later penned a detailed letter to Elise describing the most important elements of the space. The walls of the studio, he wrote, "were covered with burlap (over rough plaster) up to about three feet of the ceiling and paneled vertically with a shelf-like molding at the top, the panels being about thirty inches wide and stained dark, the burlap being buff colored." Harleston closely examined every detail in the Tuskegee studio, not for flaws, but for ideas he could incorporate into the design of their new studio in Charleston. By the time he was ready to leave Tuskegee's campus, Battey had agreed to give Elise private instruction beginning in the fall of 1921.[14]

When Harleston returned home, ideas and plans for the new Harleston Studio filled his head, but he soon realized that what he really needed were clients. The Atlanta exhibition had not generated any portrait commissions, so Harleston attempted to create interest in his artwork by sending letters to prospective patrons in Atlanta. "To whom it may concern," he wrote:

> I shall be in your city for a few days and take this occasion to ask if you
> would be interested in the idea of having me to paint your portrait or
> that of any member of your family.
>
> If you are interested, I shall be glad to have you see some specimens
> of my work which were brought to Atlanta for a recent exhibition held
> in connection with the Business League.

At the end of the letter, he signed his name and under it wrote "Portrait Painter."[15] There is no way of knowing how many of these solicitations Harleston sent or to whom, but there is no indication that any requests for portraits were received as a result of this communication.

In September of 1921, Elise traveled to Tuskegee and began working with Cornelius Battey, while Harleston remained in Charleston struggling against the gravitational pull of his funeral home responsibilities and his art career. He had hoped that Elise's time with Battey would rekindle her passion for photography, but her slow progress and limited time with the photographer proved to be unbearably frustrating. In an attempt to free herself from this situation, Elise wrote to her husband expressing her desire to leave Tuskegee and return home, but Harleston insisted she remain. To boost his wife's spirit, the artist told her that while he was a student at the SMFA, his teachers never talked to him for more than twenty or twenty-five minutes a week.[16] But this anecdote did little to inspire Elise to keep going. Finally, in a firm but compassionate tone, Harleston told her "to work like blazes and come back when you are perfectly sure you have it. I shall be very much disappointed if anything brings you home before you are quite independent. No one can miss you as I do . . . it is just as if I had lost my right hand, but I had my heart set upon your doing just that thing and you will do it, now won't you?"[17] Not wanting to disappoint her husband, Elise stayed until the semester ended in December. Before she left the campus, Harleston penned his final Tuskegee letter to Elise while sitting in the hearse waiting for a funeral service to end. In it, he asked her to make a stop in Atlanta for a day or two so that she could visit the fashionable Paul Poole Photography Studio to get some additional ideas for their new venture before coming home.[18] Although they had been apart for nearly three months, Harleston felt a few more days would not make a difference, but for Elise, it felt like an eternity.

By January of 1922, construction on the Harleston Studio had been completed. This two-story structure was the only arts facility in South Carolina and perhaps in the country built specifically for the production and formal display of painted and photographic African American portraiture.[19] There was another Black photographer in the city, Michael Francis Blake, who had been producing portraits in his home studio on West Sumter Street for more than a decade, but his photographic enterprise was small and offered little, if any, competition for the Harleston's atelier.[20] The best ideas Edwin Harleston had gathered on his trips to New York, Tuskegee, Atlanta, and elsewhere had been incorporated into the design of the new building. On the ground floor, glass display cases stood near the entrance prominently exhibiting Elise's photographs. Another section on this level held a workshop for framing and crating Harleston's paintings. Since the funeral business was still the major source of income for the couple, a portion of the facility provided casket storage and garage space for the business's fleet of motorized Cunningham hearses. On the second floor, at the top of the stairs, was a comfortably furnished foyer, which served as the receiving area for visitors and business associates. Just beyond this area was a wide hallway that functioned as Harleston's picture gallery. The hall began at the foyer and ran parallel to the family's living and dining rooms, terminating at the studio door located in the rear of the building. The studio was a large open space that housed Elise's darkroom and Harleston's easels. It also contained a raised platform with a black backdrop and skylights covered by gauze-like shades that could be adjusted for varying degrees of light to accommodate the artists' needs.[21]

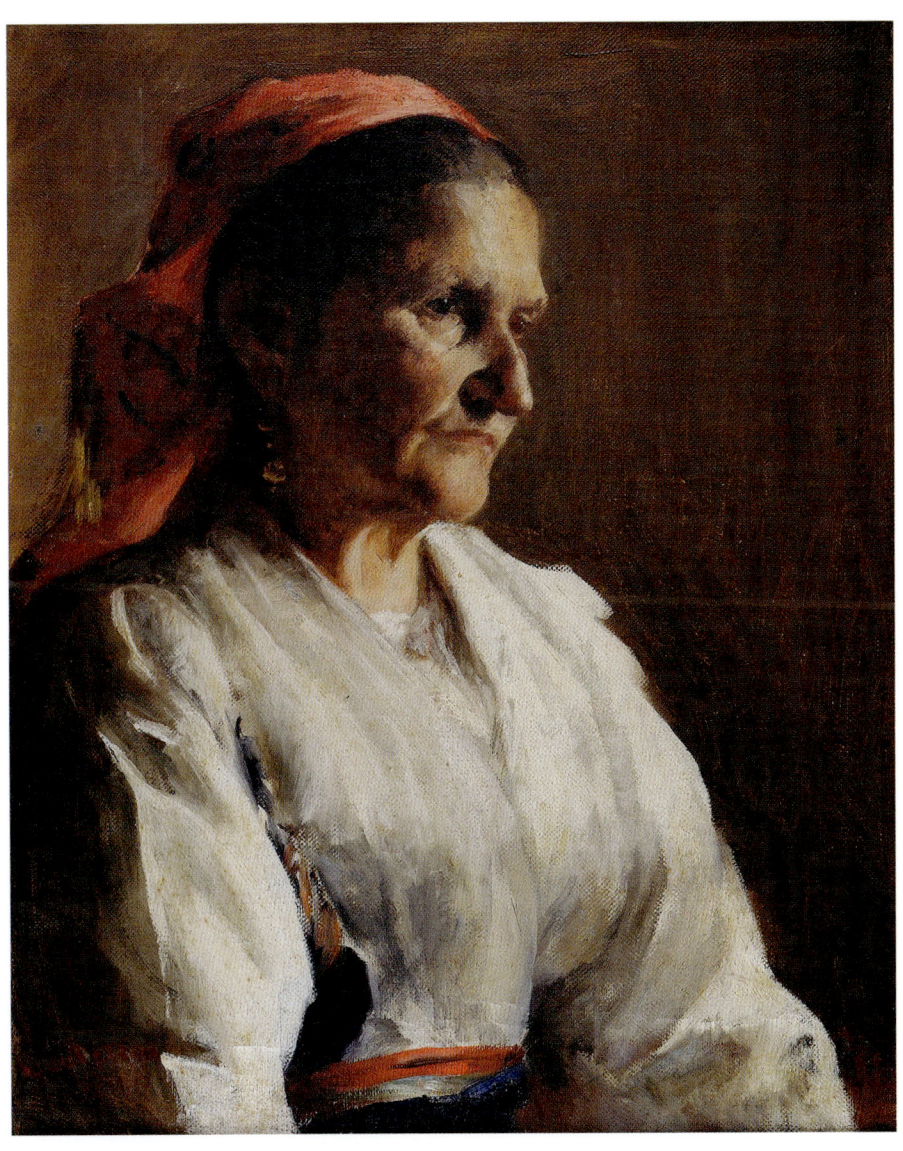

Plate 1. Edwin Augustus Harleston, *Italian Woman with Kerchief*, ca. 1912.
Howard University Gallery of Art, Washington, DC, licensed by Art Resource, NY.

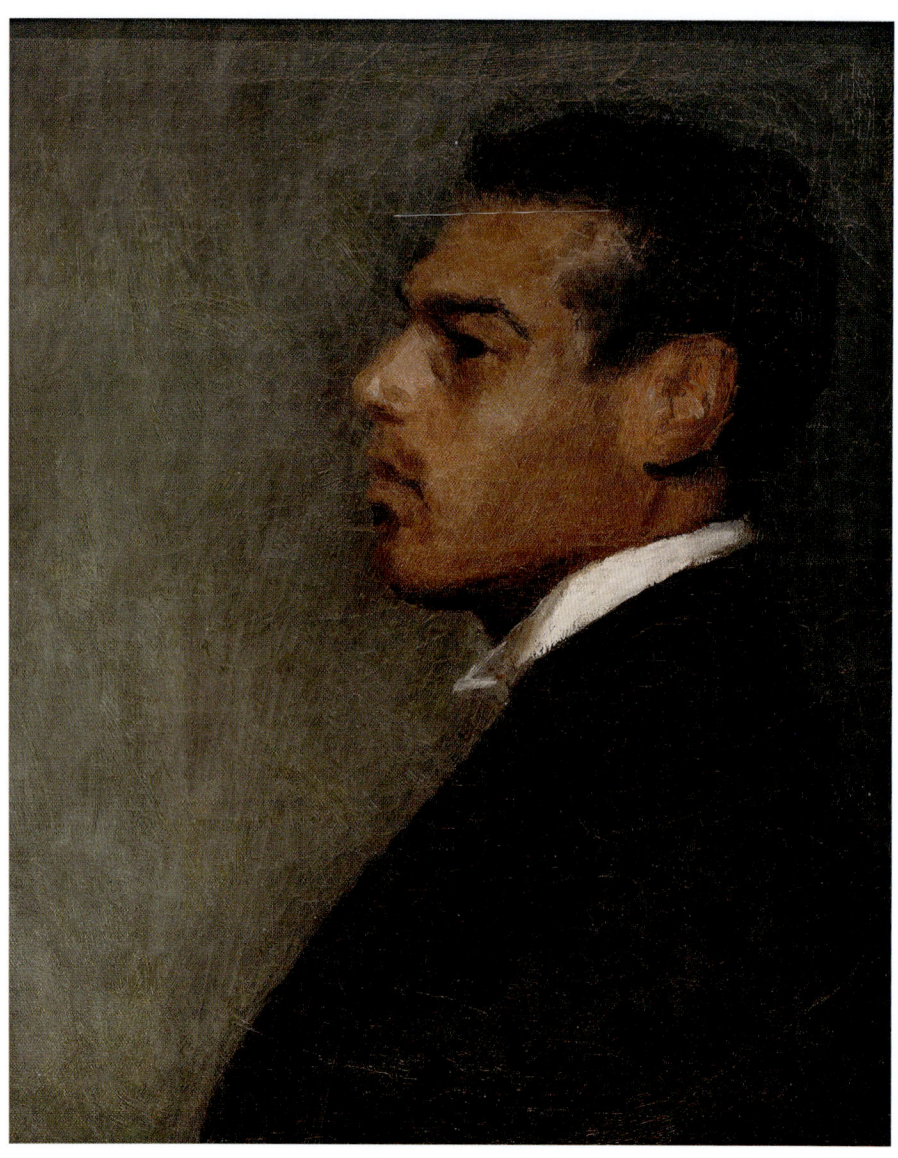

Plate 2. Edwin Augustus Harleston, *Self-Portrait, Boston*, oil on canvas, ca. 1911.
Collection of Steven L. Jones, Philadelphia and Chicago.

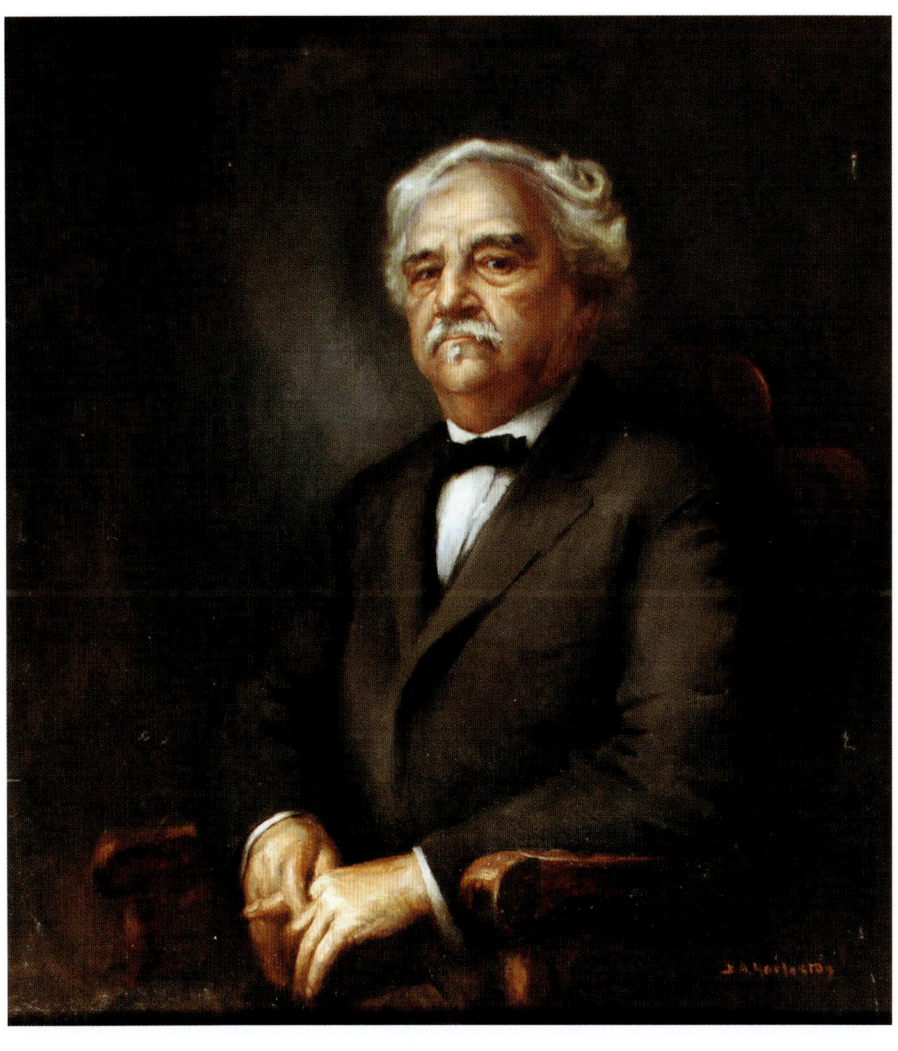

Plate 3. Edwin Augustus Harleston, *Portrait of Thomas E. Miller*, oil on canvas, 1919.
Courtesy of Avery Research Center for African American History and Culture, Charleston, SC.

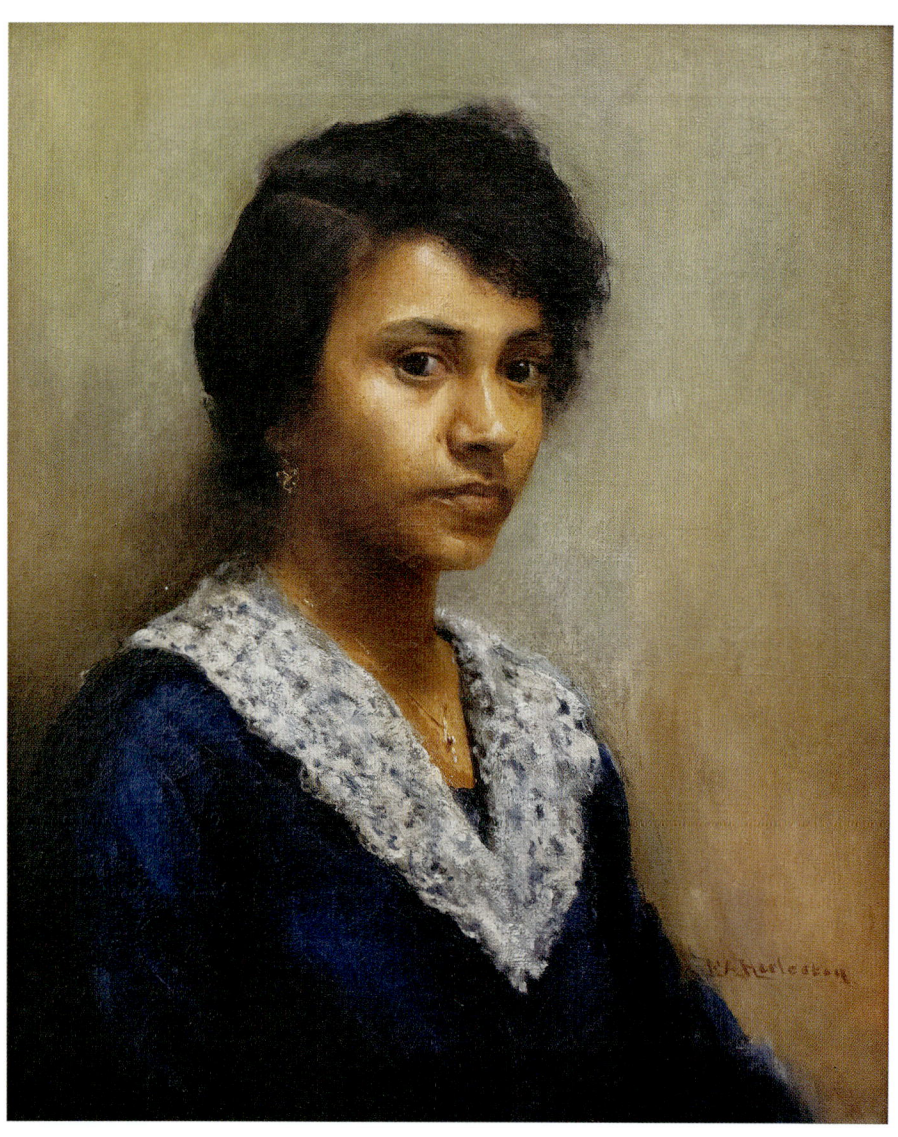

Plate 4. Edwin Augustus Harleston, *Portrait of Elise*, oil on canvas, 1920.
Collection of Mae Whitlock Gentry.

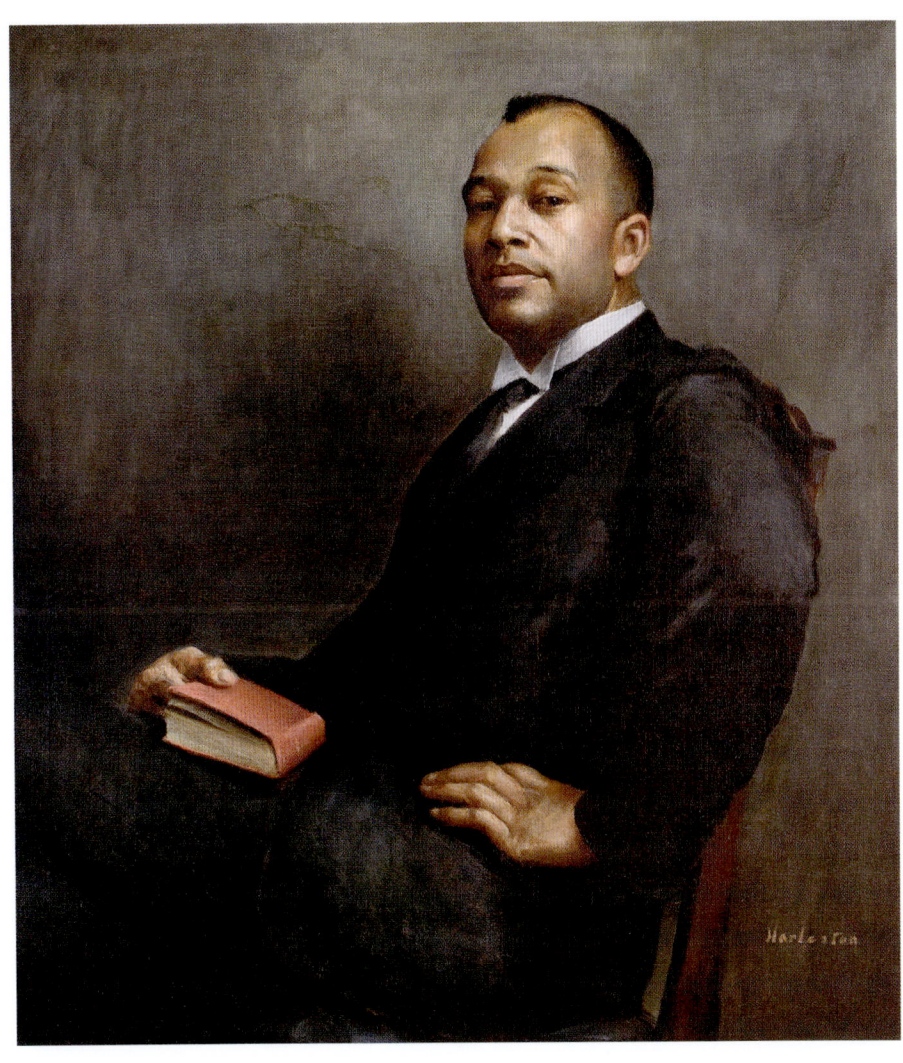

Plate 5. Edwin Augustus Harleston, *Portrait of Reverend Caesar S. Ledbetter*, oil on canvas, ca. 1920. Collection of Patrick and Katherine Ledbetter.

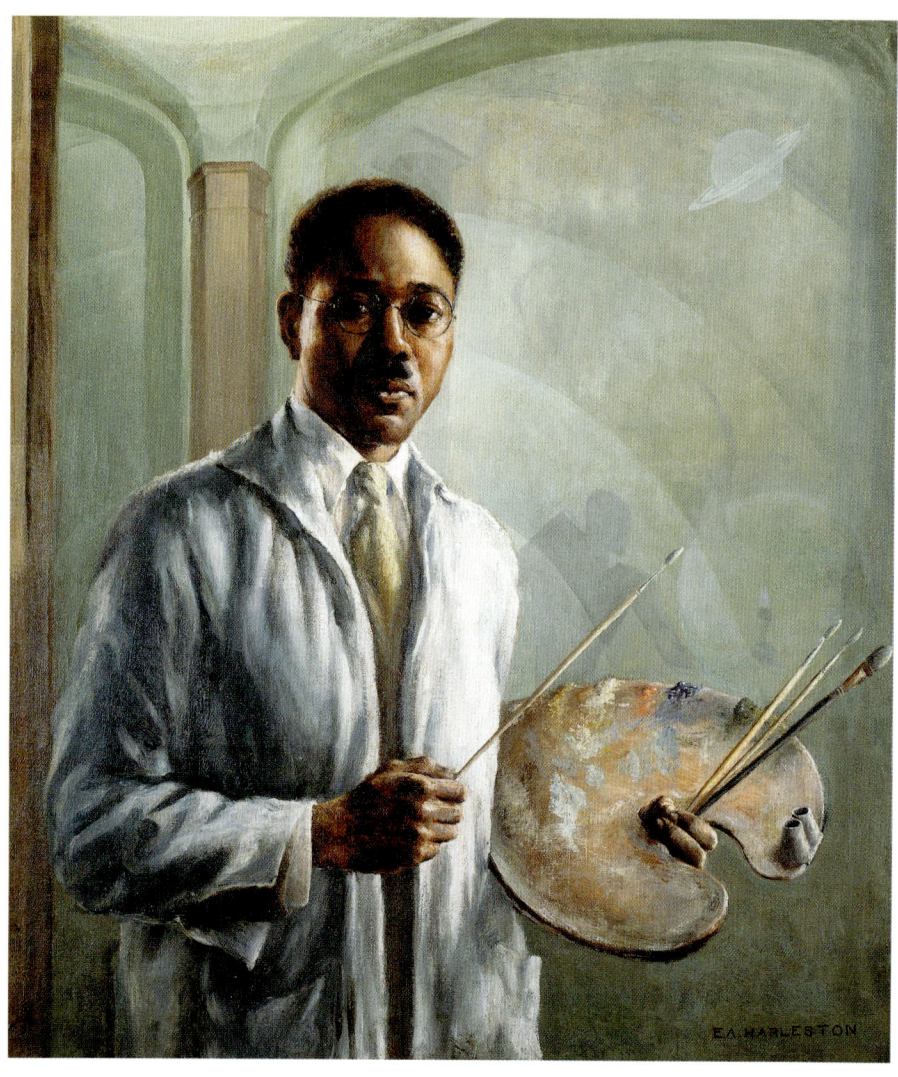

Plate 6. Edwin Augustus Harleston, *Portrait of Aaron Douglas*, oil on canvas, 1930.
Gibbes Museum of Art, Charleston, SC.

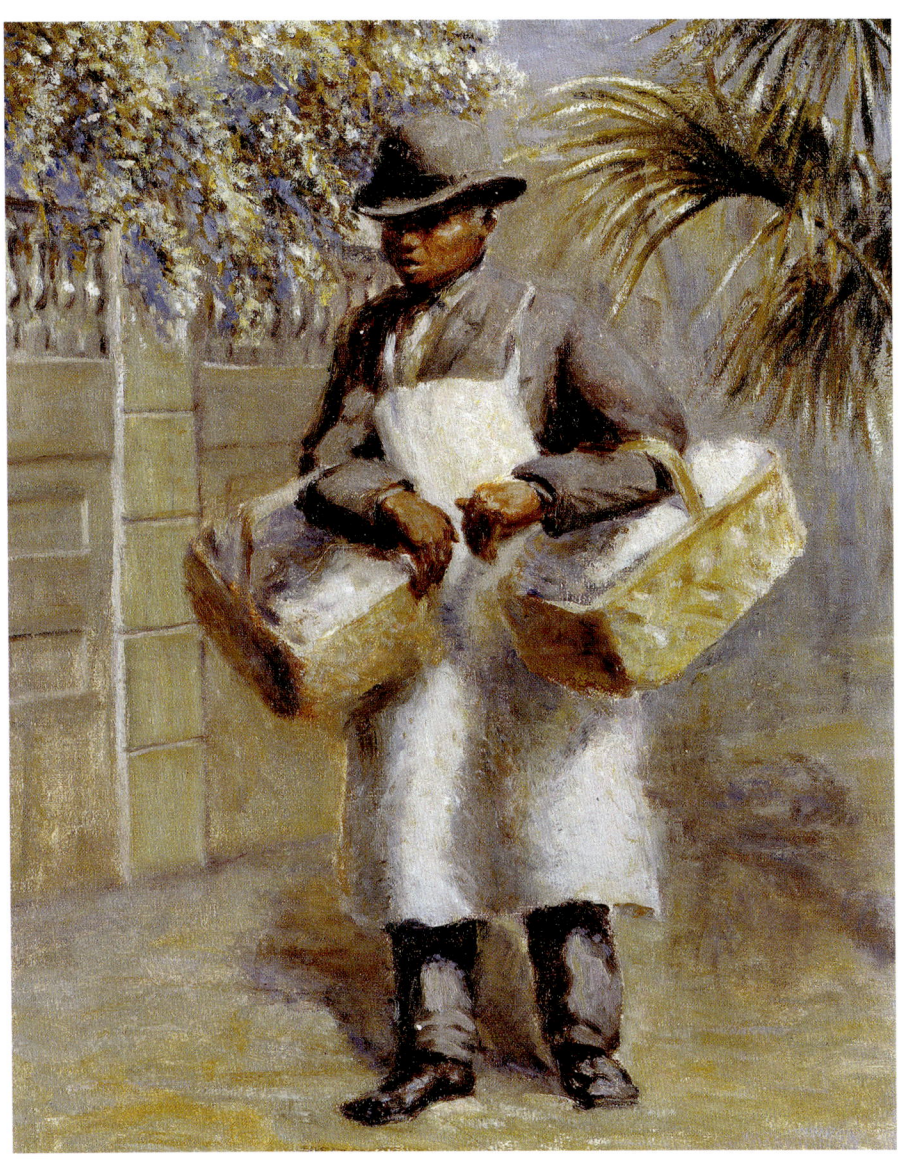

Plate 7. Edwin Augustus Harleston, *The Honey Man*, oil on canvas, 1930. Gibbes Museum of Art, Charleston, South Carolina.

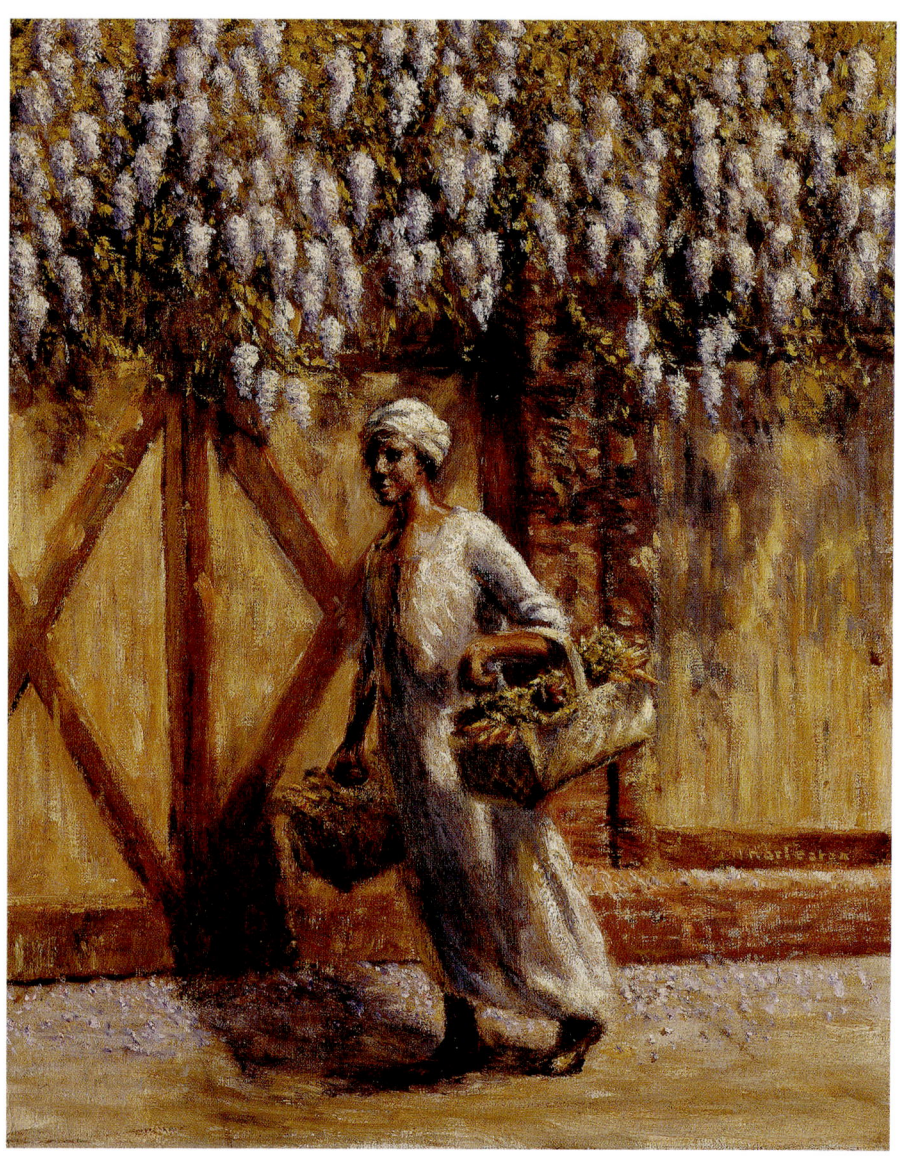

Plate 8. Edwin Augustus Harleston, *A Vendor (aka Lady Passing a Wall)*, oil on canvas, 1930. Gibbes Museum of Art, Charleston, SC.

Now that the studio was fully established and word of its existence was beginning to circulate, those who knew Harleston began to think of him as a serious artist rather than a businessman and civic leader with artistic talent. This shift in his public persona fostered new interest in his artwork among his friends as well as the general public. To show the versatility of his skills as a draftsman and portrait artist, Edwin Harleston added a series of portraits to his portfolio focusing on children in an effort to increase his clientele. One of the more successful works from this collection is *Ras*, a sensitively rendered charcoal and French crayon drawing on paper of his six-year-old niece, Gussie. The artist presents the young girl in a three-quarter length profile pose wearing a wide collared jacket with sleeves pleated at the shoulder. Her hair has been pinned up so that the graceful curve of her neck can be clearly seen. Harleston has successfully given the figure a feeling of volume and mass through a gradation of tone from the highlighted area of the face to dark areas found at the back of her head and shoulders. By using charcoal and French crayon as the media for this artwork, Harleston has been able to accurately capture Gussie's essence by focusing the viewers' attention on her delicate features and the wispy texture of the hair framing her face, an undertaking that would have been extremely difficult to achieve in an oil portrait.

Evidence of this new level of interest in his work can be found in a 1923 letter from Ernestine Rose, 135th Street Branch librarian of the New York Public Library, inviting him to participate in an exhibition in New York during the fall of 1923.[22] For the previous two summers, a *Negro Arts Exhibit* had been held in this Harlem library branch under the direction of Harleston's Atlanta University classmate, Augustus G. Dill. The first show, held in 1921, featured works by important artists such as Henry O. Tanner, one of the few artists of color who had earned an international reputation and whose name was widely known among educated African Americans during the early 1920s; along with Laura Wheeler (Waring), William E. Scott, Palmer Hayden, Albert Smith, James L. Wells, Cornelius M. Battey, and Meta Warrick Fuller. In addition to contemporary art, there were displays of rare books, prints, and African art from private collections. Copies of works by old masters such as Velázquez, Rembrandt, and Rubens were

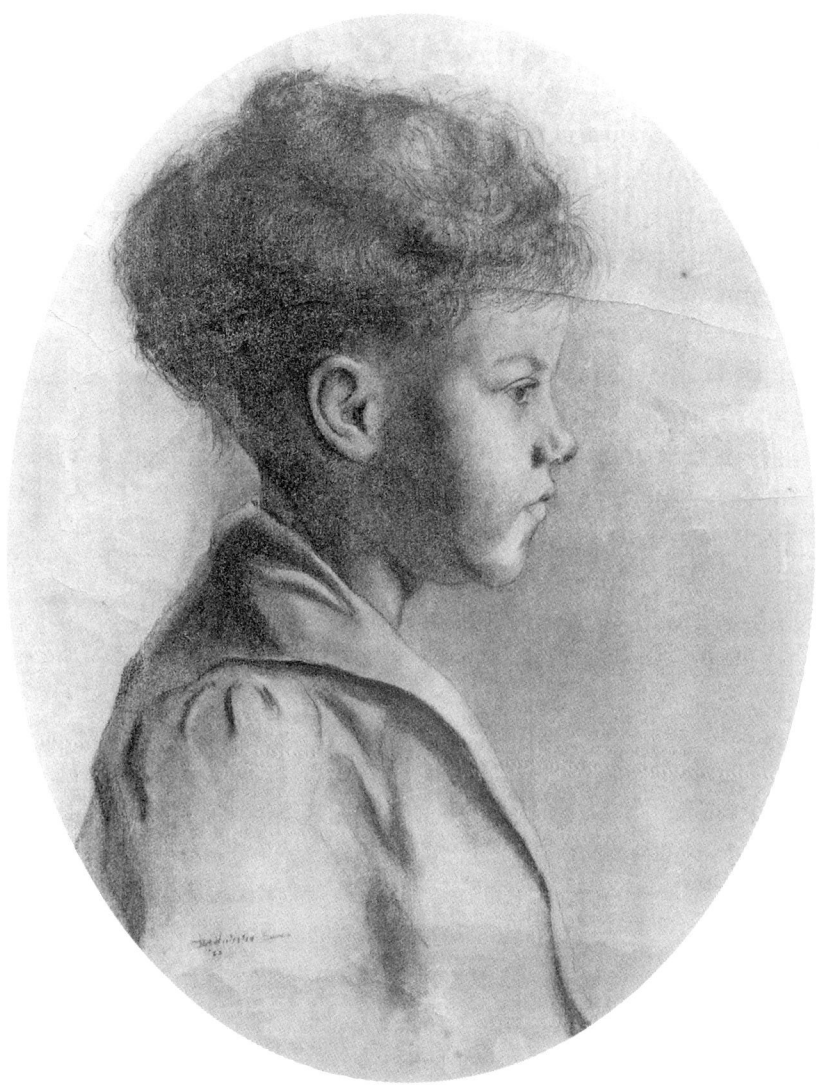

Edwin Augustus Harleston, *Ras (Gussie Harleston)*, 1922, charcoal and
French crayon on paper. Collection of Mae Whitlock Gentry.

also included. Dill had invited Harleston to participate in the inaugural group show, but the artist had already agreed to take part in the Negro Business League Exhibition and was, therefore, unable to attend.[23] This time, Harleston was not going to let anything interfere with the chance to show his work in Harlem, "the Negro capital of the world."[24]

Like several American cities in the North, Harlem was poised to become a leading "colored district" at the turn of the century. By 1915, the stream of southern African American migrants heading to New York had swollen into a mighty torrent, reshaping Harlem's character. The sudden growth in population gave this section of New York City economic power that afforded aggressive businessmen the opportunity to convert white middle-class real estate into the "biggest and most elegant Black community in the Western world."[25] In addition to having economic muscle, Harlem was also recognized as a center of political thought. For more than a decade, W. E. B. Du Bois and the NAACP had challenged the nation and the world on the issues of race. As a result of their effort, other crusaders, such as Marcus Garvey, would join those seeking to establish racial pride and social justice. Therefore, it is not surprising that young African American intellectuals, writers, and artists in search of a greater sense of self would be drawn to Harlem, the birthplace of the "New Negro."[26]

Because of the importance of this burgeoning cultural center, Edwin Harleston took great care in selecting his best portraits, character studies, and drawings for his New York debut. Among those works chosen for the exhibition was the *Portrait of Reverend Caesar S. Ledbetter*, the Harleston family minister and pastor of Plymouth Congregational Church in Charleston (see Plate 5).[27] Born in Macon, Mississippi, in 1876, Caesar S. Ledbetter has been described as a tall, self-assured man, whose deep baritone voice, quick wittedness, and dynamic preaching style never failed to capture the attention of his congregation. Critics consider this portrait to be one of Edwin Harleston's finest works, for the artist has not only captured the reverend's likeness, but he has also gone beneath his exterior to convey a sense of the sitter's personality. Edwin Harleston presents Ledbetter in a casual pose in front of a loosely painted charcoal-colored background. Seated in an armless, straight-back chair with legs crossed and his body turned at an angle parallel to the picture plane, the reverend is clothed in a conventional black suit, with a white butterfly-collared shirt, and black tie. There is nothing in the painting to distract the viewer from Ledbetter's gaze for unlike the introspective expressions displayed by the subjects in Harleston's earlier paintings, the reverend looks down at the viewer with an air of confidence.[28] Harleston has achieved this by placing the minister's image above eye level and in doing so, the artist has imbued the figure with the kind of panache rarely seen in African American portraits of this period. The feeling of superiority has been reinforced by Ledbetter's nonchalant, almost cocky facial expression and punctuated by the left hand, which rests on the subject's hip. To some, this pose might be considered unbefitting a preacher, but, in this case, the attention Harleston gives this aspect of Ledbetter's personality has made the painting even more compelling.

This psychological component was first introduced in Harleston's *Self-Portrait* and more fully developed in his World War I character study, *The Soldier;* however, the kind of bold self-confidence shown in the *Portrait of Reverend Caesar S. Ledbetter* was a new development in Harleston's portrait style. But what could have inspired him to break from the formal Boston School tradition and incorporate such an emotional element into this painting? The postwar era and the migratory surge to the North had brought about a reassessment in the African American community regarding their worth within the society as a whole. In doing so, old ideas which had previously determined "their place" in America were now being challenged. New concepts concerning the issue of race, which were being discussed in both Black and white intellectual circles, included new approaches to the issue and a commitment from some to break with the old way of thinking. This was the first generation of scholars, critics, and artists who, having written off American culture of the early twenties for lack of integrity, turned to African American art, music, and literature as a source of rejuvenation, because it "had been spared the larger white society's degradation, its obsession with mechanization, [and] its emotional repressiveness."[29] As a result, African American images began to appear that were more representative of Black life than any that had been previously produced. It is likely that Harleston's *Portrait of Reverend Caesar S. Ledbetter* was a by-product of this new way of thinking.

This painting of Ledbetter is particularly engaging because of Ledbetter's unusual pose. In the artist's earlier painting of the soldier, the subject is presented with arms folded across the body in a gesture of defiance. Reverend Ledbetter, however, is shown with his left hand on his hip and the traditional symbol of a learned man, a book, has been placed in his right hand. The positioning of the hands and open ease with which Ledbetter looks at the viewer suggests that the pose may have been conceived after Harleston studied the works of other portrait painters, a habit Harleston established as a student. When in New York, the artist never missed an opportunity to visit museums, galleries, and the photograph collection of portraits in the New York Public Library. Therefore, it is possible that he may have seen Agnolo Bronzino's *Portrait of a Young Man* and used aspects of it for the Ledbetter portrait.[30] *Portrait of a Young Man* went on display for the first time in the United States at M. Knoedler and Company in New York City in April of 1915, and later at the Metropolitan Museum, raising the possibility that Harleston could have seen that painting at one of these locations.[31] This work has been singled out because of the similarity of the pose and haughtiness of the subject in Harleston's portrait and the young man in Bronzino's painting. While Harleston may have been influenced by this Italian Mannerist, he infused his subject with a kind of spontaneous, almost playful vitality that is missing in Bronzino's contemptuous nobleman.

Another painting that was featured in the *Negro Arts Exhibit* was *The Old Man Reading* (ca. 1922), a work that would later be renamed the *Bible Student* (whereabouts unknown). This painting is particularly significant because it is one of the earliest collaborative efforts by Elise and Edwin Harleston. The basis for the painting was a sepia-toned photograph of their neighbor, Mr. Jefferson Wigfall, taken by Elise in the Harleston Studio. The elderly man, who is dressed in a suit and tie, is seated on a small bench holding a large book. Because his head is tilted in a downward position, the intense light coming from the upper-left corner of the setting has cast heavy shadows around the sitter's eyes, cheeks, and the lower portion of his face. In comparing the photograph with a reproduction of the painting, it is clear that Harleston has been faithful to major sections of Elise's photograph. But in transferring this image to canvas, Harleston made some modifications in the compositional structure.

The most noticeable difference is his use of space. The artist has placed the figure to the far right of the picture plane, establishing greater balance between the negative and positive space, creating the perception of a quiet atmosphere. Next, he reconstructed the shadows by taking the most expressive areas of the subject's face and raising the values in the darkest areas so that the eyes, cheeks, and mouth could more clearly be seen. Furrows from Mr. Wigfall's brow were also removed along with minor lines near the eyes. Harleston's altered interpretation of light marks a shift in approach not seen in his earlier works. In previous portraits, areas of reflected light were subtly developed, leaving the impression that the source of illumination was rather low in intensity. But in the *Old Man Reading* much of the subject's face is structured with broad areas high in intensity and dark shadows with minimal tonal gradation in between. Because the areas representing reflected light are loosely painted and void of the careful modeling seen in his other works, this painting seems to have the feel of an illustration rather than a formal portrait. With these changes, Harleston idealized the image of the old man and transformed his rather solemn expression, as seen in the photograph, into a softer, gentler appearance in the painting. The final touch is the shawl which the artist has placed around the old man's shoulders, giving the work the kind of sentimental quality that was popular near the end of the nineteenth century.

This change in style was well received by patrons who came to the exhibition's opening reception at the Harlem Library on September 18, 1923. Wilfred Russell, who assisted with the installation of the show, was a cartoonist for *The New York Age* newspaper and a member of the exhibition's executive committee.[32] He had seen some of Harleston's early works and was pleasantly surprised by the growth displayed in these new drawings and paintings. As a gesture of encouragement, Russell sent a congratulatory letter stating that the artist's work had "greatly improved."

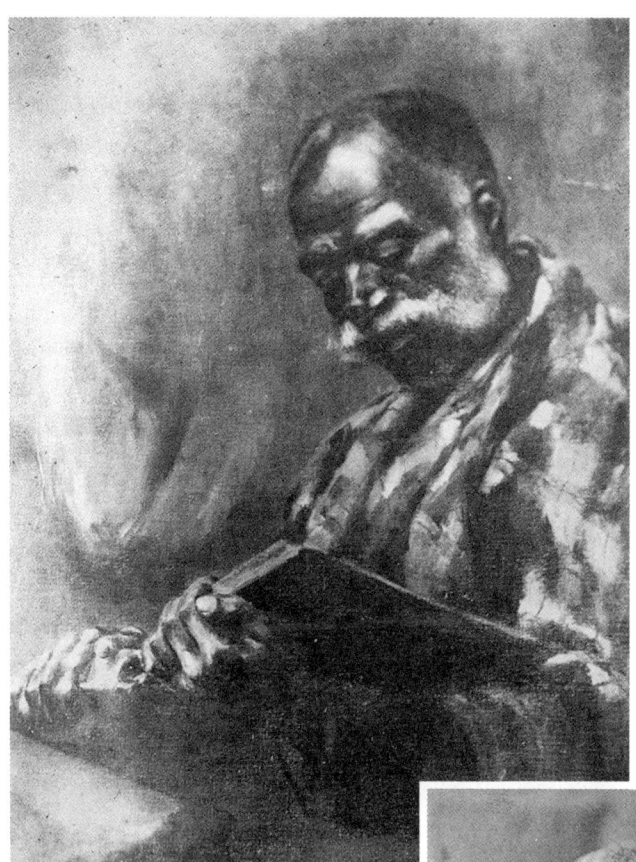

Edwin Augustus Harleston, *Bible Student*, cover art, *Opportunity: A Journal of Negro Life*, January 1924 (*above*); Elise Forrest Harleston, *Bible Student (Mr. Wigfall)*, photograph, 1923. Collection of Mae Whitlock Gentry (*right*).

He wrote, "Individuality is unmistakably seen in your work. That, I assure you is a great achievement. Your work is being appreciatively received especially your character studies. . . . As an exhibitor, I am glad to say you have 'arrived!'"[33] Before the opening of the show, Harleston had written to Russell requesting a list of potential clients who might be interested in portrait sittings."[34] Russell had initially hesitated to recommend Harleston to friends but after fully examining his paintings, he concluded that the artist deserved the title of gifted portrait painter.[35] To prove his support, Russell enclosed a list of some of New York's most important luminaries including Dr. Wiley Wilson, the second husband of heiress A'Lelia Walker; the Reverend Adam Clayton Powell Sr., pastor of Abyssinian Baptist Church; and Reverend Hutchins C. Bishop, priest of the oldest Black Episcopal parish in New York City and a political activist who helped organize the Negro Silent Protest Parade of 1917. At the end of the letter, Russell encouraged the artist to contact these patrons immediately and invite them to the exhibition to see his portraits.[36]

Edwin Harleston was so elated with Russell's praise and the public's positive response to his work, that he immediately sent letters of solicitation to the prospective patrons his friend had recommended. In the correspondence, Harleston mentioned he was planning a fall tour of his work and encouraged those interested in portrait sittings to reply as soon as possible.[37] He then wrote to various institutions in the northeast that regularly held art exhibitions to explore the possibility of additional showings of his drawings and paintings. Still not satisfied that he had done enough to promote his career, the artist decided to travel to New York to see the exhibition and hear some of these accolades for himself.

When he arrived, Harleston was pleased to see his pictures hanging beside works by some of the most outstanding African American artists of the period. Included in the exhibition were paintings by Laura Wheeler (Waring), Albert Smith, William E. Scott and prints by William M. Farrow. Although he considered the quality of their work to be excellent, Harleston felt his Boston School painting style made his work superior to the others.[38] This perception was reinforced by the attention he received from the public. Charles S. Johnson, editor of *Opportunity: A Journal of Negro*

Life, published monthly by the National Urban League, had visited the exhibition and considered Harleston's work to be "a masterful expression of real art." One of Johnson's objectives as editor was to promote the concept of "racial advancement through artistic creativity" in his publication.[39] Literary writers such as Claude McKay, Jessie Fauset, and Jean Toomer had already been featured in the magazine, and now the editor was looking for visual artists. Because Harleston's images fit his criteria, Johnson had written to the artist prior to his arrival, requesting permission to feature an illustrated story about him in the January issue of the magazine so that "thousands of others . . . [could see] the best work by [one of] our best artists."[40] At the appointed time, Johnson and Harleston met in the exhibition hall for an interview, and several photographs of the paintings were taken for the magazine.

Later that same day, Walter White, the assistant secretary of the NAACP and a man with whom Edwin Harleston had worked on several civil rights projects, brought Herbert Seligmann, a reporter for the *New York Evening Post* and publicist for the NAACP, to see the artist's work. Harleston was more familiar with Seligmann's essays on American artists such as Marsden Hartley and John Marin, published in *International Studio* magazine, than he was with his work as a newspaper reporter. But having an established art critic such as Seligmann see the exhibition raised Harleston's hopes that his works might possibly be mentioned in a review of the show.[41] But nothing about the exhibition ever appeared in the *New York Evening Post* or any of the other local newspapers.

This snub was probably not race related but a reflection of Seligmann's preference for American mainstream aesthetics. Before the Great War, many artists who had studied in Paris returned to the United States as converts to modernism. On this side of the Atlantic their new appetite for the avant-garde was nurtured by Alfred Stieglitz, the undisputed apostle of modernism, who aggressively worked to expose the American public to this new form of expression through exhibitions at his "291" gallery in New York City. Stieglitz not only educated the public and critics about European modernism, but he also developed a reputation for being the singular refuge in America where avant-garde artists such as Marsden

Hartley, Arthur Dove, Max Weber, Arthur B. Carles, Abraham Walkowitz, and Georgia O'Keeffe could show and discuss their works. With the opening of the Armory Show in 1913, where, for the first time, the public was given the opportunity to view the wide range of trends in European modernism, interest in the avant-garde spread. After the war, however, this newly kindled interest began to fade. Many of the American artists who had experimented with abstraction were now stepping back, preferring instead to concentrate on a more naturalistic portrayal of urban subjects and experiences closer to home.[42]

These fair-weather modernists rejoined the loyal majority of American realist painters who had ignored the arrival of abstract expression, preferring instead to remain faithful to established academic standards. Most of the artists in the *Negro Arts Exhibit*, as well as Edwin Harleston, were a part of this group. Although there may be many reasons why these artists preferred realism over abstraction at this phase of their careers, it is probable that their adherence to the artistic status quo developed as a means of survival and acceptance in a system that did not welcome their presence. Only a few African American artists were enrolled in art institutions nationwide, and only a fraction of that number had studied in Europe. Therefore, it was in their best interest, both professionally and monetarily, not to deviate from realism, the bedrock of American artistic style. But a more likely reason why Harleston and other Black artists of this period preferred realism over the new avant-garde styles was their need to paint accurate, empowering images of African Americans to counter the negative stereotypes saturating popular culture. To these artists, image making was "a domain of hope and an area of possible progress," not only for themselves but also for their race as a whole.[43]

Even though no reviews were published in the mainstream press, Harleston's spirits were lifted by the positive reaction from those who visited the exhibition. One of the library members was so impressed that she invited the artist to a private reception in honor of Henry O. Tanner, who was visiting the city on business. In a letter to Elise, Harleston confided to his wife that all this attention was so overwhelming that it almost seemed as if he were "dreaming."[44]

His euphoria was further heightened by an invitation from the Tanner Art Students League to show his work in Washington, DC. The exhibition was to be held in the new Paul Lawrence Dunbar High School, "one of the most complete and beautiful institutions for Negro youth in the country."[45] Although it functioned primarily as an educational facility, the school was also an important cultural center for Washington writers, musicians, and artists. Since Harleston did not have enough work for both shows, he would have postponed the Washington exhibition under ordinary circumstances, but an exhibition at Dunbar High School was another opportunity not to be missed.

More important, Harleston was in a desperate financial situation and could not afford to bypass a chance to sell his work or receive a commission.[46] His father had not seen the need to make his son a partner in his funeral business or pay him more than an employee's salary. Instead, Captain took advantage of his son's loyalty by doling out any extra money to the artist and his wife as he saw fit. This untenable situation had forced Harleston to remove his paintings from the New York show and send them to Washington for an eight-day exhibition at the high school.[47] At the behest of the artist, William D. Nixon, instructor of drawing and president of The Tanner Art Students League, sent out a flyer to Washington art lovers inviting them to the exhibition and encouraging them to book a portrait sitting as a "Christmas gift."[48] After the show closed on November 28, Harleston shipped the work back to the library in New York for the formal opening planned for the first Saturday in December.[49] All this was done with the hope that such widespread publicity would boost his career and sales of his work.[50]

Unfortunately, the stress of shuttling his artwork between the two venues and worry over his lack of money caused an old stomach ailment, which had probably become a perforated ulcer, to become too painful to ignore. Because he needed specialized medical care, Harleston contacted his trusted friend Dr. William Augustus Hinton, a graduate of Harvard Medical School and member of the faculty, to make the arrangements for his surgical procedure. On November 19, 1923, he entered Boston's Roxbury Hospital.[51] Elise was unable to be at his side during his hospitalization because of the numerous duties she had assumed at the funeral home along with the responsibility of caring for Harleston's niece, Gussie. In recognition of the burden he had shifted to his wife, Harleston wrote to Elise on the night before his surgery apologizing for overlooking her "interests . . . and wishes: This situation had not occurred, he said, out of "a lack of love" for her, but as a result of trying to repay a family obligation.[52] The artist felt immensely indebted to his father for allowing him to attend art school and therefore believed it was his duty to try to balance his own desire for a successful art career with his obligation to the family business even though his status and pay were that of an employee rather than an owner. As a result of trying to balance these two seemingly incompatible demands, Harleston was paying a heavy price, physically, emotionally, and financially. While he was recuperating at the home of Dr. Hinton, Harleston received several letters from Elise asking for money to cover daily expenses and holiday shopping. Since there had been no response to his solicitations for portrait commissions in New York or Atlanta, there was no money to send.[53] A few days before Christmas, Harleston sent his wife a melancholy letter declaring that this would be their "last POOR Christmas." He hoped that his recovery would be enough to make her holiday cheerful and sent forth a wish for a "happier . . . more prosperous New Year."[54]

Edwin Harleston's desire for artistic recognition finally met with success at the dawn of 1924 when the article Charles Johnson had promised appeared in the January issue of *Opportunity* magazine. "Harleston! Who is E. A. Harleston?" written by Madeline G. Allison, introduced the artist to the National Urban League's readership as well as members of northeastern cultural circles who may not have been familiar with his work. In her essay, Allison identified Harleston as "a man of . . . genius . . . [who] should most certainly be widely known." Photographs of two artworks from the exhibition, *The Soldier* and the portrait of an African American woman titled *A Type*, accompanied the review so that readers could appreciate his talent for themselves. The article ended with a brief overview of his career and her assessment of Harleston's gentlemanly presence followed by a notation that "unlike some artistic folk, Mr. Harleston is a well-groomed person."[55] The appearance of the article in *Opportunity*, along with the cover featuring the *Bible Student*, had given Harleston the type of national exposure that had eluded him for so long. Soon after the magazine appeared on newsstands, letters of congratulations and requests for information about the artist's work began to arrive.

One such inquiry came from Jesse Binga, the Chicago realtor and South Side developer who was also president and founder of the Binga State Bank, located near the corner of 35th and State Streets on the city's South Side. Binga's life was a rags to riches story and for many Black Chicagoans, he was the personification of the American dream.[56] Mr. Binga had seen the *Bible Student* on the cover of *Opportunity* and was so taken by the image that he immediately reached out to Edwin Harleston with an offer to buy the painting. Without hesitation, the artist accepted the agreed-upon price, and within a few months the artwork was shipped to Chicago. When the painting arrived, Binga sent a note to Harleston asking for the story behind his subject.[57] In response, Harleston stated that there was really no story behind the work; it was a study of a characteristic "Negro type." Harleston was trying to capture the essence of a man who had been mellowed by the years following the "dark days of slavery" and had turned to the Scriptures for solace. The Bible verses he reads provide him with some measure of comfort, for he knows he will be compensated in the next life for the material things denied him during his time on earth. At the end of the letter, the artist conveyed the hope that the "old man" would become as dear to Binga as he had become to Harleston and his wife, Elise.[58]

In a matter of four months, Edwin Harleston made his New York debut, had an article written about him in a national African American publication, and sold a painting to one of the most important businessmen of the race. To keep the momentum going, Harleston decided to take commercial advantage of his good fortune by having a promotional brochure printed featuring his best works and most recent accomplishments. On the front of his 8½″ × 6″ pamphlet was a reproduction of the *Bible Student* with a reprint of the *Opportunity* article inside. The back page of the brochure stated that "the artist greets the public in the name of art and offers his faithful and painstaking service to those who are interested in the rendering of portraits in oil, done from life in any part of the United States." This salutation was followed by a description and list of his commissions with the address of the Harleston Studio at the bottom.[59] All this activity, in such a brief period of time, must have encouraged Harleston to reevaluate his situation and question whether his career could continue to flourish from Charleston. After a few weeks of contemplation, he concluded that if he were ever going to succeed as an artist, he had to leave South Carolina.[60]

———

EDWIN HARLESTON WAS NOT ALONE in his desire to abandon the South. After World War I, there were those who expressed the hope that the South would rise from poverty and transform itself into a place of productive farms, bustling cities, and innovative industries during this period of change. Yet, by the dawn of the 1920s, few changes had occurred in this section of the country. Mismanaged farms, low wages, poor working conditions, and inadequate education continued to be the rule rather than the exception. Although conditions in the South affected all its citizens, African Americans sustained a disproportionate measure of poverty and persecution. Their service and support of the Great War had led Black soldiers to believe that they had earned the right to full and equal citizenship for themselves and their families. But instead of receiving access to equal opportunities as tribute for their valor, these returning men were seen as a threat to society. White people were convinced that Black veterans were planning to arm themselves to forcibly take what they perceived to be rightfully theirs. The fear in the white community surrounding this issue was so pervasive that Black soldiers were often lynched while still in uniform and their families driven from homes that were then burned to the ground. In most cases, their land and personal property were also confiscated during midnight raids. Concerns over this "Black risin'" were fueled by the Ku Klux Klan, the white supremacist organization that had been revived in 1915 and had grown to more than one hundred thousand members by 1920.[61] This reign of terror accelerated the northward migration of African American citizens.

——

FOR MANY OF THOSE FLEEING TO THE NORTH, large cities such as New York and Chicago promised well-paying factory jobs and service opportunities. But Harleston was a middle-class, well-educated artist who had been nurtured by the slower-paced academic atmosphere of Atlanta and Boston. Therefore, he set his sights on Washington, DC, a place that offered the perfect combination of intellectual and artistic stimuli. A pivotal part of the capital city's well-developed cultural life was Howard University, an African American institution known for producing outstanding writers, poets, artists, and scholars. Alain Locke, professor of philosophy at the university and author of numerous articles on racial issues and African American culture, would later be recognized as the leading interpreter of this new wave of race consciousness. Other notable associates included Kelly Miller, professor of mathematics and sociology and dean of the College of Arts and Sciences, and Carter G. Woodson, a renowned historian who had written articles and books concerning the race question. The list of writers and poets who either studied or taught at Howard University included Jean Toomer, Zora Neale Hurston, Lewis Alexander, Waring Cuney, and Sterling A. Brown.[62] The idea of living and working among such talented intellectuals filled Harleston with exciting possibilities of what his life could become if his talents were nourished and cultivated in the shadow of Howard University and among those who shared his creative desires.[63]

To make this relocation happen, Harleston had to be gainfully employed. He began his search with the Washington, DC, public school system, which had a good reputation for hiring African American teachers and paying them well. In addition, he received word that an arts administrator position requiring teaching experience and training in outdoor painting might soon be available. Since Harleston had not taken any outdoor painting classes while studying at the SMFA, he decided to enroll in summer courses at the Art Institute of Chicago to qualify for the new post.[64] The process by which Harleston selected the Art Institute for advanced study is difficult to determine, but he probably knew that the school accepted students of color because William Edouard Scott, a prominent African American artist, had studied there in the early 1900s. However, the fact that his cousin, Richard Mickey, and several Atlanta University classmates lived in Chicago may have provided the impetus needed for the artist to spend his summer there.[65] When his friend, T. K. Gibson, heard that Harleston was thinking about coming to the Windy City for the summer, he wrote to his friend and enthusiastically encouraged him to ". . . come on. Chicago is here waiting for you . . . and be sure to bring your spring overcoat."[66]

In late June 1924, Harleston arrived in Chicago full of excitement and anticipation as to how his summer would unfold. As he exited the Englewood train station at 63rd and State Streets, he hailed a taxi and asked the driver to take him to 4439 Calumet Avenue, located in the Black section of Chicago known as Bronzeville. When Harleston reached the third-floor apartment, he knocked on the door and was warmly greeted by his landlady, Mrs. Farley, who escorted him to the room he would be renting.[67] A few days after settling into his temporary living quarters, Edwin wrote to his wife describing his first impressions of this burgeoning Midwestern metropolis. This is "a spacious, breezy, drab town, an overgrown frontier city with sooty building . . . not dingy, inky black buildings . . . wonderful avenues full of flying motor [cars] going 30 to 40 miles per hour."[68] Only five years prior to his arrival, the city had erupted into one of the bloodiest race riots in American history, which left thirty-eight people dead. Fortunately, the scars were beginning to heal, in part, because of the abundance of well-paying factory jobs and as Harleston described it in a note to his wife, "Negroes by the tens of thousands . . . intelligent, refined, thrifty, course, vulgar, filthy, crooked . . ." were pouring into Chicago to take advantage of these opportunities. Harleston had never seen "such a motley crew" in any of the cities where he had lived or visited, but within a brief time, he was confidently interacting with all these varied groups.[69]

On registration day, Edwin Harleston quickly walked up Michigan Avenue toward the classical beaux-arts style building looming ahead. When he reached the steps leading to the school's entrance, he briefly glanced at the two large bronze lions flanking each side of the stairs as he passed. Upon entering the lobby of the Art Institute, he joined the long line of students, both young and old, who were waiting to pay the registration fee of $27.50 per class.[70] Harleston had initially paid for three courses, but the overflow of students that summer forced him to eliminate one of his choices, leaving him with only two classes: outdoor painting and compositional illustration.[71] His instructor for the outdoor painting class was Carl R. Krafft, an artist who had received his training at the Art Institute and was a well-respected landscape artist and printmaker in the local arts community.[72] The class gathered on the steps in front of the school at nine o'clock each morning and walked from Michigan Avenue to their designated painting site for the day. Since he had never painted outdoors, Harleston knew he would have to adjust to the bright natural light, but he did not anticipate having to contend with the strong Chicago wind coming off Lake Michigan. He often struggled to keep his canvas on the easel as the debris-laden wind swept around him. On one occasion, while working near the Illinois Central Railroad, the wind deposited a drizzle of coal dust onto his canvas and in his eyes.[73]

These small inconveniences, however, did not seem to impede his progress. At the end of each session, he usually had a fairly decent oil sketch to show for his trouble. By the end of the summer, success in his landscape class was confirmed by his mastery of outdoor sketching and painting which added to his growing sense of accomplishment.[74] One of his more impressive paintings from this period is *Landscape with Painters*. This Impressionistic work shows two artists in smocks with easels standing in a grassy clearing surrounded by trees. An unidentified female figure in a pink dress leans against the tree in the foreground with her back to the viewer in a manner that suggests she might be a model. Sunlight filtered through the trees covers the female figure and the artists with broken patches of dappled light, leaving the grassy clearing in the painting's middle ground bathed in full sunlight. The strong play of light against dark gives this *plein air* painting a dramatic intensity that is absent from Harleston's other landscapes from this period, and it is obvious his use of Impressionistic color and light in this work is not an accident. Even though the artist had been exposed to Impressionism by his teachers Benson and Tarbell while studying in Boston, the most immediate influence was one of his teachers, Henry Gilbert Foote, a local artist who was a disciple of this technique. In the Chicago area during the twenties, Impressionism was the most popular style among landscape painters.[75]

Harleston's morning class ended at 12:45, giving him just enough time to make it back for his afternoon composition class. At 4:30 in the afternoon, he routinely went to the school library to examine newly acquired books and art magazines, while his evenings were spent tending to personal tasks, writing letters to Elise, or sketching.[76]

Edwin Harleston's leisurely life as an art student quickly disappeared when Jesse Binga commissioned him to paint his portrait. The businessman knew Harleston was a skilled and reputable artist, but it was Inez Canty, a Binga Bank employee and college classmate of the artist, who urged Mr. Binga to follow in the tradition of other prominent businessmen by sitting for a formal portrait.[77] Edwin wrote to Elise about this exciting news and asked for her thoughts concerning his fee. "Please don't ask me what to charge Mr. B for I'd say 1000, four figures . . . he's used to having large sums and it would mean no more to him than 10 would to you-ha ha!" she responded.[78] Settling on a fee was difficult but coming up with a time for the sittings would prove to be even more challenging. Because Binga's daily schedule was so busy, the fifty-nine-year-old mogul agreed to have his sittings in the morning before his business day began, which meant that Harleston had to be dressed and on his way to the client's home at 5922 South Park Avenue (now Martin Luther King Drive) by 5:30 each morning in order to arrive by 7:00. Since they had never had a face-to-face meeting, Harleston was unsure what to expect, but once pleasantries had been exchanged and the two had established a routine, Harleston liked the man and admired him even though Binga talked incessantly about business during these early morning sessions. But what Harleston liked most about him was his ability to hold a pose.[79]

While he was working on the new commission, Harleston received a letter from Elise inquiring about his progress. "Hope you are getting on with the 'Great Mogul's' portrait. I pray for you continually with every thought. Be humble in you thanks to Him who guides our fate. You have worked so very hard it is time you had some measure of success." In addition to her words of support, Elise also included a request. Her brother, Tom Forrest and his wife, had fallen on hard times and could no longer care for their three-year-old daughter, Doris. Elise asked her husband if they could keep the child indefinitely and provide a home for her, as they had for Gussie. "You'll love her. . . . She'll make you."[80] His wife had made so many sacrifices to support his artistic career, it was difficult for Edwin to deny her the thing she wanted most—children. He knew Elise was sensitive about the fact that they had been unable to grow a family of their own, so he usually avoided the subject, but in one of his letters he reassured his wife by telling her, "I love you for yourself and nothing shall come between us, not even childlessness."[81]

Now that his family was expanding, Edwin Harleston knew that he had to do his best work in order to attract more paying clients like Binga. Unlike the painting of the Reverend Ledbetter, in which Harleston explored the psychological nature of his subject, Harleston took a different approach with the *Portrait of Mr. Jesse Binga*. In this painting, the artist has captured the man's placid exterior without revealing the underlying steely core that must have fortified Jesse Binga during the building of his real estate and banking enterprises, while simultaneously surviving nine bombings of his home and businesses by white vandals.[82] Although the original painting has been lost, a black-and-white photograph of the portrait appeared in the exhibition catalogue, *Primitive African Sculpture/Modern Paintings, Sculpture, Drawings, Applied Art, and Books*, which was held during the Art Institute of Chicago's Negro in Art Week, November 16–23, 1927.[83] Harleston presents Binga in a traditional dark business suit and tie, seated in a straight-back armchair against a plain dark background. The subject holds a letter or perhaps a bank statement in his right hand and looks directly at the viewer with a wide-eyed, calm, and reassuring gaze. A small table located near his left arm holds a few books and a large decorative vase, the traditional symbols of knowledge and wealth. When the painting was finished and signed on August 9, 1924, the artist proudly declared to his wife that "when it is varnished, they will think he can talk."[84] Mr. Binga was also incredibly pleased with his portrait and considered the artist to be the best in his field.[85]

Edwin Harleston's good fortune continued with the notification that he had been selected by the DuPont Testimonial Association in Dover, Delaware, to paint a portrait of Pierre S. DuPont. Seen as the driving force behind the modernization of DuPont Chemical Company and General Motors, Pierre DuPont was widely recognized for his role in establishing American industrial prominence among nations around the world.[86] In addition to his achievements in the field of business, DuPont was also widely known as a philanthropist who supported, among other things, a series of educational efforts in the state of Delaware designed to improve the educational facilities for African American children. Because of his generosity, DuPont had almost single-handedly transformed the Delaware public school system from one that was barely adequate to one of the best in the country. In appreciation for the millions of dollars given by DuPont for the construction and modernization of African American schools, teachers of color from throughout the state decided that a portrait of the philanthropist would be a lasting testimonial to his altruism.[87] Harleston had been recommended for this commission by Du Bois, who had described him to the committee as "the leading portrait painter of the race."[88] When the artist's longtime friend and teacher, George Towns, heard about the commission, he sent Harleston a letter acknowledging his award by boldly declaring that "Mr. DuPont is the more to be congratulated in getting you for the artist!" In this same correspondence, Towns informed Harleston that as soon as he finished the DuPont painting, another job would be waiting for him. The alumni association was commissioning him to paint the portrait of former Atlanta University president, Edmund Twitchell Ware."[89] When he was informed that Edwin Harleston had been selected as the artist for his portrait, Ware sent him a lighthearted note in which he expressed great pleasure at the thought of following the artist's most recent portrait client into the sitter's chair. Ware likened Harleston's task to "painting the prince and the pauper, DuPont and Ware."[90]

By September of 1924, Harleston was busy working on a concept for the *Portrait of Pierre S. DuPont*. In the early stages of planning for the painting, DuPont assumed that Harleston would be using a photograph as the basis for the portrait, with one or two sittings in the final stages for finishing details. But the artist was intent on coming to DuPont's office in Wilmington, Delaware, to work on the painting in person so that he could meet this internationally recognized industrialist and develop a sense of the man in his own surroundings.[91] As in his earlier works, Harleston's approach to the DuPont painting is based on the portrait tradition of the Boston School, which includes the use of muted Tonalist color and chiaroscuro. The artist presents DuPont in a seated three-quarter position with his face turned squarely toward the viewer. To underscore DuPont's interest in education, the artist has placed a book in the subject's left hand, and on the table to his right there are additional volumes. Harleston defines the figure using strong direct lighting. DuPont's head and hands are the highest areas in value, yet the emphasis on these light sections is increased because of the subject's contrasting navy suit and the dark brown background. In less skilled hands, these areas of high intensity might have been constructed with flat, broad strokes, but Harleston has taken great care to model them with shadow and subtle variations of color. This gradation of tone from light to dark challenges the viewer to peer carefully into the shadows to see the fine details in DuPont's face and hands. Careful attention to this important aspect of portrait painting has resulted in a sober, yet sensitive image which might not have been achieved had the artist worked exclusively from a photograph. Despite the artist's effort, some of his critics felt that the dark shadows around DuPont's eyes and mouth made him look stern rather than sensitive. When DuPont's wife saw the painting, she complained that Harleston "had painted the mouth just as Mr. Sargent had done in the one, he made on Mr. DuPont giving him two pronounced shadows under the lower lip and making him appear too severe." To be compared even with John Singer Sargent's presumed errors must have seemed almost complimentary to Harleston. But in an effort to please Mrs. DuPont, Harleston tried to soften the shadows in a way that would not weaken the image too much.[92]

One of the technical problems that was not mentioned by his critics was the slightly shortened torso of the subject. In a normally proportioned

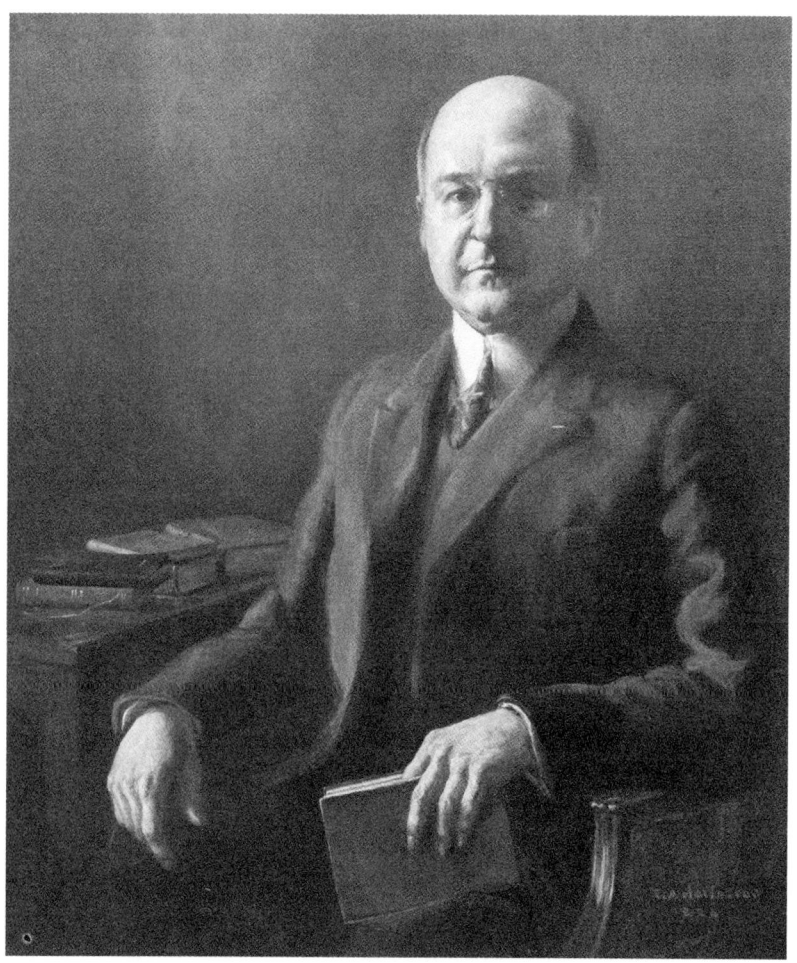

Edwin Augustus Harleston, *Portrait of Pierre S. DuPont*, oil on canvas, 1924.
Courtesy of Delaware Division of Historical and Cultural Affairs.

figure, the elbow bends at the waist. But in the DuPont portrait, his left arm is bent higher than his waistline, creating the perception that his torso is slightly shorter than normal. These minor flaws appear to have been unimportant to Pierre DuPont and the testimonial committee, both of whom expressed their genuine appreciation for the portrait. When it was presented to the public during the official DuPont tribute and unveiling ceremony at the Booker T. Washington High School auditorium on December 5, 1924, in Dover, Delaware, the public also expressed their enthusiastic admiration.[93]

Soon after the painting was completed, DuPont wrote to the artist to express his gratitude for the good work he had done and to let him know that the time spent posing had been both enjoyable and beneficial.[94] The DuPont Testimonial Association committee shared their honoree's opinion. For this group of teachers, and for the African American community at large, there was clearly a deep sense of pride that came from knowing that the portrait was painted by an African American artist. They considered Harleston's painting to be an aesthetic triumph and a cultural achievement which carried "the race one step higher."[95] This sentiment was also expressed in *The Philadelphia Tribune*, the area's largest Black newspaper. In the Saturday, November 15, 1924, edition of the paper, bold headline stretched across the entire width of the paper's front page proclaiming, "COLORED ARTIST PAINTING A PICTURE OF MAN WHO GAVE MILLIONS FOR EDUCATION."[96] Edwin Harleston had finally achieved the national recognition for which he had been striving most of his life.

While Harleston was still working on the DuPont portrait, the artist received word that the Coolidge Republican Club of Boston had submitted a proposal to the national committee commissioning a portrait of President Calvin Coolidge designating Edwin A. Harleston as the artist.[97] Upon its completion, the finished painting would be presented to Howard University or the veteran's hospital in Tuskegee, Alabama.[98] Because Coolidge sympathized with Black civic leaders on some problems regarding their plight in American society, the club thought this gesture would stimulate interest among African American voters in his 1924 bid for reelection. Their offer was favorably received by the president and the chairman of the Republican National Committee, William M. Butler. But in a letter to the club, Butler stated that Coolidge had so many speaking engagements to fulfill prior to the election that he would not have time to sit for the portrait. However, their proposal would be reconsidered after the election.[99] While it may have been true that Coolidge had other obligations, his noninvolvement with any special interest groups or individuals was part of a well-thought-out campaign strategy designed to keep the president free from controversy before the election.[100] Coolidge was elected to a second term of office; however, the portrait proposal was never mentioned again.

Harleston wasted no time lamenting the loss of such a high-profile commission because President Ware was anxiously waiting for the artist to begin work on his portrait. The day before Harleston was to meet with Ware, he made a quick visit to Washington, DC, although the reason for the trip remains unknown. Since he was still trying to gain employment with the local school board, he may have been checking on the status of his job application. Whatever the reason, during his excursion, Harleston visited the National Gallery of Art to examine the portraits for some last-minute ideas. He was particularly interested in studying Edmund Tarbell's portraits of Woodrow Wilson and Herbert C. Hoover, both completed in 1921, to refresh his memory on the methods his teacher used in rendering the skin tones of Caucasians.[101] For more than ten years, he had concentrated exclusively on mastering the subtle complexities of African American skin coloring, and in doing so, he wrote Elise that he had forgotten some of the "little things" he had learned as a student about how to paint white skin effectively.[102] Harleston must have sensed a slight loss of mastery in this area while working on the DuPont portrait, for why else would he search for this type of technical information so soon after painting a picture similar in type?

Work on the *Portrait of Edmund Twitchell Ware* began on Tuesday, November 24, 1924, at the Montclair, New Jersey, home of the former Atlanta University president.[103] This bust-length portrait is similar in compositional structure to the Adams painting that Harleston had completed five years earlier, but instead of a suit, Ware is dressed in his academic robe. However, the main element separating the Ware and Adams paintings is color. The Adams portrait is bland and pale with flecks of pale yellow, violet, and pink along with various shades of beige constructing his face, while the Ware portrait is bursting with vibrant colors. Although Harleston has used some of the same pastel hues found in the Adams painting, added strokes of green, red, and blue that are high in intensity. This subtle use of pure color seems to electrify Ware's face with a kind of rich, vibrant energy that is new in Harleston's work. Although this expressive use of color introduced a fresh vitality into Harleston's painting style, there was an anatomical problem with the painting. The artist had placed a slight bulge along the bridge of Ware's nose, but the former president did not comment on the problem immediately. However, by New Year's Day 1925, Ware decided to communicate his dissatisfaction with the portrait by writing a letter to Harleston in which he stated the following: "I suppose that it is naturally difficult for me and the family to be entirely pleased with the portrait of myself. I am too nearly related to the project to be objective, however, the line of [my] nose from the brow to the tip of the nose is nearly, if not, quite straight in line. The portrait makes it look more like a Roman nose."[104] There is no record of Harleston's response to Ware's criticism; however, it is clear, in examining the painting, that the nose was never corrected.

Although Edwin Harleston was becoming a successful portrait painter, his business acumen left much to be desired. He had entered into an agreement with the Testimonial Association for the DuPont portrait without a written agreement and the six hundred dollars he had been promised upon completion of the work had not been paid. After several letters had been sent requesting compensation with no reply, one of the artist's friends suggested that he take legal action if the money was not immediately forthcoming.[105] To make matters worse, business at the funeral home was off considerably, and his father was constantly pressuring him to come home to assist with the day-to-day management of the family enterprise. Captain Harleston only had four or five competitors when he first opened, but now there were eight other funeral parlors in close proximity competing for the business of a dwindling Black population. The exodus of thousands of African American citizens from South Carolina who had joined the

Great Migration north was a contributing factor to the economic downturn in the city and throughout the state. On top of everything else, Elise often complained that the lack of money for daily expenses had become almost unbearable, especially since Christmas was only a month away. She reminded him that the promise he made two years earlier to improve their financial situation had not been fulfilled, and his continued absences from home were beginning to strain their relationship.[106] In spite of these difficulties, Harleston was unyielding in his desire to build a career as an artist and continued to strive even harder to reach his goal.

Just when everything seemed on the verge of collapse, Edwin Harleston received a portrait commission from the Martin-Smith Music School in New York. One of the school's founders, David Irwin Martin, had recently died and to honor his contribution to the institution, the faculty and staff decided that a full-length portrait would be an appropriate memorial for this accomplished composer, violinist, and teacher. Harleston had been recommended for the commission by Du Bois, and, perhaps out of gratitude for his friend's endorsement, the artist accepted. But the most compelling reason for Harleston's acceptance of the job was money![107] The school was offering to pay him one hundred dollars in advance and four hundred upon completion of the portrait, which was reason enough to accept. Unlike his other commissions, Harleston had no sitter with whom he could work, only a photograph of the deceased. There is also a strong possibility that the artist never had the opportunity to meet David Martin or see him perform, since he was not a nationally recognized talent, thus eliminating any chance of infusing Martin's image with any personal memories. This assumption may account for the uncharacteristically stiff, wooden quality of the figure in the *Portrait of David Martin* and the lack of subtle modeling seen in this portrait.

In the summer of 1925, Harleston returned to the Art Institute of Chicago to continue his landscape classes even though the financial situation at home had not improved, and Elise's dissatisfaction with his extended absences continued to cause problems in their marriage. She had been left behind to shoulder the responsibilities of wife, mother, funeral home employee, household and studio manager, without an inordinate number of complaints, while her husband traveled the country in pursuit of his dream. Elise even took on the task of washing and ironing the dirty laundry Harleston mailed home each week to save money so he could buy brushes, paint, and other things while on the road. Yet, Edwin seemed to be taking her sacrifice for granted. After more than a week had passed without a letter from her husband, Elise poured out her frustration in a rage-filled letter. In response, Harleston did not open his correspondence with the usual endearing phrases but began by formally addressing her, "My dear Elise, I am writing to let you know I am well, working and willing to write if you will let me do so . . . , but if I have such another nightmare of a letter from you soon again I fear it will wreck me. I have gone a long time without being so thoroughly upset. Are you ill?" At the end of his letter, Harleston thanked his wife for the freshly laundered shirts she had included in the box he had received but wondered, " How can I reconcile the owner of the hands that would do this for me with the author of so bitter a letter—I am shocked—I am so sorry. Your husband." By the following week, Elise's vitriolic words had disappeared and the loving banter that usually filled their letters had returned, but their financial woes persisted.

To ease their situation, Harleston instructed Elise to make a list of all his unframed studies and sketches so that he could have them framed for sale. Chicago artist, William E. Scott, offered to assist him with the project by helping him find bargains on picture molding since he knew many of the framers and art dealers in the city.[108] Scott was a seasoned portrait and landscape painter who had studied at the Art Institute, Académie Julien, Académie Colarossi, and had been mentored by Henry Tanner while in Paris. The artist also bore the distinction of having his work accepted in the Paris Salon of 1912 and 1913 as well as London's Royal Academy. Now Scott was back in Chicago trying to determine what his next career move would be.[109]

In the beginning, the relationship between these two artists was friendly but during the summer, a gentlemanly rivalry developed. It began when Harleston and Scott both applied for the mural commission advertised by the Supreme Life and Casualty Company, headquartered in Chicago. Harleston felt certain he would be awarded the project since he had presented the original idea to his close friend, T. K. Gibson, a company executive. But when the designated artist was officially announced, William E. Scott had been awarded the commission, not Harleston.[110] The second upset involved the Miss Golden Brown Girl of America National Beauty Contest of 1925. Madame Mamie Hightower, the purported founder of the Golden Brown Chemical Company in Memphis, Tennessee, decided to launch a national competition to find the most "ravishing beauty" of the race in order to boost sales of the company's hair products, perfumes, cremes, and powders. The winner would receive an all-expenses paid trip to Atlantic City, a new Hudson automobile, and several other prizes.[111] Since none of his prospects for portraits had materialized, Harleston assured his wife that he was "going to do something . . . to get in the news again soon."[112] When the ad for the beauty contest appeared in *The Chicago Defender*, the artist saw this as the perfect opportunity to get the national publicity he wanted by awarding a painting of the winning contestant as an additional prize. During the first week of August, Harleston wrote to Madame Hightower with the suggestion.[113] In response, Madame Hightower expressed gratitude for receiving this idea from "one of the foremost artists of the world" and informed Harleston that she would take his suggestion under advisement.[114] A few weeks later, an announcement of the Miss Golden Brown Girl commission appeared in the newspaper designating William E. Scott as the artist. Harleston was understandably disappointed after losing twice to Scott, but he probably took comfort in knowing that he was the source of both commission ideas.[115] One year later, it was discovered that Madame Mamie Hightower was, in fact, a fictitious character developed by a white cosmetic company as a marketing ploy to gain a portion of Madam C. J. Walker's beauty products business and, to date, there is no evidence a Golden Girl portrait was ever completed by Scott.

Fortunately, the summer did not pass without Edwin Harleston experiencing victory for himself. On Wednesday, August 11, 1925, Du Bois sent a telegram to the artist announcing that he had won the seventy-five-dollar NAACP Amy Spingarn First Prize in Art for Illustration along with Albert A. Smith and Hale Woodruff, who received the forty-dollar second prize and the ten-dollar third prize, respectively.[116] The mission of this annual award was to recognize the achievements of literary and visual African American artists and "to bring to light the infinite riches that lies [*sic*] hidden in the soul of a gifted race."[117] Each Spingarn Prize applicant was required to sign the work on the back with a pseudonym to shield their identity from the judges. In this instance, Edwin Harleston chose the Greek pseudonym "Outis," meaning "no one," for his entry to the competition. The painting he submitted, *Portrait of a Woman*, was not a "character study" or commissioned portrait but an attempt by Harleston to break free from his conservative Boston School style to experiment with a more modern approach to portraiture. Things had changed since the war and so had the art world. As he traveled from Charleston to the museums and galleries in New York, Boston, and Chicago, Harleston could see and feel the social and aesthetic shifts occurring and wanted to make every effort to keep up with these rapidly changing trends. In the Black community, some of these ideological changes were being fueled by Alain Locke's book, *The New Negro*, an anthology of essays, poems, and short stories that sought to erase old African American stereotypes and replace them with a more realistic, multilayered interpretation of Black life and culture. Locke, a Philadelphian who had been educated at Harvard, the University of Berlin, and Oxford University, was the first African American Rhodes Scholar. In his position as professor of philosophy at Howard University and an art and literary critic for *Opportunity* magazine, Locke was inspired by the efforts among many African American writers and visual artists working in New York to tell their own stories by abandoning the stereotypes fabricated by those outside the race.[118] Scholars have considered the collection of essays, short stories, and poems to be a defining document of the period, which would later be known as the Harlem Renaissance.

To encourage this aesthetic shift, Locke subscribed to the idea that artists should be free to interpret ideas in their own unique way without having to adhere to a political agenda.[119] Edwin Harleston seems to have embraced this notion in *Portrait of a Woman*. In this painting, for which Elise was probably the model, the artist presents the image of a young Black woman who looks over her right shoulder to visually engage the

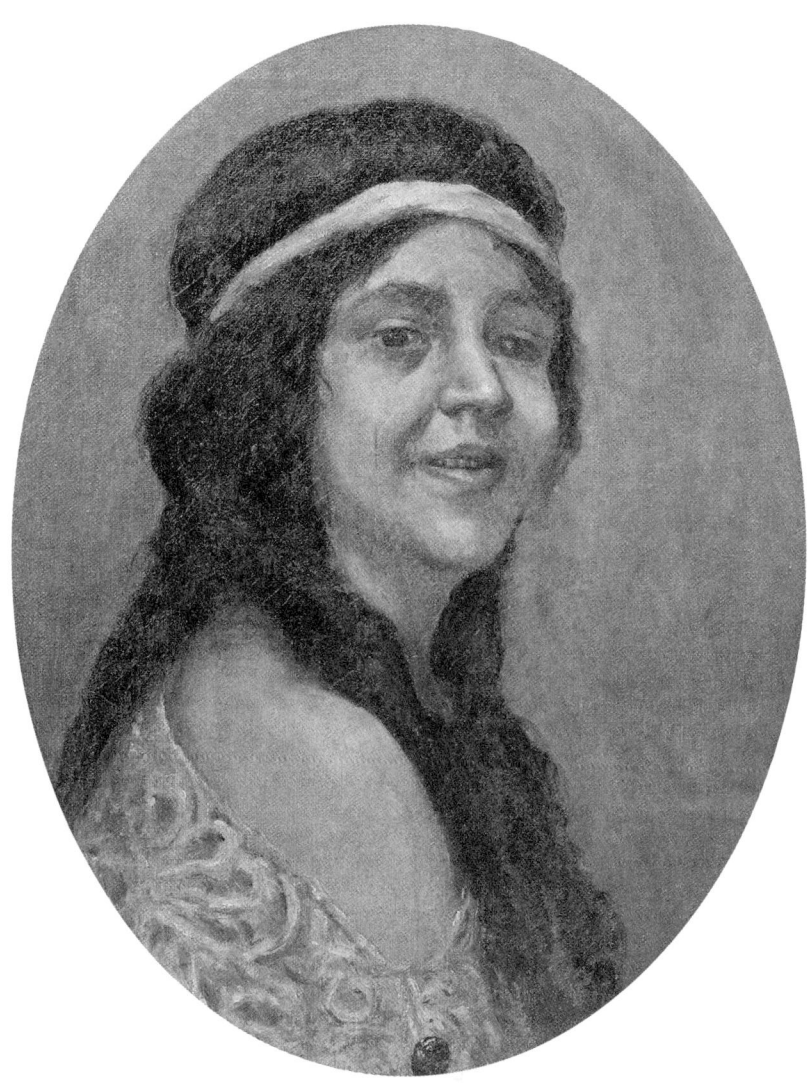

Edwin Augustus Harleston, *Portrait of a Woman*, oil on canvas, 1925.
Courtesy of SCAD Museum of Art, Permanent Collection Gift
of Walter O. Evans and Mrs. Linda J. Evans.

artist and the viewer with a coquettish smile. She wears a lacy, off-the-shoulder chemise and a gold-colored headband which holds her long black hair in place. Unlike the somber hues used in his earlier Tonalist portraits, Harleston has infused this painting with a golden glow created by the layering of yellow and brown oil paint of varying values. His choice of color may have also been a subtle response to his commission rejection by the Miss Golden Brown Girl of America selection committee. Whatever the reason, the result is a warm, vibrant image of a modern woman who reflects the free spirit of this new era, and like the Ledbetter painting, *Portrait of a Woman* represents another important shift in Edwin Harleston's style.[120]

When the title of the winning artwork was finally announced, Edwin and Elise were shocked to discover that one of his earlier character studies, *A Colored Grand Army Man*, had won the prize. This drawing is similar in style to the *Bible Student* because it exhibits the same quiet, introspective façade. The sitter for this drawing was fellow Charlestonian, Smart Chisolm, a former Civil War soldier who was now a member of the Grand Army of the Republic (GAR).[121] Based on a three-quarter-length photograph taken by Elise, the photo shows a dark brown, aging soldier posed in front of a light backdrop. His weatherworn, deeply lined face looks confidently into the camera's lens with a self-assured gaze that is softened by the slightly upturned corners of his mouth that are partially hidden by the white stubble of his mustache and beard. A heavy shadow has been cast by his wide-brimmed hat, making the circles under his eyes and the wrinkles across his forehead and cheeks seem even more dramatic. In comparing the photograph with the drawing, it can be easily discerned that Harleston has altered the image of Chisolm in a manner that imbues him with a softer, more sensitive appearance. The harsh lines that defined Chisolm's face in the photograph have been dissolved into smoothly modeled tones in the drawing. These changes help to create a sentimental portrait of the formerly enslaved man who was willing to fight for his freedom. Chisolm, who was in his mid-eighties when the portrait was made, felt so strongly about the cause for which he fought that he often said that if the United States Army ever needed him, he would gladly fight again![122]

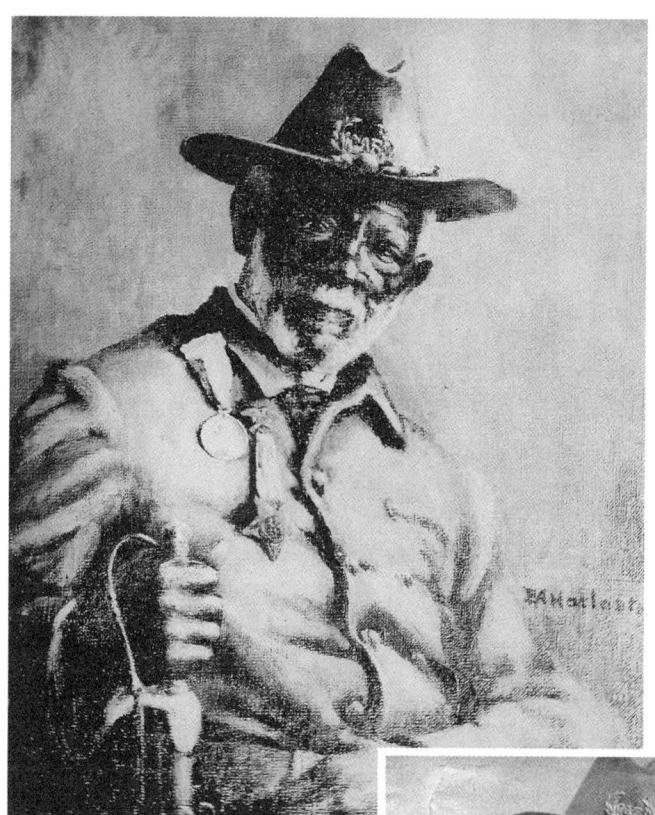

Edwin Augustus Harleston,
A Colored Grand Army Man,
graphite on paper, 1925.
Collection of Mae Whitlock
Gentry (*above*). Elise Forrest
Harleston, *A Colored Grand
Army Man* (Smart Chisolm),
photograph, 1925. Collection of
Mae Whitlock Gentry (*right*).

In a letter to her husband, Elise expressed her disbelief. "What is this?" she exclaimed. "How did the old man get in the contest? I was all puffed up over the result as I was sure it was your golden brown girl. I am so very disappointed . . . I suppose Dr. Du Bois entered it. Did you know he would?"[123] It is unclear how the drawing came into Du Bois's possession, but there is little doubt as to why he entered Harleston's *A Colored Grand Army Man* into the competition. Since the inception of *The Crisis*, Dr. W. E. B. Du Bois had used the magazine to promote his ideas about race in the articles, stories, and illustrations that filled the pages of the publication. He believed that art was to be used as a propaganda tool for the purpose of racial uplift and that artworks such as *Portrait of a Woman*, which were appreciated primarily for their beauty, were frivolous and would lead to "decadence."[124] Du Bois made no secret of the fact that the visual arts played an important role in his multifaceted campaign to redefine the Black image in his effort to instill racial pride. With the dawning of the New Negro movement, however, Alain Locke and his acolytes challenged this notion by promoting the idea that art should be appreciated "for its own sake" and that individual creativity should take precedence over social or political ideologies.[125] Unwilling to give this idea credence, Du Bois took it upon himself to enter *A Colored Grand Army Man* on Edwin Harleston's behalf. To him, this image supported his efforts to depict accurately the pride-filled image of Black men, such as Smart Chisolm, who had fought for the liberty of enslaved people and, in doing so, had done their part to earn full citizenship rights for African Americans. In comparison, *Portrait of a Woman* was a pretty picture that had little, if any, political value as far as Du Bois was concerned. In the opinion piece, "Criteria of Negro Art," which appeared in *The Crisis*, he emphatically declared that he did not "care a damn for any art that is not used for propaganda."[126] Du Bois also had a reputation to protect. Over the years, he had recommended Harleston for important commissions and in doing so, considered the artist to be a standard bearer in Du Bois's crusade to redefine the Black public image. Therefore, Du Bois could not allow an artwork that did not reflect his mission to be considered for such an important cultural event.

Soon after the Spingarn Prize winner was announced, articles detailing Harleston's accomplishments appeared in the African American press. Even white neighbors, who had never shown interest or taken his art career seriously, were now asking Captain Harleston about his son "the artist."[127] Although Edwin Harleston was pleased with the recognition surrounding his achievement, he realized that his success would never have been possible had it not been for the many sacrifices made by his wife, Elise. In a letter to her, Harleston acknowledged her role in winning the Spingarn Prize by declaring that the award was not his alone, but it belonged to both of them.[128]

As the summer drew to a close, Edwin Harleston was shaken from his aesthetic reverie with a notice from the State Board of Embalmers that he would have to take an examination on the third of September in Columbia, South Carolina, to renew his license.[129] Working as a mortician had not been a priority for Harleston for quite some time. In fact, he was hoping to abandon the profession altogether and devote himself to his art if the position in Washington ever materialized. But now, these plans seemed in serious doubt. The funeral home was still his primary source of income, and his father's control over his life, tying him to the business all these years, seemed just as strong as ever. Reluctantly, Harleston agreed to set aside his artwork to prepare for the examination. He confided in Elise that "it is rather unfortunate for us as I had just started on the furtherance of a very definite campaign to get some portrait work, but now, I must give it over."[130] In the perpetual struggle between the family business and his art career, the business seemed to be winning.

7

HOPES CRUSHED TO EARTH

WITH THE STATE EMBALMER'S examination successfully behind him, Edwin Harleston was back in New York by early November. His mission on this trip was to visit as many exhibitions as possible so he could gather new ideas for his artwork and assess current trends. But what he enjoyed most about being in the city was strolling the streets of Harlem. In one of his weekly letters to Elise, he expressed his excitement at being back in a place where African American pride and creativity were on display at every turn.[1] As far as Harleston was concerned, being in the presence of Black intellectuals was the best of all possible worlds, but it was also becoming evident that he was rapidly falling out of step with those who populated the land of the New Negro, especially the visual artists.[2] This fear was supported in Alain Locke's article, "Legacy of the Ancestral Arts," in which he calls attention to those artists whom he believed had fallen short of their creative greatness because their artwork was not grounded in African aesthetic principles. The absence of such ancestral tenets, according to Locke,

> explains why the generation of Negro artists succeeding Henry Tanner
> had only the inspiration of his great success to fire their ambitions,
> but not the guidance of a distinctive tradition to focus and direct their
> talents. Consequently, these artists have fumbled and fallen short of their

international stride. The work of W. E. Scott, E. A. Harleston, W. Braxton, W. Farrow, and Laura Wheeler in painting, and of Meta Fuller and May Howard Jackson in sculpture, competent as it has been, has felt this handicap and wavered between abstract expression which was imitative and not highly original, and racial expression which was only experimental. Lacking group leadership and concentration, they are wondering amateurs in the very field that might have given them concerted mastery.[3]

The publication of Locke's essay came at a time when white intellectuals were criticizing the provincialism of American life, while offering up the Black artist as a curiously refreshing cultural personality in modern America.[4] As a result, new attention was given to the thoughts and images produced by these artists. Many of the painters and sculptors who read Locke's words had studied in Europe and were beginning to experiment with a combination of African imagery and abstraction. But Harleston remained faithful to realism, the gold standard of academic tradition, despite Locke's criticism. Although he had been relegated to the fringe of this movement by Locke and others, Harleston felt he could benefit from the ripple effect caused by this cultural phenomenon.

This new wave of interest in African American aesthetics seemed to provide the perfect opportunity for Harleston to breathe fresh life into his faltering career as a portrait painter. But rather than send random requests to patrons with the hope of receiving a positive response, he decided to ask personal friends and acquaintances for their patronage. Meta Vaux Warrick Fuller was one of the first people he contacted. Fuller was a trained sculptor who had studied in Paris at the Colarossi Academy, maintained a close friendship with Henry Tanner, and had received critical evaluations of her work from Auguste Rodin. Upon her return from Europe in 1905, Fuller exhibited her work extensively, and in 1907, she was commissioned to create a tableau illustrating the achievements of African Americans for the Jamestown Tercentennial Exposition. Because of her talent, race, and gender, the young sculptor was widely known in art circles throughout the United States. Meta Fuller and Edwin Harleston probably met while he was a student at the SMFA in Boston. Three years after her marriage to Dr. Solomon C. Fuller, the nation's first African American psychiatrist and chief of pathology at the Boston University School of Medicine, Meta Fuller's studio was destroyed by fire in 1910 along with much of the artwork she had produced in Europe. Although devastated by the loss, Fuller continued to produce small sculptures in her home and limited her artistic pursuits to the Boston area in order to care for her family.[5] Yet, her career limitations had not diminished her standing in the community for Meta Fuller was respected and well connected with access to a small but influential circle of the city's African American citizenry. What began as a casual association eventually developed into a genuine friendship during Harleston's recuperation from surgery at the Hinton's home in Canton, Massachusetts. The Hintons and Fullers were close friends who visited each other frequently and because of their relationship, Harleston had no qualms about asking Meta Fuller if she would be interested in having her husband's portrait painted. Unfortunately, Dr. Fuller had not been well and was looking "rather thin and tired;" therefore, Meta Fuller thought it best to wait until another time.[6] The year ended with promises from Fuller and other friends for commissions, but nothing materialized.

Harleston spent much of his time during the early months of 1926 working with his father at the funeral home. The monotony of his daily tasks was occasionally broken by small exhibitions of his work at local civic club gatherings and schools in the area. Claflin University, an African American institution in Orangeburg, South Carolina, invited him to deliver a talk at the unveiling ceremony of a Tanner painting that had been recently acquired by the school.[7] Other than these minor distractions, there was little that sparked Harleston's interest.

In March he was visited by Mrs. Clelia P. McGowan, chairman of the South Carolina Inter-Racial Committee headquartered in Columbia, South Carolina, and the mayor of Charleston, Thomas P. Stoney.[8] McGowan was representing Dr. George E. Haynes, secretary of the executive board of the Federal Council of Churches of Christ in America and a nationally recognized African American civic leader. Hayes had been given the responsibility of identifying candidates for the Harmon Foundation's first annual Awards for Distinguished Achievement Among Negroes.[9] Harleston was being considered for one of these prestigious awards; therefore, McGowan wanted to see his works firsthand. The reason for Stoney's presence during this visit is unclear, but he was undoubtedly impressed with Harleston's work after seeing the studio, so much so that he contacted Laura Bragg, director of The Charleston Museum to investigate the possibility of organizing a showing of Harleston's artworks. Although the museum was primarily a science and natural history institution associated with the College of Charleston, rooms in the building were often converted into art exhibition spaces. In his letter to Bragg, Stoney expounded upon his reason for wanting the show by stating how impressed he was by the artist and thought that the citizens of Charleston would be interested to know that the supportive cultural environment of the city had "so impressed a member of the colored race that he had gone out and perfected himself in the art of painting and crayon drawing." In closing, Stoney asked if an exhibition of Harleston's artwork could be arranged for doing so would promote "a worthy individual of the opposite race."[10] Since Stoney was fully aware of the fact that African Americans were prohibited from attending most of the city-sponsored cultural events, it is ironic that he credited Harleston's success as an artist to Charleston's cultural environment.

Bragg received Stoney's suggestion with enthusiasm, for she was a New England Progressive who had grown up with a sense of empathy for people of color. This race consciousness had been cultivated during her formative years on the campus of Rust College, a historically Black institution in Marshall County, Mississippi. Bragg's father, a Methodist minister and missionary who taught mathematics at the college, resigned his position and returned to his home in Massachusetts in 1892 because of rising Klan violence.[11] This experience informed Bragg's initiatives to encourage the African American community to visit the Museum and saw this exhibition as an opportunity to reach this segment of the city's population.[12] But in her response to Stoney, Bragg approached the importance of this show from a business point of view by bringing to the mayor's attention that the South was frequently criticized for its supposed lack of appreciation for the attainments of "the negro race." He should, therefore, take the opportunity to point to this exhibit during the next meeting of the Foreign

Trade Council, and let the members know that he had taken the initiative, as mayor of the city, to mount this exhibition.[13]

An objective of Stoney's mayoral campaign had been to establish Charleston as a main port of the eastern seaboard. Such a designation could have multiple benefits including increased shipping trade, which would give the city's sagging economy a much-needed boost, and eventually improve the quality of Charleston's cultural life, thereby making this art show even more appealing.[14] For Harleston, it meant that he would finally be recognized for his talent by the white arts community. But more important, it provided him with the opportunity to exhibit his works to family and friends in his home city's largest and most prestigious facility, the "first museum founded in America," The Charleston Museum.[15]

Edwin Harleston met with Bragg to select the works for his exhibition in early April of 1926. After carefully examining the artist's paintings and drawings, she selected several oil portraits along with some works on paper, which Harleston readily agreed to frame for the show. As she sifted through his portfolio and chatted with him about his experiences as an artist, Bragg discovered that the two of them had quite a bit in common. Laura Bragg, who was a senior at Simmons College the year Harleston arrived in Boston, was familiar with the SMFA and spent much of her free time in the museum and often traveled to New York to visit the Metropolitan Museum.[16] By the end of the studio visit, the date of April 25 had been agreed upon. Harleston's two-week exhibition would follow a showing of watercolor paintings by Margaret May Dashiell, a resident of Richmond, Virginia, known for her genre scenes of the Old South.

Edwin Harleston shared the news of his upcoming exhibition with family and friends, and he also made a list of eighteen Charleston ministers who could be counted on to spread the word about his show.[17] But by the end of the month, preparations for his Charleston debut had taken an unsavory turn. Members of the white arts community who had gotten wind of Harleston's impending exhibition were outraged that an African American artist, no matter how talented, was actually being invited to display works in The Charleston Museum. Their reaction should not have been a surprise for two of the city's most prominent artists, Alice

Ravenel Huger Smith and Elizabeth O'Neill Verner, thought of "Charleston as a world where all the whites were aristocrats and all blacks were servants," and of course, servants could never be allowed to occupy their most important cultural space.[18] To make sure the show did not occur, local artist groups, such as the Carolina Art Association and the Charleston Etchers Club in which both Smith and Verner held membership, along with those who "aspired to paint," pressured the museum director and members of the board of trustees to abandon the idea. Out of fear that this negative reaction might develop into a larger upheaval, the invitation to exhibit was withdrawn. However, none of this information was made public.[19] Bragg tried to explain the cancellation of the exhibition in a letter to the artist which read:

> My dear Mr. Harleston:
>
> Unforeseen circumstances made it necessary for me to have a conference with the Mayor in regard to your exhibit and we decided that, in consequence of this, the exhibit would hurt and not help you at the present time. I, therefore, have to tell you that it will be necessary to postpone an exhibit of your portraits until a time when it can be given with benefit to you.
>
> I am afraid you may have been at some expense for frames that you would not have incurred otherwise. In this case, if you will let me know the amount, I will pay it personally.[20]

Unfortunately, the letter from Laura Bragg was sent to the wrong address, making Harleston unaware of what had taken place. Bragg realized the mistake when she received a package from the artist containing some of his exhibition catalogues along with the list of local ministers.[21] She quickly dashed off a note enclosing a copy of the original communication as proof that it had been sent earlier. At the end of this letter, she reiterated that his exhibition had been deferred, not cancelled.[22] When Harleston finally received the official notification that his show had been "postponed," the words hit him like a punch to the gut, for he knew that he would never have an exhibition at the museum. This news was so devastating that nearly two weeks passed before he was able to respond. When he finally gathered his thoughts to express his dismay, Harleston conveyed his regret over the misdirected letter and in a gentlemanly manner, explained that if he had been called or otherwise notified,

> I should have been a little better prepared for the disappointment caused by the postponement of the exhibit of some of my work at the Museum. I beg you to be assured, however, that this delay in replying to your kind letter has not been due to discourtesy on my part but rather to the disconcerting statement of the postponement without my knowing the cause of it. It might not make much difference whether I know or not, but you will understand that I have been very much embarrassed.
>
> Thank you very much for your kind offer in regard to the framing but as that is an ordinary item in our line I would not think of bothering you with it.
>
> Please keep the catalogues for me as they are the only copies I have.[23]

This letter communicated his disappointment and embarrassment. Yet, none of the bitterness caused by this rejection or the self-recrimination he must have felt for believing his talent had given him the power to transcend local views about race was never conveyed to his friends or the larger community.

It is difficult to believe that Edwin Harleston was unaware of the circumstances that resulted in the cancellation of his exhibition, for he had never been recognized by the white arts community for his artistic achievements during the decade following his return. Although race was the primary reason for his exclusion, Harleston's professional training and choice of subject matter also helped to fuel the campaign against him.

One of the best-known local artists of this period, Alice Ravenel Huger Smith, who frequently exhibited at The Charleston Museum, was a self-taught artist.[24] In spite of this lack of formal training, Smith and her close-knit circle of friends, which included Elizabeth O'Neill Verner, had successfully gained local and national recognition along with impressive financial profits for their images of the Old South.[25] In many of their paintings, watercolors, drawings, and prints, familiar city landmarks and landscapes were conflated with imaginary depictions of anonymous working-class African Americans in their roles as laborers, domestic servants, and street vendors. Their presence was not only supposed to add a sense of exoticism to these images, but it was also presumed that these Black bodies represented the majority of the city's African American population. Their inclusion, therefore, was meant to reinforce their status as part of a permanent underclass in an attempt by members of the white elite to reenvision Charleston's past.

In stark contrast to Smith and her cohorts, Edwin Harleston was a professionally trained artist whose portraits and drawings affirmed his superior knowledge of the human form and mastery of painterly techniques. But it was his subject matter that probably caused the white arts community the most angst. The body of work Harleston had planned to exhibit focused on Charleston's Black middle class, which included portraits of Reverend Ledbetter, Congressman Thomas E. Miller, African American soldiers who had served their country during the Civil War and World War I, along with other prominent citizens, including members of his own family. If Edwin Harleston had been allowed to display the artworks that he and Laura Bragg had selected for the exhibition, those images would have shattered the myth of Black inferiority perpetuated by Smith, Verner, and other Charleston artists. Under no circumstances could they allow such a bold and public assault on this white fictionization of Blackness to go on public display, therefore the invitation to exhibit at The Charleston Museum had to be withdrawn.[26]

A few days after receiving Bragg's communique, Harleston received a letter from Clelia P. McGowan informing him that he had been nominated for the first Harmon Foundation Award in the area of fine arts. In order to qualify, six photographs of his most recent works along with the enclosed application form needed to be sent to New York immediately.[27] Because he was still deeply wounded by the withdrawal of the museum's invitation, Harleston ignored the request. However, McGowan was determined to have this nationally recognized South Carolina artist enter the competition, so a second invitation was sent, but this time Harleston responded.[28]

The foundation sponsoring the award competition had been organized by William Elmer Harmon, a philanthropist who had earned his fortune in real estate at the turn of the century.[29] By 1920, Harmon had turned the business over to his son so that he could dedicate more time to philanthropic efforts. The original purpose of the Harmon Award was to recognize the accomplishments of individuals in business and industry, science and invention, education, race relations, religious service, literature, music, and fine arts. The arts category also gave special recognition to the best painting by a first-time exhibitor at the National Academy of Design exhibition. Prize money, which ranged from one hundred to three hundred dollars, was to be used to further the work of each recipient. Earlier drafts of the proposed program made no mention of race, but by October of 1925, the focus of this initiative had shifted to the achievements of African Americans.[30]

The excitement surrounding the New Negro movement had influenced this change in the awards plan and at the urging of Alain Locke, Harmon was now looking for the best African American artists in the country to participate in the competition.[31] To make sure the quality of the works met with his standards, Harmon called on some of the candidates to see their work for himself. While he was in the Charleston area overseeing the restoration of a South Carolina plantation house he had recently purchased, Harmon made an appointment to visit Harleston's studio on Friday, June 18, 1926.[32] On the appointed day, Harmon, along with his wife, Helen, entered the Harleston home without knocking or ringing the bell, came upstairs to the studio, and announced himself. Although Harleston was probably startled and maybe even a bit annoyed by this display of unwelcome familiarity, the rest of the afternoon went well. As Harmon looked around the studio admiring Harleston's work, he identified several paintings he wanted the artist to send to New York for the judging. *The Soldier, Portrait of Reverend Caesar S. Ledbetter, Portrait of Mr. Miller, A Colored Grand Army Man,* and a recent portrait of Elise that Harleston had not yet finished were among the works selected.

Harmon and his wife had developed a particular fondness for portraiture because of their association with William Paxton, who had painted both of their portraits while they were living in Boston. Perhaps it was this experience, coupled with his general appreciation of art, which made Harmon believe he had an eye for art and was, therefore, qualified to be on the awards panel of judges. At the end of the visit, Harmon expressed his earnest admiration for the artist's work and confided to Harleston that some of the works by other artists were in no way comparable to his. Even though Harmon would have only one vote as a judge, he sincerely hoped that "one of the awards, especially the first [prize] would come to Charleston."[33] After such an enthusiastic endorsement, Harleston felt he had a better than even chance of winning the Harmon Award. In addition, Mayor Stoney, conceivably as a gesture of redress, sent a special letter of recommendation to the foundation in support of the artist's nomination, which probably raised his hope even higher.[34]

The fine arts panel, which convened in New York in the fall of 1926, included two artists, two architects, and the award's founder, William Harmon. National Academy artists Gifford Beal and Howard Butler were originally asked to serve as judges; however, they were unable to participate. George Haynes then invited Francis Coates Jones, an academy member who also taught still-life painting, and sculptor Meta Warrick Fuller to participate in the selection process. Jones accepted the invitation, but Fuller was unable to come to New York on the day the panel convened. Fortunately, Laura Wheeler Waring, a painter who had been trained at the Pennsylvania Academy of the Fine Arts and who had participated in several exhibitions with Harleston, was willing to serve. William A. Boring, dean of the Columbia School of Architecture, and architect Grosvenor Atterbury rounded out the group of artists invited to review the works submitted by the twelve applicants.[35]

After a general discussion of the works, the field of award candidates was narrowed to Palmer Hayden, Hale Woodruff, and Edwin Harleston. The first candidate, Palmer Hayden, was a thirty-six-year-old artist who had taught himself to paint through correspondence courses and night classes while he performed odd jobs around Greenwich Village during the day. It was here that he met Victor Perard, a French artist who was teaching at Cooper Institute (now Cooper Union). Although Perard encouraged Hayden's artistic aspirations, it was Alice Miller Dike, a wealthy textile heiress, who suggested that Hayden enter the Harmon Foundation Award competition while he was away, studying in Paris.[36] The second nominee, Hale Woodruff, who was also living in Paris at the time, was a twenty-six-year-old artist who had studied landscape painting at the Herron Art School in Indianapolis, Indiana, under William Forsyth and had studied part-time at the Art Institute of Chicago.[37] Even though these two candidates seemed promising, William Harmon was still in full support of Edwin Harleston as the first-prize winner.

When the written evaluations of the panelists were submitted to George Haynes for final tabulation it became clear that the others did not share Harmon's enthusiasm for Edwin Harleston's artwork. Francis Jones dismissed Harleston's portraits as being nothing "more than the work of a photographer. Of course, not bad, but they have not the painterly quality. He is 46 years old and may be considered to have done his best work."[38] An artist that Jones considered promising was Hale Woodruff. Compared to the other artists, Jones felt that Woodruff had the greatest potential and saw him as someone who "might be expected to develop in a fine way as he [went] along."[39] The landscapes and seascapes of Palmer Hayden also appealed to Jones but not enough to convince the judge that the artist deserved more than an honorable mention.[40] But William Boring considered Hayden to be the strongest artist in the group, with Woodruff placing a close second. The architect did, however, share Jones's opinion about the Harleston paintings. Boring thought that the artist could "paint well [but] he did not have the poetic soul of what he considered the real artist" and should, therefore, be eliminated from the competition.[41] In Laura Waring's communique there is no mention of Harleston's work. Rather than speak unflatteringly of an artist with whom she had exhibited over the years, perhaps she believed it would be better to remain silent. However, she did endorse Hayden "because his subjects seemed to have required much more restrained painting."[42] Atterbury agreed with Boring and Waring in their praise of Hayden and stated that the artist "showed a real appreciation of beauty and a respect for Nature, as well as a keenness of observation, that . . . puts it above the work of Mr. Woodruff."[43]

After the judges' assessments of the artists were reviewed, it was clear that Palmer Hayden had won the first prize, a gold medal, and a $400 honorarium. The second-place winner, Hale Woodruff, would receive one hundred dollars and the bronze medal.[44] Unfortunately, Edwin Harleston's works were rejected by the panel.

When William Harmon received the final results, he was genuinely dismayed that his candidate had been eliminated and, in a personal letter to the artist, shared his dissatisfaction with the results of the judging by saying, "I am truly disappointed that you did not get one of the awards. I was on the Committee but fear I am hopelessly old-fashioned. As you said and I contend, your pictures were painted with sincerity and skill, but the other judges were, in my opinion, saturated with modernism and I being at best an unschooled judge, had to yield to them."[45]

The award-winning paintings submitted by Palmer Hayden included *St. Servan, The Schooners*, and *A Home in Bretagné.* Hale Woodruff's second-place entries *Along the Eure at Chartres, Old Farmhouse in the Beauce Valley*, and *The Road from Chateau Neuf* also bore titles underscoring their French connection.[46] In examining these artworks, it is clear that these two artists were influenced by European modernism, for both had abandoned representational painting methods in exchange for the expressive use of color, abstract shapes, including the application of thick paint and visible brushstrokes, as a means of interpreting their subject matter for the viewer.

Harleston's loyalty to the academic tradition of realism, his embrace of the human figure, and his rejection of the dramatic stylistic changes that had taken place in the world of art since the advent of modernism were some of the reasons his paintings were overwhelmingly rejected by the panel. Another reason was the content of his work. Instead of continuing to explore themes of empathy and social recompense, New Negro artists were directing their attention toward subjects that reflected "a bold assertion of self."[47] This new brand of race consciousness imbued their work with the kind of visual power that made Harleston's work seem rooted in the past. Losing the Harmon Award was an unanticipated disappointment for the artist, especially coming so soon after the cancellation of his

Charleston Museum exhibition. He had placed all his hopes of winning on Harmon's strong endorsement, but Harleston had clearly misjudged the extent of the philanthropist's power. A national award of this magnitude would have given his stalled career new life and perhaps a pathway out of Charleston, but the Harmon panel had not seen fit to give him so much as an honorable mention. This wound to his confidence was made even deeper by the fact that most of the artists in the competition were half his age and not nearly as experienced.

Edwin Harleston became so distraught that he withdrew from his art, redirecting his energy toward the family business and local civic organizations. He had recently been elected to the Inter-Racial Committee of South Carolina and was presently serving as president of the local branch of the Independent National Funeral Directors Association, secretary of the Advisory Committee of the Avery Institute, and clerk of the Unity and Friendship Society, while also working with the NAACP and YMCA.[48] As if that were not enough, Harleston took on the added responsibility of assisting his sister Kate Fleming and brother Robert with their new funeral business in St. Augustine, Florida.[49] All of this activity helped to dull the pain caused by the mounting setbacks to his art career.

The year 1927 came and went without producing any significant artwork. Harleston did, however, honor a few requests to show his paintings. The Art Institute of Chicago organized an exhibition of works by African American artists, which included his *Bible Student* along with works by William Harper, Henry Tanner, Hale Woodruff, William Farrow, J. W. Hardwick, and William E. Scott. Asa H. Gordon also contacted the artist about illustrating his book, *Sketches of Negro Life and History in South Carolina*, in which both Harleston and his father are mentioned.[50] However, the artist must have refused Gordon's request because no illustrations appear in the book. He also received several invitations to art competitions including a request from sculptor Augusta Savage and a proposal request for a mural design for the National Training School for Women and Girls in Washington, DC.[51] Each applicant was to submit a design based on the theme: "The Spirit of the Negro Womanhood of America." Harleston's reluctance to enter and lose another competition coupled with the fact that the commission award was only one hundred dollars may explain why he did not bother to respond.[52]

Try as he might, Harleston could not ignore his artistic aspirations because, for him, it was the only thing that kept him going; it was his life's mission. In 1928 he began to take on small art projects. The first was a portrait of Du Bois's daughter, Yolande, which he sent to his mentor and friend as a gift. Unfortunately, the painting has been lost, making it impossible to judge the quality of his work during this period.[53] Harleston also delivered a lecture and demonstration, "The Building of a Portrait," in February of 1929 at Claflin University, showing the audience how a painted portrait evolves.[54] The university president J. B. Randolph was so impressed with Harleton's ability as a speaker and an artist that he offered him a position at the school teaching European history and the history of art. But in a letter to Randolph, the artist respectfully declined the offer because he was still holding on to the hope that one day, he would secure a teaching job in Washington, DC.[55]

That summer Harleston received a letter from the Harmon Foundation asking him to submit his work to the 1929 awards competition and art exhibit. The 1926 show had been such a success for the Harmon Award fine art winners that the foundation decided to expand the exhibition to include juried works by a larger group of African American artists. With this show, the Harmon Committee on Admissions aspired to establish ongoing support for these artists by creating a wider audience for their work and encouraging purchases by the public.[56] George Towns sent Harleston an invitation to participate in the show, and Dr. George E. Hayes, chair of the committee that administered the awards, sent a second appeal, but Harleston ignored both requests. Finally, Dr. Haynes made a personal plea to the artist knowing he was still harboring resentment toward the foundation because of his earlier rejection. In his letter, he argued that not only would Harleston be a part of one of the most important shows of the year, but the committee would also be promoting sales of the artists' works.[57] Although money was still at the center of many of his problems, the prospect of a purchase was not enticing enough to persuade him to submit any of his work.[58]

Edwin Harleston did not enter the 1929 competition, but a newspaper clipping and a list of the gold and bronze award recipients for that year was found among his papers indicating that he was interested in knowing who won prizes that year. At the top of the list was William H Johnson, who received the gold award for his expressionist landscapes described by the judges as the work of a "real modernist . . . spontaneous, vigorous, firm, direct."[59]

The fact that another modern landscape painter had won the Harmon Foundation's top prize forced Harleston to rethink the direction of his own artwork and whether he would adjust his subject matter and stylistic approach to reflect this modernist trend. In August of that year, Harleston went to St. Augustine, Florida, to consult with his sister Katherine about her funeral business. While there, he wrote to Elise requesting his folding easel, paint box, and canvas so that he could make oil sketches of Florida's beautiful surroundings.[60] Harleston found his landscape painting challenging but thoughts of portraiture were never far away. A few weeks into his visit, he decided to take a day trip to Daytona to call on Mary McLeod Bethune, the Florida educator who had recently merged her Daytona School for Girls with Cookman Institute, a local men's college. Bethune started her school with one dollar and fifty cents in capital, the sum total of her assets.[61] Now, as president of the new Bethune-Cookman College, Mary Bethune was in the process of moving the institution away from its nonacademic past to a future as an accredited liberal arts college. During this visit Harleston toured the campus and met with the school's art teacher. It is difficult to determine why the artist initiated this visit, but there is a strong possibility he may have come to the campus to visit a niece who was attending the school at the time or perhaps he intended to approach the internationally recognized educator about having her portrait painted. Harleston greatly admired Mrs. Bethune and considered her twenty-five years of effort at the school to be exemplary.[62] But no commission ever developed from this visit.

Harleston did, however, receive a portrait request from a friend who wanted a painting made of a relative from an old tintype. It was not a major commission, but it helped to keep him busy, and as he complained to Elise, he needed the extra money because he was nearly broke. The Florida funeral home had not had much business and the same was true for the Charleston establishment. The continuing northern migration plus a faltering economy had forced many in the Black community to forgo expensive church and funeral home ceremonies in favor of home or graveside services. But since death is ever present, the Harlestons were able to make enough money to keep the family solvent, but not enough to eradicate the artist's unending financial woes.

Yet, he and his community were not the only ones suffering financially. Working-class Americans in the North as well as the South had been the first to experience the nation's withdrawal pains brought on by an over-extended market economy, the growing gulf between rich and poor had been expanding at an alarming rate since the mid-1920s. As the next decade approached, manufacturing plants began to lay off thousands of workers because of overproduction, especially in the automobile industry, while stocks soared to artificial heights. On Wednesday, October 23, 1929, the stock market crashed, depleting individual assets, bank holdings, pension funds, and real estate investments, leaving millions of broken lives in its wake. The Great Depression that followed brought suffering to every corner of the nation and Charleston's African American community did not escape unscathed.

In spite of these challenging times, Harleston's desire to revive his art career had become his main focus. As more Black artists began showing works in exhibitions across the country, Harleston had become painfully aware of the fact that his name was fading from Northeastern art circles and invitations to show his work had become increasingly rare. In an effort to reestablish himself, it is conceivable that he may have discussed problematic aspects of his career with Sue Bailey (Thurman), a New York intellectual who was well connected in Harlem's cultural circles. She had recently been appointed traveling secretary for the national staff of the YWCA and had come to Charleston to establish a YWCA high school chapter for African American girls. Since there were no hotels in the city that accepted Black guests, out-of-towners stayed in private or tourist homes and were entertained by a network of friends, churches, and social organizations. Because Edwin Harleston was such a charming host, the Harleston Studio was high on the list of places to house and entertain visitors, thus making it the place where every one of prominence visited at one time or another.[63] During Sue Bailey's tour of the artist's studio and gallery, Harleston asked if he could paint her portrait, and she agreed. While Bailey posed, Harleston questioned her about the current New York art scene and shared with her his struggle to show and sell his artwork. At one of the sittings, Bailey suggested that he contact Alain Locke for assistance in promoting his artwork.[64]

Even though Alain Locke had been critical of Edwin Harleston's approach to painting, Bailey encouraged the artist to contact this influential critic and art patron for guidance in moving his career forward.[65] To garner Locke's support, Harleston gifted the cultural critic a landscape painting from his *Magnolia Gardens* series. At the time, this famous South Carolina landmark was off-limits to African American visitors and as a result, the artist had to disguise himself as one of the carpenters assisting Thomas Pinckney, builder of the park's bridge, to gain entry to the gardens.[66] The painting was probably an attempt by Harleston to impress Locke with his versatility and to remind this important cultural scholar that he was more than just a portrait painter. But beneath the thinly veiled effort was Harleston's desire to prove that his Harmon Award rejections had not marked the end of his career as an artist. It seems that Harleston's efforts were successful because in December of 1929, he received a letter from Locke expressing his sincere appreciation for the painting and his surprise at his excellent skills as a landscape artist. Locke asked the artist to consider having a one-man show and offered to help in any way he could to further his career.[67]

This offer of support gave Harleston the encouragement he needed to focus on his artwork again. But this time, he planned to supplement his income by capitalizing on his ability as a speaker. "The Building of a Picture" lecture and demonstration presented the previous year at Claflin University had been successful. Harleston felt certain that other historically Black colleges and universities in the South would be anxious to present his artistic demonstration on their own campuses. He began his new venture by sending an introductory letter, on Harleston Studio stationary, to several college presidents. In this communication, he described an "enjoyable evening program" that would appeal to the college community as well as the general public, which included an artist talk and painting demonstration using a live model, for a fee of $75.00. As a bonus, Harleston offered to exhibit his drawings and paintings for an additional $25.00. At the end of his correspondence, he encouraged the schools to make copies of an enclosed flyer to assist with publicity and to respond as soon as possible to secure a desired date.[68]

This letter had all the characteristics of a well-developed marketing campaign, complete with institutional and student benefits and ideas for audience development, along with the promise of viewer satisfaction.

Edwin Augustus Harleston, *Magnolia Gardens*, ca. 1929. Gibbes Museum of Art, Charleston, South Carolina.

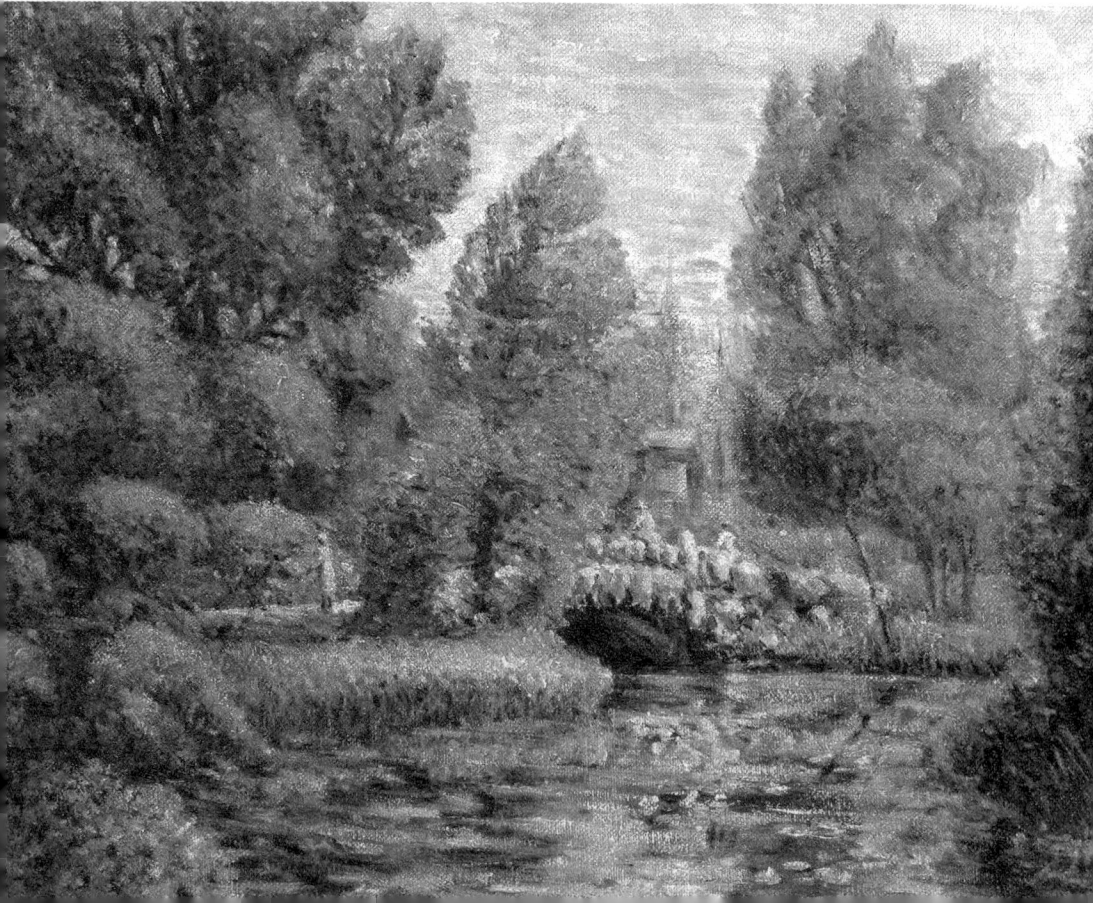

What Harleston outlined had the potential to attract academic and cultural audiences; therefore, he was certain that the response to his solicitation would be positive. Within a few weeks, replies to his letters came from Shaw University in Raleigh, North Carolina; Livingstone College in Salisbury, North Carolina; Edward Waters College in Jacksonville, Florida; Straight College in New Orleans, Louisiana; and Talladega College in Talladega, Alabama.[69] Regrettably none of their replies contained the invitations he had expected. The collapse of the American economy had left all these schools in dire financial need, making it difficult for them to pay faculty and cover daily operating expenses, not to mention guest lecturer's fees.

Edwin Harleston was surprised to discover that not a single school was able to accept his offer. But considering all that he had suffered in the past few years, this small setback was not enough to deter him from exploring other possibilities. In his search for the means to make his art career profitable, Harleston turned, as he had in the past, to his friend Truman K. Gibson, who was now an executive with Supreme Liberty Life Insurance Company in Chicago, for assistance in identifying prospective clients. Gibson volunteered to explore the possibility of having a portrait made of Oscar De Priest, an African American politician who had recently been elected to the Seventy-first US Congress from the Illinois First Congressional District in Chicago. Gibson also suggested organizing a group of supporters similar to that which commissioned the DuPont portrait with the goal of honoring Julius Rosenwald. This Sears, Roebuck & Company vice president had earned much of his fortune in clothing manufacturing and in recent years, his financial generosity had included the support of several African American schools in the South as well as a two-million-dollar gift to the Provident Hospital fundraising campaign in Chicago. Although Gibson's ideas had enormous potential, he admitted to Harleston that "things have been quite tight with . . . people in this city, and . . . I could [not] offer you very much hope other than along a few personal lines."[70]

Since Gibson could provide little in the way of assistance, Harleston decided to make his own opportunity. At the end of April 1930, he received a letter from Walter White asking for a contribution to the Moorfield

Storey-Louis Marshall campaign. The memorial fund was being organized in recognition of Storey's service as the NAACP's first president and Marshall's contribution as adviser to the organization's legal committee. Since Harleston's finances were always anemic, he decided to donate a drawing from his Grand Army veteran series in lieu of money. In the letter to White, Harleston requested that "the drawing be sold (for at least $100) and the proceeds given to the Fund or the Association. This kind of drawing reproduces well and cheaply, so that it might be appropriately used on *The Crisis* cover if it is desired."[71] Although Harleston's gift was offered with the deepest sincerity, there can be little doubt that he also hoped the NAACP would afford him the opportunity to recapture some national attention by placing his work on the cover of their publication. The NAACP thanked him graciously for his gift and acknowledged his generosity in the press, but Harleston's artwork never appeared on the magazine's cover.[72]

Even though Harleston was having difficulty advancing his national career, he did receive regional exposure with "The Building of a Picture" lecture at the Southern Regional YWCA Conference held during the week of June 6, 1930, at the Lincoln Academy (an American Missionary Association institution) in King's Mountain, North Carolina. Sue Bailey had invited him to give his presentation as part of the conference activities along with luminaries such as A. Philip Randolph, Benjamin E. Mays, and Herbert T. Delany. When he arrived, Harleston was impressed with what he found. The Blue Ridge Mountains were not only breathtakingly beautiful, but there were also over a hundred college women in attendance, each of whom could serve as the ideal model for his lecture and demonstration.[73] One of these young ladies, Frances Johnson, was so smitten by the handsome artist that she asked him to draw something in the back of her autograph book and he complied by doing a quick landscape sketch while they were waiting for the next session to begin.[74]

The week following the conference, Harleston was back in New York searching for portrait commissions. This time several possibilities were discussed but, as usual, no firm commitments were made. During his visit, Harleston was also determined to meet the artist Aaron Douglas. The two had never been introduced, but Harleston knew Douglas was a bright star in the New Negro firmament and he had been impressed by his illustrations in *The Crisis* and *Opportunity* magazines. Although Harleston may have considered Douglas a resource in his search for new commissions, more than likely, he was eager to gain insight into the world of modern painting and find out how Douglas was able to successfully transition from realism to modernism.

Douglas had only been living in New York for six years, but during this brief period he had risen to considerable heights in the world of art. Before coming to New York, Douglas had studied painting at the University of Nebraska in Lincoln and briefly taught in a Kansas City high school. At the dawn of the Harlem Renaissance, Douglas moved to New York and quickly established himself as an artist and illustrator. It was during this period that he met Winold Reiss, whose fame as an interpreter of folk types captured Douglas's attention. As their relationship developed, Reiss encouraged Douglas to abandon realism and incorporate African art and its cubist forms into his work. The results of Reiss's suggestions can be seen in a series of illustrations Douglas completed for James Weldon Johnson's book, *God's Trombones: Seven Negro Sermons in Verse*.[75] The works, which included *Judgement Day*, *Let My People Go*, *Go Down Death*, *Noah's Ark*, and *The Crucifixion*, captured poignant moments in Bible stories, Negro spirituals, and various aspects of African American life. When they were first published, critics praised these illustrations because of the unique way Douglas was able to evoke a "quality of movement through abrupt changes in line and mass in a lateral direction, which effectively complemented the rays and arcs of light geometrically plotted and abstractly illuminated within the given shape."[76] This fresh stylistic approach established Douglas as one of the most sought-after African American artists in New York.

Word of Douglas's recently awarded mural projects: the dining room of the Sherman Hotel in Chicago and the new library at Fisk University in Nashville, Tennessee, had been announced in the press, and Harleston, being one who was constantly looking for new ways to expand his skills, may have been seeking Douglas's technical advice on mural painting to pursue a future mural project of his own.[77] Whatever the reason, the meeting did not occur because Douglas had left the city on a trip to visit relatives in Kansas by the time Harleston had arrived.[78] But instead of brooding over this failed attempt as if it were another lost opportunity, Harleston pushed aside his pride and wrote to the artist offering to assist him with the two commissions. Initially, Douglas's response seemed hesitant, but near the end of the letter the artist admitted that the responsibility of working on two mural projects simultaneously had become burdensome and he could use the help of a professional artist, especially when it came to mixing colors. With the time constraints of these tasks in mind, Douglas asked if Harleston could assist with the project until September 15 with the understanding that he could only pay him $300 even though he knew his time was worth much more.[79]

Without hesitation Harleston accepted Douglas's offer and by August 1, 1930, he was on a train heading for Nashville to work as the New York artist's assistant on the Fisk University library mural project.[80] When he arrived in Nashville, Harleston was struck by the deteriorating condition of the city. In a letter to Elise, he described the place as being "surprisingly dilapidated, dirty and tumbled-down, even the neighborhood around the State Capitol looks like the foot of Calhoun Street."[81] But on the university campus the artist found conditions a bit more favorable. Perhaps it was Douglas's easy manner that made Harleston feel at home, for when he arrived the artist was diligently working on the Chicago panels but set aside his work to greet his new assistant. After this initial chat, Harleston concluded that Aaron Douglas was a "very cordial and affable fellow" and a man with whom he could easily work.[82] During the next few days Harleston resided with Douglas in the home of Fisk University President Thomas E. Jones, who was vacationing in Canada.[83] But when the chief administrator returned to campus, Harleston moved into a small house across the street where he received room and board for ten dollars a week.[84]

On the morning of August 4, 1930, Aaron Douglas and Edwin Harleston entered the Erastus Milo Cravath Memorial Library. Along with the two master artists, there were three university students, one of whom was Cornelius "Connie" Lunceford, the brother of the famous big band leader, Jimmy "Piggie" Lunceford, a recent Fisk graduate, and Mr. Foster, the neighborhood mailman who had been recruited to assist with the murals.[85] The building was a gift to the university from John D. Rockefeller's General Education Board, the Julius Rosenwald Fund, and the Carnegie Corporation. The library was a steel and masonry structure of Gothic design but modified by African decorative elements.[86] When it was completed in the spring of 1930, the building was "pronounced by competent authorities to be one of the finest college buildings in the country."[87] The finishing touch to this edifice was to be the mural series designed by Aaron Douglas, *Build Thee More Stately Mansions*, the title of which was taken from "The Chambered Nautilus," a poem by Oliver Wendell Homes. However, the title was selected "not so much to reveal or describe the content of the pictures as to provide a springboard or starting point around which pertinent symbols might be collected in the hope of giving greater illumination to the work."

With "the progression of cultures and civilizations from the dawn of recorded history to the present" as his theme, Douglas's plan called for each of the decorated rooms to represent a phase of this progression. Murals in the north and south reading rooms on the second floor depicted "the pageant of the Negro from Central Africa to contemporary America," while the seven panels in the adjacent catalogue room present the dawn of cultural and intellectual pursuits such as philosophy, drama, music, poetry, and science. In the Periodical Room on the third floor, Douglas used typography and outstanding monuments from Asia, Africa, Europe, and the Americas to underscore how magazines and newspapers bring news from around the world. On the same floor, the Negro Collection Room recounts aspects of African life including hunting, metal forging, weaving, and architectural achievements ranging from simple huts to elaborate mosques.[88] In each of these sections, the artist employed the same flat, two-dimensional stylistic approach that had brought him acclaim on his *God's Trombones* series. But instead of using violet tints exclusively, as he had in his earlier work, Douglas used tints and shades of pink, yellow, blue, green, and violet to structure his images in these murals. In a letter to Elise, Harleston described the mural design as a "scheme of many figures silhouetted in a kind of smoky blue-gray against a background of tones (seven or eight) divided into geometric shapes and running from pale yellow through the lighter greenish blues to violet."[89] Although Harleston did not personally care for Douglas's style, he recognized the beauty inherent in his designs and was therefore able to appreciate them from an objective point of view.[90]

The schedule Douglas and Harleston set for themselves was grueling. Douglas arrived at the library at eight o'clock each morning to give Harleston and the other assistants the instructions for the day. He would then retreat to his studio and labor over the Sherman Hotel panels until evening. At five o'clock Harleston would break for dinner, then from seven until nine-thirty he usually helped Douglas with the hotel panels. These extended periods of work were made even more difficult by the blistering heat wave that had held Nashville in its grasp for the past seventy-nine days. During the day, temperatures usually hit the one-hundred-degree mark, and although evening brought some relief, the high humidity prevented any noticeable improvement. Everything in sight was burnt and brown including the grass, trees, and even the weeds.[91]

Despite this apparent hardship, Harleston was pleased and stimulated by the work. The team had nearly completed most of the two large reading rooms by August 25 and Harleston had decorated much of the 25" × 6' friezes, which adorned the top sections of these walls. He proudly announced to his wife that he had painted part of the American section and all the African section himself. Execution of these segments seemed effortless compared to the ceiling designs which placed considerable strain on the painters' necks and backs.[92] They endured the same physical strain during the painting of the Periodical Room and the Negro Collection Room on the third floor, but their discomfort was exacerbated by complaints from the architect and librarians about Douglas's choice of color. In the estimation of these laypeople, there was too much color on the overhead beams in the ceiling. They advised Douglas and Harleston to remove some of the red in the design. To suggest that the design be altered seemed absurd to the artist because "the red [was] nothing but a pale pink in a stencil which would spoil the design if tampered with."[93] Douglas stood his aesthetic ground and the "red" remained.

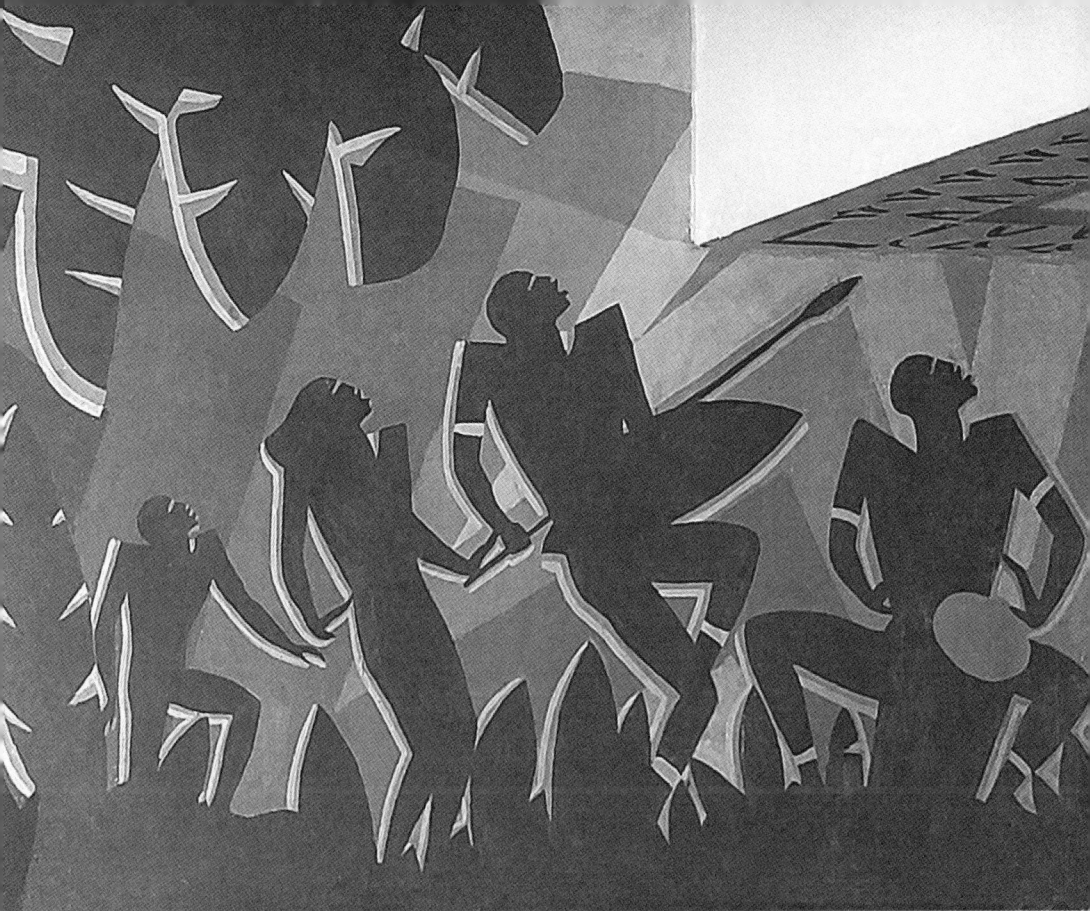

Aaron Douglas, *murals in Cravath Hall, Fisk University*, oil on canvas on plaster walls, 1930. Fisk University, Nashville, TN; photography by Micheal Ruzga.

During the last week in August, Douglas and Harleston began working day, night, and Sunday in an effort to finish the murals.[94] Even though the work was hard and the hours long, Harleston was enjoying the process immensely. Being able to paint twelve to fifteen hours a day without interruption brought him great satisfaction but learning the steps of mural painting was the most rewarding aspect of the job.[95] Harleston was also introduced to new painting materials, new methods of painting, new policies, and new friends, making this innovative addition to his repertoire all the more exciting.[96]

As always, Edwin Harleston was anticipating how he could incorporate these recently acquired skills into a project of his own. The opportunity came when he received word that a new library serving Atlanta

University, and the neighboring colleges was being planned. Harleston wasted no time in writing to John Hope, president of Atlanta University and chairman of the library project, to ask if provisions had been made in the design of the facility for a mural. If so, Harleston felt that as an Atlanta University graduate, he should be given first consideration for the job, not only because of his skill but also for his unique ability "to interpret the spirit of the place."[97]

While waiting for a reply from John Hope, Harleston continued blissfully working on the mural project. Elise, however, was trapped in Charleston struggling to keep the funeral business going and caring for two children. Robert Harleston had been the primary assistant and manager of the funeral home's daily operations, but after his death in July of 1929, much of the administrative responsibility was shifted to Elise's shoulders. Business had been poor for quite some time and the Depression had caused those who would normally patronize their business to look elsewhere for less expensive services. Those who did use the Harleston Funeral Home were often unable to pay.[98] Having removed himself from the day-to-day strife of the business, Harleston was more convinced than ever that the debt to his father had long since been paid and now was the time to break from Captain's control to concentrate solely on his artistic career. With the full support of his wife, Harleston decided to try his "Building of a Picture" lecture tour again. In a letter, Elise bitterly reminded Harleston that he had worked for his father for more than ten years and played a major role in building and maintaining the business, yet, the elder Harleston, who was now in his seventies, was still unwilling to turn the funeral home over to his son or offer him partnership in the establishment he helped build. But what seemed to aggravate her even more was the fact that during all of these years, Captain Harleston had refused to pay his son a decent wage, thus keeping the couple at his mercy. Elise urged her husband to ask for his inheritance so they could leave Charleston and get on with their lives. She ended the letter with softer words by declaring that "through it all, I love you . . . it is all that keeps me, it is all that constrains me. When the cruel iron turns in my heart and my thoughts are black, I think I feel your arms, hear your voice, I remember sublime moments and I hold on . . ."[99]

An energized and determined Harleston forged ahead with plans to regain his place in the art world by reaching out to some of the schools he had contacted earlier. But in addition to his standard talk, the artist offered to include a discussion of his working experience on the Fisk University murals with Aaron Douglas as a bonus. In only a few weeks, Harleston had received several responses to his letter; but unlike his previous solicitations, this time, they were positive. One of the recipients who expressed delight at having Harleston speak at the school was James V. Herring, head of the Department of Art at Howard University.[100] J. T. Carter, dean of Talladega College in Alabama, also accepted his offer, however, Shaw University in Raleigh, North Carolina, was still financially unable to accommodate the artist.[101] But the school's president, Benjamin Brawley, was able to suggest some other colleges in the area that might be interested in his presentation.

Excited by the favorable responses to his lecture tour, Harleston asked Elise to send the portrait of Sue Bailey so he could work on it during his spare time and perhaps include it in his touring exhibition.[102] He also decided to answer the Harmon Foundation Awards and Exhibition Committee's plea for his assistance "in making this Exhibition representative of the best work that in being done by Negroes today" by mailing in his application.[103] Harleston may have been motivated by this personal appeal but what probably had greater bearing on his decision was the fact that this would be the last year of the five-year experimental period for the awards, thereby, raising doubt as to the future of the competitions and exhibitions.[104] Another reason for entering was the new level of confidence Harleston had in himself. The physical and creative demands placed on him during his summer in Nashville along with his association with Aaron Douglas had rejuvenated Harleston's creative energy and sharpened his painting skills. Now, he seemed ready to take advantage of any opportunity that could potentially move his career forward.

On October 4, 1930, Harleston wrote to Elise proclaiming, "We ARE DONE! Finished! Completed!!! 670 linear feet of mural decoration of a unique type done by Us, of Us and for Us in the home of the famous Jubilee Singers. Two months of strain and concentration have left us a little tired but happy . . . Yours truly played second fiddle this time and was not the one to go to the front, but I have seen all along that without me it could not have succeeded so well."[105] Douglas also realized the importance of Harleston's contribution to the project. After returning to New York, Douglas sent Harleston a letter in which he stated that "your decision to come over and give me a hand last summer was little short of cosmic. I don't know how I could have made it through without your skill, your sound judgement and your helpful, friendly attitude."[106]

With the successful Fisk University mural project at the top of his list of accomplishments, Edwin Harleston returned to Charleston with renewed artistic fervor. This momentum was kept alive by a visit from Sue Bailey, who had come to South Carolina on official YWCA business, but took time to come to the Harleston Studio so he could apply the finishing touches to her portrait.[107] Based on a sepia-toned photograph of *Miss Sue Bailey* (Thurman) taken by Elise, the *Portrait of Miss Bailey with the African Shawl* has been considered by critics to be one of Harleston's finest works. Although the photograph of Bailey is nearly full length, the artist presents her in the traditional three-quarter seated pose with her face turned toward the viewer. Bailey is framed by a background streaked with royal blue, violet, and charcoal gray. The strong light on the left side of the photograph, beyond the picture plane, creates heavy shadows under the subject's right eye, across the left side of her face, and at the corners of her slightly down-turned lips. These dark areas create the impression that Bailey's demeanor is stern and businesslike. But instead of focusing on this aspect of her character, Harleston chose to alter this feeling by softening the shadows in her face and turning the curve of her mouth upward, giving Bailey a demure appearance.

Compositionally, this painting is similar to Harleston's other portraits but what separates it from his earlier works is his strong use of color. In the Ware portrait and in his landscapes the artist occasionally used colors high in value for emphasis, but in the Bailey painting Harleston has enlivened the entire surface of the painting with short strokes of Impressionistic color. For example, in the shawl and bodice of the subject's dress Harleston has constructed the areas with short strokes of yellow, violet, and

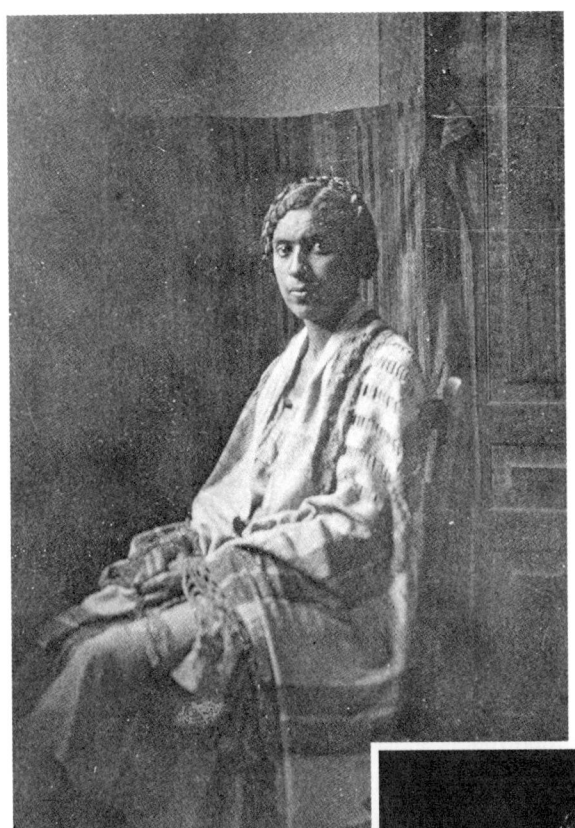

Elise Forrest Harleston,
Miss Sue Bailey (Thurman),
photograph, ca. 1929. Collection
of Mae Whitlock Gentry (*above*).
Edwin Augustus Harleston,
*Portrait of Miss Bailey with the
African Shawl*, oil on canvas,
1930. The Johnson Collection,
Spartanburg, SC (*right*).

scattered specks of pure red. In addition, Harleston used yellow under-tones in concert with a gradation of brown tones laced with touches of pink and violet to construct Sue Bailey's face. In doing so, the artist has transformed Bailey's cool exterior, as seen in the photograph, into an image that radiates a pleasant, mellow warmth.

Edwin Harleston was so pleased with the *Portrait of Miss Bailey with the African Shawl* that he entered it in the 1930 "Exhibition of the Work of Negro Artists" sponsored by the Harmon Foundation and the Federal Council of Churches. The fact that he describes her shawl as "African" in the title was probably his way of trying to incorporate the heightened interest in Africa that characterized the New Negro movement. Along with that painting, the artist also submitted the recently completed *Portrait of Aaron Douglas.* Like the Bailey portrait, the painting of Douglas was constructed from a photograph but in this instance, the picture was taken by Harleston while the two were working in Nashville, not in a studio (see Plate 6).[108]

The painting of Douglas is unusual in that he is not presented in the traditional seated position, formally dressed, or placed against a dark background in an unidentifiable space with a few symbolic references. Instead, Aaron Douglas is seen wearing Harleston's smock and holding his palette and brushes while standing in front of *The Scientist*, a segment of the Fisk murals, located in the rotunda of Cravath Memorial Library.[109] Douglas looks directly at the viewer, delivering a thoughtful glance, leaving the impression he has stopped momentarily to recognize the presence of his observer. However, the awkward manner in which he holds the brush in his right hand is more like an orchestra conductor than an artist, exposing the fact that the setting is not the result of a chance encounter but a carefully planned pose. The informality and contrived sense of the moment was an element in Harleston's work that he had not explored for more than a decade, but it was one that he would expand upon in the months ahead. There is no evidence that the two men collectively made a decision to use this segment of the mural as the background for the portrait, but it is likely that Harleston saw Douglas's visual record of the Africans' journey from the old world to the new as an attempt by the artist to expose unknown and forgotten worlds to the students as well as the public.

Another aspect of this painting that separates it from the artist's earlier portraits is the presence of two light sources. In addition to the standard light, located in the upper right corner beyond the picture plane, illuminating the right side of the subject's face, the artist has placed a secondary light source to the left of Douglas's shoulder. The shadows and highlights created by these separate sources of illumination reinforce the sculptural solidity of the figure and dramatically define its boundaries, thus adding to the sense of staging. When Douglas saw the painting, he was quite pleased with the results and congratulated Harleston for the "splendid job" he had done despite the subject.[110]

For the third entry to the competition, Edwin Harleston returned to the subject with which he was most familiar, the African American elder. Like the *Bible Student* and the *Portrait of a Colored Grand Army Man*, the artist has focused on a local Black woman whom he felt personified his traditional "character type" in *The Old Servant*. Elise, who was always looking for interesting subjects to photograph, saw the woman as she passed the funeral home one morning and asked if she could take her picture. Although her name has been lost to history, the woman Harleston captured in this painting agreed to be photographed and while posing she disclosed to Elise that during the Civil War, she cooked breakfast for Robert Smalls, the African American boat captain who stole the Confederate vessel, *CSS Planter*, and sailed with his family, his crew, and others, up the Atlantic coast to Union lines and freedom. Her amazing story made the photograph and Harleston's painting even more meaningful, for he felt that in this artwork he was paying tribute to the nameless and faceless thousands still living who had experienced slavery and emerged from it as productive members of society.[111] In the overall composition, Harleston has returned to the dark background and the use of a single light source to illuminate the old woman who is shown sitting in an unadorned chair, dressed in a plain white sweater with a royal blue shawl wrapped around her shoulders. Her working-class status is underscored by the textured bandana covering her hair and the small split-oak market basket supporting her left arm. Although the lines on her face tell the story of her hard life, the old servant's erect posture and calm, introspective gaze convey her determination to survive despite the difficulties she has encountered. Her regal air is reinforced by the crimson drapery in the background, a symbol of nobility often seen in eighteenth-century European portraiture. In using this approach, Harleston has made a subtle yet important connection between colonial hegemony and the African American demand for full citizenship. By using the colors of the American flag throughout the painting, he links his subject to a sociopolitical form of modernity, which elevates her status from that of a formerly enslaved domestic worker to patriotic citizen.[112] When the painting was finished, the artist was so pleased with the results that Elise took a photograph of the old woman with her portrait and probably gave her one of the pictures as a keepsake for being a willing model and sharing her story.

In addition to the three portraits, Harleston included an unidentified painting from his new series of genre works depicting Charleston street scenes and vendors.[113] It is difficult to determine what motivated him to include images made popular by the same group of Charleston artists who had rejected him, but perhaps Harleston had hoped that he too could benefit financially from the growing interest in these popular imaginings of the city's past. It was also common knowledge that Elizabeth O'Neill Verner had been hired by DuBose Heyward to illustrate his book, *Porgy*, which had become a successful Broadway play and would later serve as the basis for Geroge Gershwin's opera, *Porgy and Bess*.[114] Because these visual and literary art forms had generated national interest in the folkways of African Americans living in the South, it is plausible that Harleston may have wanted to be prepared in case an illustration offer or some other lucrative opportunity came his way. There is also the possibility that he may have chosen to increase his chances of winning the Harmon prize by entering a painting that was different from his formal portraiture and more in keeping with the current trend. By selecting street vendors as subject matter, Harleston may have thought of himself as joining the growing number of American artists who were painting scenes from everyday life. This approach was associated with a movement known as American Scene

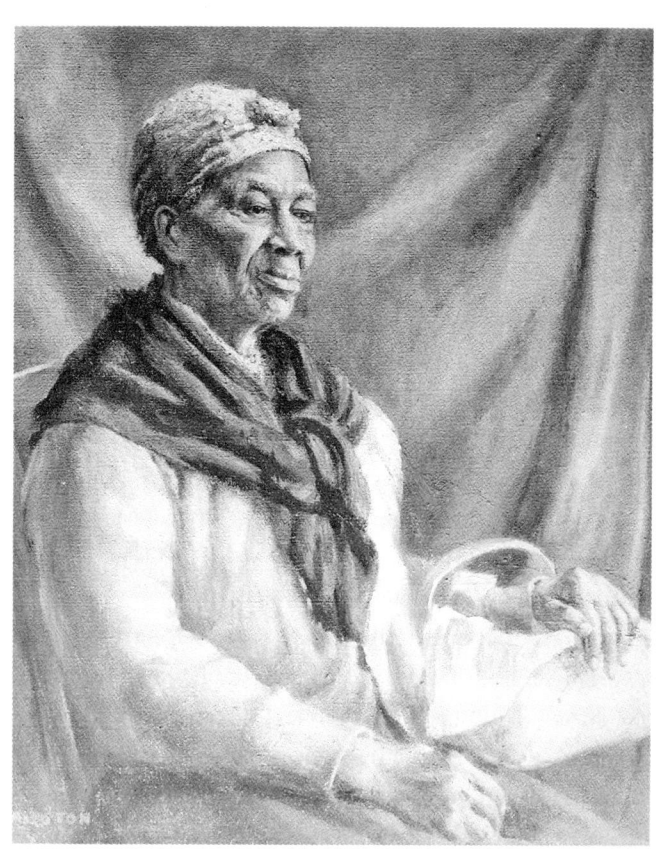

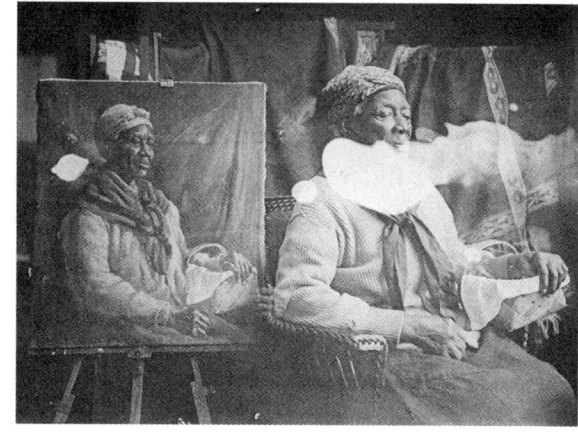

Edwin Augustus Harleston, *The Old Servant*, oil on canvas, 1930. Alamy Stock Photo (*above*). Elise Forrest Harleston, *The Old Servant*, photograph, 1930. Collection of Mae Whitlock Gentry (*right*).

Painting, a style that became popular during the early to mid-twentieth century. Artists who embraced this approach thought of themselves as rejecting modern European influences in favor of realism, rooted in the academic tradition, to capture images from their environment.[115]

But a more likely reason for Edwin Harleston's sudden interest in Charleston street merchants may have been his desire to imbue his subjects with a measure of dignity and agency that is absent from the popular images of street vendors, domestics, and field laborers, produced by the city's white elite. Two examples of his efforts are *The Honey Man* and *A Vendor* also known as (*Lady Passing a Wall*). In *The Honey Man*, Harleston has captured the image of Ralph Bennett, a local street merchant, who is wearing a spotless white apron over a gray suit and tie, with matching fedora, and shined black shoes.[116] On each arm he carries a split oak basket filled with honey concealed under white cloth coverings in an effort to shield his valued product from menacing insects. Using a palette of varying shades of blue, gray, violet, and brown the artist has given the viewer a hint of Charleston's architectural charm by placing this solitary African American male figure in front of a wall with decorative balustrades covered by lush regional flora, which includes blue flowering vines and palm fronds. In this painting, Harleston has abandoned any attempt to individualize the physical characteristics of his subject in favor of a generalized figure that is emblematic of the enterprising spirit and self-pride displayed by members of the city's Black business community (see Plates 7 and 8).

In *A Vendor (Lady Passing a Wall)*, the artist uses a similar compositional approach, but in this instance, he presents the viewer with a slender, brown female figure captured in mid-stride, carrying baskets brimming with vegetables in her left hand and on her right arm. Her ankle-length white dress and matching head wrap are framed by clusters of lavender wisteria blossoms cascading over a nearby wall, adding to her graceful appearance. Mrs. Edwina (Gussie) H. Whitlock, the artist's niece, identified this work as *Lady Passing a Wall* which raises a question as to whether she is, in fact a vendor, or simply a woman returning from the market with food for her family?[117] The female subject's status is being questioned because Edwin Harleston has eliminated the traditional symbols used by

Smith, Verner, and other artists of this period to classify working-class African American women. These artists typically presented their female subjects as dark skinned, full-figured, wearing tattered work clothes covered by an apron, and presented as objects void of an identifiable sense of place rather than individuals. To counter this stereotype, Harleston has lightened the complexion of his subject, removed the apron, and carefully placed her in a beautiful environment in which she is actively engaged. In both *The Honey Man* and *A Vendor*, the artist created a bond between realism and the ephemeral memory of those people who had worked so hard to support their families and their community. The interpretation of these genre scenes as sites of memory for the artist underscores the fact that these paintings are idealized interpretations of his experiences rather than a physical record of a particular person or place.

Harleston packed, crated, and shipped the works during the Christmas holidays to ensure their arrival by the January 5, 1931, deadline. The judges gathered at the Harmon Foundation office a few days later to examine the works and select the prize winners.[118] Among those making the decisions were James V. Herring of Howard University; Walter M. Grant of the American Art Association/Anderson Art Gallery; Arthur Schomburg, bibliophile and curator of Negro Collections at Fisk University; Alon Bement, educator and director of the Art Center of New York where the exhibition would be held; and Aaron Douglas's teacher and friend, artist Winold Reiss.[119] Unlike the panel of 1926, most of the judges in this group were familiar with Harleston's work, which probably made him feel more confident in his chances of winning an award.

For more than a month the artist anxiously waited for the judges' decision. Finally, on February 16, 1931, he received a letter from Mary Beattie Brady, director of the Harmon Foundation, announcing that he had won the one-hundred-dollar Locke Portrait Prize for *The Old Servant*. This was an inaugural award which was being given "in honor of Dr. Alain Locke . . . in recognition of his very splendid services in opening up greater cultural opportunities for Negroes."[120] Harleston must have felt a measure of satisfaction knowing that the competitors for this prize included William H. Johnson, Archibald Motley, and Lois Mailou Jones—artists who had been medal winners in the past and were widely celebrated for their modernist approach to African American subject matter.[121] Winning the Locke Prize represented vindication for Harleston but in a self-effacing letter to William Burke Harmon, son of the Harmon Foundation founder, W. E. Harmon who had died two years before, he considered the award to be "the greatest encouragement . . . as it might well be to any quiet worker in the fine arts."[122] Yet, his euphoria must have been edged with the disappointment of knowing that his vendor painting had been rejected by the committee and as a result he had been denied, for the second time, the gold medal award, which had been won by James Lesesne Wells. There is nothing in the committee records to indicate why the painting from his vendor series was not accepted, but the judges may have considered his artwork more representative of late nineteenth-century European genre painting or more reflective of sentimental antebellum scenes of the Old South rather than socially conscious work of the current movement. Whatever the reason, this rejection was inconsequential, for Edwin Harleston had finally regained some of the national recognition that had eluded him for so long.

Soon after the names of the winners had been announced, Douglas wrote to Harleston congratulating him on his success and expressing regret that the artist had not been awarded the first prize.[123] The critics, however, did not share Douglas's opinion. Although one reviewer did praise Harleston for his "native understanding and objective rendering of Negro character," press coverage of the forty-six works on display at New York's Art Center focused primarily on the more modern works.[124] James Wells was praised for "the rhythmical feeling of his race that . . . combines individual naivete with accumulated wisdom for an old and ripe tradition" and Hale Woodruff received recognition for his "cubist structure" in *Head of a Woman*.[125] But of all the artists, William H. Johnson received the highest acclaim. *The Art News* found his portrait, *Sonny*, to be executed with "surprisingly subtle use of Cezannish accents and angles" and his *Landscape with Setting Sun* was made so alive by expressionistic color "that [it] would require the genius of a Van Gogh to pull it out of the fire."[126] These reviews made it clear to Harleston the reality that the

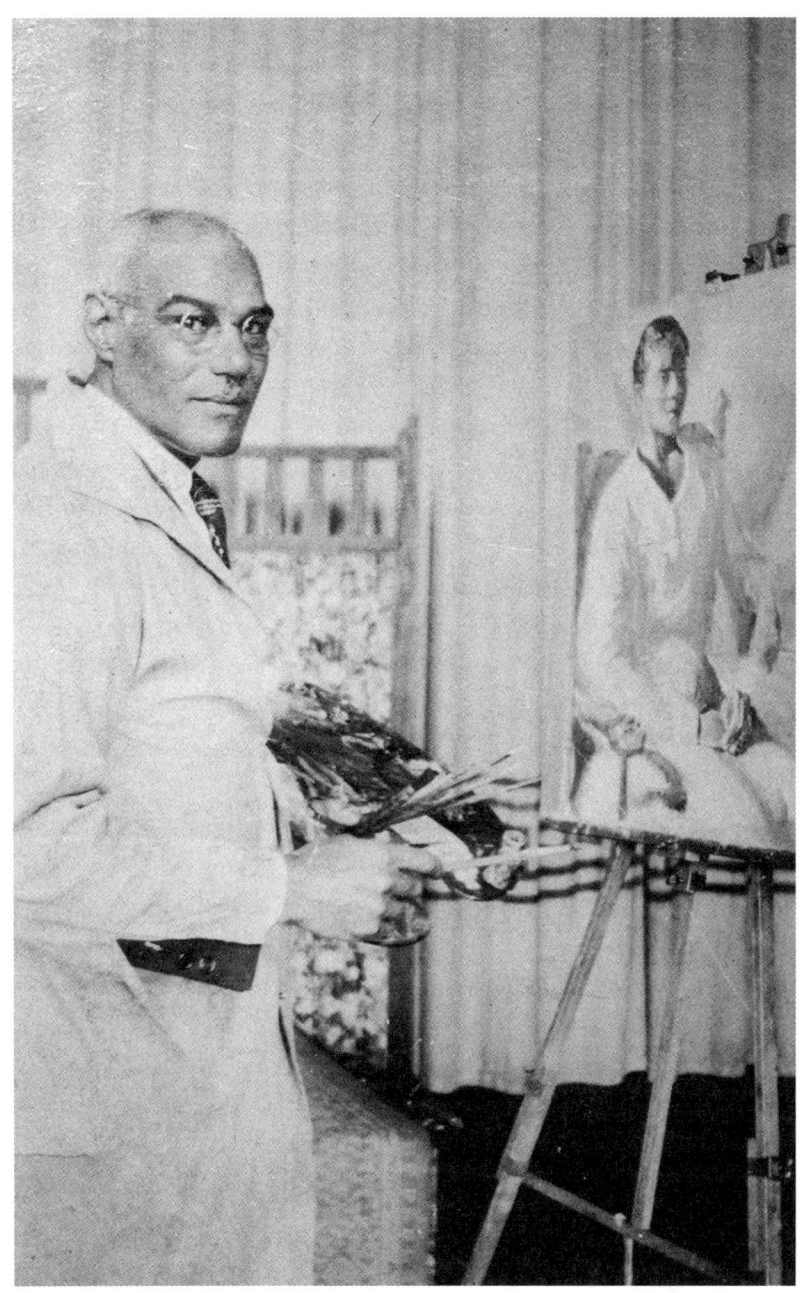

Elise Forrest Harleston, *Edwin A. Harleston with Easel*, photograph, 1931.
Collection of Mae Whitlock Gentry.

works of older, academically trained painters such as himself were rapidly being eclipsed by younger artists who were eagerly integrating realism with modernism and infusing their works, in some cases, with the energy of urban African American life.

Nevertheless, this awareness did not seem to diminish Harleston's zeal to make his career as a full-time artist a reality. "The Building of a Portrait" lecture series was in its early stages but was well received, and he was working on ideas for new works.[127] While on tour in April of 1931, Edwin Harleston was forced to abruptly cancel his speaking engagements and rush home to Charleston because his father had fallen seriously ill with pneumonia. By the time the artist reached the bedside of the seventy-nine-year-old patriarch, he was barely clinging to life. During those final hours, Edwin Harleston refused to leave his father's bedside, maintaining a constant vigil over the man whom he dearly loved, the one whom he owed unconditional allegiance, and who had held an unyielding iron-clad grip on his life. On April 21, 1931, Edwin Gaillard Harleston took his last breath.[128] With Captain's passing, a clear pathway to the new life his son and daughter-in-law had always hoped for was now a reality. Yet, the sudden loss of his father overwhelmed Harleston with such grief that he quickly became physically ill and despondent. In the days following the funeral, the family physician expressed growing concern over the fact that Harleston was not responding to treatment and that mentally he seemed "to have given up . . . there was no more fight in him."[129] The stress of his father's passing, coupled with the rigors of keeping business and family solvent had finally overtaken him. On Sunday, March 10, 1931, at approximately 4:39 PM a little more than two weeks after his father's death, Edwin Augustus Harleston, who was just four days shy of his forty-ninth birthday, also succumbed to pneumonia. Tragically, the life of the South's first academically trained African American artist, whose career had been hovering on the edge of greatness for more than a decade, had come to an untimely end.[130]

EPILOGUE

THE SHOCKING NEWS of Edwin Harleston's death swept through the city on a dark cloud of disbelief. It was difficult for the citizens of Charleston to accept the fact that both father and son, two men who were "held in high esteem by both white and colored who knew them, had died within days of each other."[1] From across the United States, African American newspapers praised Edwin Harleston for his skill as an artist, as well as his leadership in religious and civic affairs. In a condolence note to Elise, Joseph B. Randolph, president of Claflin University, described her husband as "one precious jewel in the crown of our race."[2] While Alain Locke expressed his deep regret that such an important artist had been lost at a time when "Negro art was just on the threshold of a larger audience." In facing such a tragedy, Locke hoped that Elise would draw comfort from the knowledge of the important pioneer work Mr. Harleston did for the movement and real joy that distinctive recognition came to him in the later days of his career.[3] Unfortunately, Harleston's teacher and mentor, W. E. B. Du Bois, did not think it was necessary to send words of sympathy to the artist's grieving widow, instead, he chose to send a telegram to Edward Mickey, the funeral's director. In the message he stated: WE ARE SENDING OUT NOTE OF HARLESTON THROUGH OUR PRESS SERVICE. I AM VERY SORRY TO HEAR OF HIS DEATH GIVE MY CONDOLENCES TO HIS FAMILY.[4]

On Wednesday, March 13 at 2:00 PM, family and friends gathered at Plymouth Congregational Church on the corner of Pitt and Bull Streets to bid farewell to the younger Harleston. Although the business of death had been the primary source of income for the artist and his family for nearly two decades, he thought extravagant funerals with expensive coffins were a waste of money. As a result, Elise chose a simple pine casket for her husband's remains. Despite Harleston's desire for simplicity, the crowd at the church was so large that mourners who had arrived late to the service could only get as close as the steps of the building while others were turned away. Inside the sanctuary, Black dignitaries from across the city and neighboring states gathered to pay their final respects to this nationally recognized artist and civic leader. The first tribute, delivered by Reverend J. E. Beard of Emanuel AME Church, extoled Edwin Harleston's sterling character and artistic talent as well as his accomplishments as a trailblazer in the fight for civil rights, while the second eulogy, given by Reverend Caesar Ledbetter, attempted to inspire hope among the grief-stricken family members of the deceased.

After the funeral service, the casket was carried through the crowd and placed in the hearse by pallbearers for a short drive to Unity and Friendship Cemetery. A brief graveside service was held in the family plot under a cloudless, blue sky with music provided by singers from Avery Institute.[5] After the spiritual, "Ain't Gonna Study War No More," had been sung and the final prayers uttered, a carload of friends from Atlanta, who had missed the service, pushed through the crowd just as the grave attendants were lowering the body into the ground. Edward Mickey knew them as friends of the deceased and, as a gesture of goodwill, the pine box was raised and the wooden casket was pried open so that Harleston's friends could see his face for the last time, while Elise silently watched in stunned disbelief.[6] When the coffin was finally lowered into the open grave, hundreds of mourners who had gathered for the final rites dispersed quietly, taking their personal memories of Edwin Augustus Harleston with them.

Five months later, Alain Locke authored the essay, "The American Negro as Artist," for the September issue of *The American Magazine of Art*, using Harleston's prize-winning painting, *The Old Servant*, as the frontispiece for his article. Unlike his earlier critique, Locke attempted to give an evenhanded analysis of the distinct types of art being produced by African American artists of this period. Locke began his investigation by dividing the artworks into three stylistic categories: the traditionalists, the modernist, and the Africanist or neo-primitive. Harleston was classified as a traditionalist. But instead of continuing to label him as a "wandering amateur," as he had in earlier writings, Locke commended the artist for the socio-political and artistic significance of his paintings in their ability to capture the "Southern Negro peasant types," a subject that Locke concluded was absent from the panorama of American art.[7]

Now that the funeral was over and most of the mourners had departed, Elise seemed lost without her husband. The relationships she had shared with the Harleston family for more than a decade had become strained and her connection with Edwin's siblings began to show signs of tension without him there to smooth over perceived slights or stand up for her when disagreements occurred. The warm bond she had shared with Harleston's youngest sister, Eloise Harleston Jenkins, had waned. While Elise's dealings with his oldest brother, John Moultrie, who had never been interested in the funeral business but was now in charge, had become insufferable because of inappropriate advances and financial disputes over business matters. Although Edwin had provided a small insurance policy to cover his wife's needs in the event of his death, demands from Moultrie for money to pay expenses soon left her with nothing. According to Gussie, Elise signed some of her husband's paintings and tried to sell or give them to friends, but the profits from these sales were not enough to provide the financial support she needed.[8] After mulling over her options, Elise Forrest Harleston sent Gussie to live with her Aunt Eloise who was still secretary at the Jenkins Orphanage, then packed her belongings, including what remained of Harleston's letters, papers, and artwork, and in January of 1932, with Doris in tow, she left Charleston. Elise enrolled in the Atlanta School of Social Work in Atlanta, Georgia, and in doing so, she left her photography and her life as a Harleston in the past.[9]

In less than a year, Elise would remarry, yet the interest in Edwin Harleston's artwork continued to grow. In 1933, the National Gallery of Art in Washington, DC, held a Harmon Foundation exhibition which included several Harleston portraits, landscape paintings and drawings.[10] A few years later, Alain Locke fulfilled his promise to promote Harleston's artwork by including his paintings in two exhibitions at the Howard University Art Gallery in Washington, DC, in 1935 and 1937. When the 1937 exhibition closed, Elise donated *The Old Colonel*, a seascape, and a series of figure studies on paper to the university collection in appreciation for their continuing interest in Harleston's artwork. Nearly a decade later, Howard University professor and art historian, James A. Porter, would praise Harleston in his book, *Modern Negro Art*, for perfecting a sensitively rendered, humane, African American image at a time when few conventional institutions, publications, or individual artists were willing to do so.[11]

Although there were other Black artists who were also striving toward the same goal during the early1920s, the superior training Harleston had received at the School of the Museum of Fine Arts in Boston, coupled with his strong determination to make a name for himself as an artist, contributed to the success of his formal and folk portraits. However, the root cause of his unwavering dedication to a realistic, dignified interpretation of the Black image was embedded in the fact that he was, first and foremost, a race man. Shaped by the philosophies of W. E. B. Du Bois and other civil rights activists of the period, Harleston believed that portraits of his family, friends, and neighbors would be his way of bearing witness to the fact that African Americans were not the inferior beings whom society had unapologetically relegated to the rank of a second-class citizen.[12] Consequently, the depth of his commitment can be measured not only in his selection of imagery but also in the political and civic leadership he willingly extended to the citizenry of Charleston.

Under ordinary circumstances an artist living in the South, away from the northern aesthetic mainstream, would have been powerless to capture the attention of New York art enthusiasts. Yet, Harleston was adept at expanding and maintaining his career because of a curious combination of race pride, self-determination, business acumen, and the unwavering support of his wife, Elise, along with a network of friends. It was also his desire to prove to his father that, if given the opportunity, he had the ability to become successful in the art world. These incentives motivated him to travel to northern art centers, despite the peril associated with Black mobility, so that he could exhibit his artwork and stay abreast of the latest trends in painting. As a result of his efforts, critics often compared some of the early portraits of Edwin Harleston with those of turn-of-the-century painter, Henry O. Tanner.[13] As realists, both artists shared, as Tanner put it, a desire to "represent the serious" African American subject.[14] However, Tanner's interest in Black genre scenes faded after settling in Paris, while Harleston's commitment to the race lasted throughout his life, affecting his aesthetic choices as well as his civic concerns.

It is ironic that during the twenties, when race consciousness was at an all-time high, interest in Harleston's ability to "do the dignified (African American) portrait" began to dwindle. In an age "of rum and racism, of jazz and jalopies, of frenzy and frolic," Harleston's "elegiac art, retrospective in tone, tinged by philosophical melancholy" seemed strangely out of place.[15] New Negro artists had rejected the artistic standards of his generation by transforming the embarrassment associated with "colored" stereotypes into positive characteristics.[16] This reversal in values caused the most aesthetically attuned segment of Harleston's audience to reject his work because it was seen as too sentimental and lacking in visual linkages to modernism or to Africa in his depiction of the race. This opinion was upheld by the Harmon Foundation panel of judges and reinforced later by James A. Porter. In a critique of Harleston's work, Porter concluded that the artist was no more racially motivated than "Winslow Homer and Eastman Johnson in their pictures of Negroes."[17] This assessment indicates that Porter was unaware of the fact that Harleston had dedicated nearly a decade of his career to the perfection of African American imagery nor was he cognizant of the artist's civic engagement and leadership in the NAACP, or the fight to integrate Black teachers into the South Carolina school system. Unfortunately, what seems to have been the primary concern of Porter, the Harmon Foundation panelists, and other critics was Edwin Harleston's perceived inability to abandon the traditional conventions of representation and infuse his subject matter with modernist qualities associated with the New Negro movement. The artist's heavy reliance on photographs, which often produced stiff, overworked figures in his later paintings, also influenced the public's assessment of his skills. Despite these criticisms, Edwin Harleston held fast to the belief that he had a moral obligation to create distinguished portraits of Black people for the purpose of uplifting the race, while demonstrating to all Americans that people of African descent were worthy and deserving of the advantages and protections of full citizenship.

From the late 1940s to the mid-1970s, the pioneering artwork of Edwin Harleston was rarely mentioned by Elise or anyone else. To keep his name and memory alive, the artist's niece, Gussie Louise Harleston, who was fifteen years old at the time of her uncle's death, decided to change her name to Edwina Augusta Harleston as a tribute to her beloved uncle. Elise encouraged Edwina, who was now married with four children and working as a journalist for the *Gary American*, a Black newspaper in northern Indiana, to write about her uncle's life and work. In conversations with family members, she began to uncover pieces of the Harleston family's remarkable history.[18] But in 1960, Edwina was forced to put aside her research to focus on her children because of the sudden death of her husband, Henry O. Whitlock. In the aftermath of this tragedy, she uprooted her family and moved them to California so she could be close to Elise—the only mother she had ever truly known.

Edwina soon found employment at the Family Savings and Loan in Los Angeles, but her job did not pay enough to make ends meet so she decided to sell some of her uncle's artwork, including *The Old Servant*, which was purchased by Mr. Earl Grant, the bank's president.[19] On July 15, 1970, at the age of seventy-nine, Elise Forrest Harleston Wheeler died, leaving behind a steamer trunk filled with Edwin Harleston's letters, notebooks, sketchbooks, photographs, newspaper clippings, and other memorabilia. Edwina was the recipient of this treasure trove and over the years she poured over these documents to better understand her uncle's achievements and sacrifices.

As she researched Edwin Harleston's life and discovered the importance of his contributions as an activist and artist, Edwina never missed an opportunity to tell others about her "Uncle Teddy." The success of her one-woman campaign to educate the public was impressive. In 1976, Edwin Harleston's painting, *The Old Servant* and *Portrait of Aaron Douglas* were included in *Two Centuries of Black American Art* (1750–1950), the first comprehensive survey exhibition of African American art held in a major United States museum. Organized by the Los Angeles County Museum of Art and curated by African American artist and scholar David Driskell, the exhibition is considered a turning point in the art world for it broadened the range of creative expression associated with the canon of American art. The exhibition, which traveled to the High Museum in Atlanta, Georgia; the Dallas Museum of Fine Arts, Dallas, Texas; and the Brooklyn Museum in New York was seen by record crowds at each location.[20]

In 1983, Edwina collaborated with her friend, Josephine Harreld Love, the founder of Your Heritage House, an important cultural center in Detroit, Michigan, to mount the exhibition "Edwin A. Harleston: Painter of an Era." In the accompanying exhibition catalogue, Edwina Harleston Whitlock wrote an illuminating essay that outlined the Harleston family history and highlighted the artist's achievements.[21] In December of that same year, the show traveled to the Gibbes Art Gallery in Charleston, South Carolina, where it was described in *the News and Courier/The Evening Post* as "both historically and artistically surprising."[22] Six years later, Harleston's *Portrait of Aaron Douglas* and *Miss Bailey with the African Shawl* were included in "Against the Odds: African-American Artists and the Harmon Foundation," a show presented by the Newark Museum in Newark, New Jersey.[23] In 2006, The Avery Research Center for African American History and Culture at the College of Charleston presented "Edwin Augustus Harleston: Artist and Activist in a Changing Era," an exhibit and symposium which included more than twenty-two artworks and artifacts highlighting his career.

This assembly of academics, independent researchers, and family historians offered a comprehensive overview of Edwin Harleston's achievement in capturing the unique characteristics of southern African American folk images as well as members of the Talented Tenth. The presentations concluded that Harleston was able to achieve what many others could only aspire to because of his family's wealth and his unwavering desire to present an accurate Black image to the public. This aspiration, coupled with the support of his wife, Elise, enabled him to travel beyond the typical limitations faced by most people of color during this period. Although he was forced to exist at the margins of the white arts community in Charleston, Harleston's exposure to the arts and ideas of the Northeast significantly influenced his artistic ambitions and sustained his hope of becoming an independent artist.

It has been said that "the arc of the moral universe is long, but it bends toward justice."[24] This held true for Harleston. Eighty years after The Charleston Museum withdrew its invitation, the artist's work made its return to Charleston and Avery, the very place where his artistic talent initially developed. Although it occurred posthumously, in this powerful full-circle moment Edwin Augustus Harleston's aspiration of exhibiting his artwork in his hometown was finally achieved.

ACKNOWLEDGMENTS

This book was inspired by stories shared while in the company of the late Mrs. Edwina Harleston Whitlock, Edwin A. Harleston's niece, and Dr. Richard A. Long, my mentor. Special thanks must be given to Mae Whitlock Gentry for her unwavering support of this project and her willingness to share family history and photographs. A deep sense of gratitude must also be extended to the following people for their support, assistance, advice, and encouragement throughout this process: Dr. Amaila Amaki, Dr. Earl Clowney and Dr. Ruby Thompson, Dr. Walter Fluker, Faye and Chester Goolrick, Dr. Shawnya Harris, Dr. Melanee Harvey, Dr. Tuliza Fleming, Steven Jones, and Carla J. Friend. I must also give special recognition to my loving family members, Agai B. and Vuyani M. Jones, Norman L. Jones, and Judy B. White, who have always provided open hearts, willing hands, and honest critiques when needed. A special note of gratitude must be given to my dear friend, Joan Barnes Ross, who was with me from the beginning of this project and cheered me on through each phase but was called home to be with the ancestors before it was finished.

I am grateful to the following institutions for their librarians and collections managers who provided assistance in accessing their archives and giving permission to use their materials: Allison Whitted, Atlanta University Archives Research Center, Robert W Woodruff Library, Atlanta, GA; Aaisha Haykal and Georgette Mayo, Avery Research Center for African American History and Culture, Charleston, SC; Harlan Greene, Special Collections, Addlestone Library, College of Charleston; Katherine Little, Delaware Division of Historical & Cultural Affairs; Christine Gostowski, Fisk University, Nashville, TN; Sara Arnold, Teresa Muñoz, and Maggie Claytor, Gibbes Museum, Charleston, SC; K E Coney-Ali, Howard University Gallery of Art, Washington, DC; Sarah Tignor, The Johnson Collection, Spartanburg, SC; Lela Sewell-Williams, Moorland-Spingarn Research Center, Howard University, Washington, DC; E. Kathleen Shoemaker and staff, Stuart A. Rose Manuscript, Archives, & Rare Book Library, Emory University; Jessie Ward, SCAD Museum of Art, Savannah, GA; Deborah Shapiro, Smithsonian Institution Archives, Washington, DC; Molly Silliman, South Carolina Historical Society, Charleston, SC; Tamia Thompson, South Carolina State Museum, Columbia, SC; Pamela Hopkins, Tufts Archival Research Center, Medford, MA, and special thanks to Charles Kaufmann, Starflower Film, Portland, ME.

NOTES

Chapter 1: The Black Branch

1. Alfred V. Frankenstein and Ann C. Van Devanter, *American Self-Portraits* (International Exhibition Foundation, 1974), 8.
2. "US, Passport Application, 1795–1925," Ancestry.com, National Archives and Records Administration (NARA), Washington, DC, Roll 071-24, May 1858–1923, June 1858.
3. "1840 United States Federal Census, Sixth Census of the United States, 1840," Ancestry.com, NARA microfilm publication M704. Records of the Bureau of the Census, Record Group 29. National Archives, Washington, DC.
4. "William and Kate," Ancestry.com, Family Stories, Family Tree files submitted by Mae Gentry, Posted 22 March 2008.
5. Edward Ball and Edwina Harleston Whitlock, *Sweet Hell Inside: A Family History* (HarperCollins, 2001), 11.
6. Henry Louis Gates, Jr., *Life upon These Shores: Looking at African American History (1513–2008)* (Alfred A. Knopf, 2011), 144.
7. Francis B. Simkins, "The Ku Klux Klan in South Carolina, 1868–1871," *Journal of Negro History* 12, no. 4 (1927): 608–9. www.jstor.org/stable/2714040.
8. Bernard E. Powers, Jr., "Community Evolution and Race Relations in Reconstruction Charleston, South Carolina," *South Carolina Historical Magazine* 95, no. 1 (1994): 28.
9. Powers, "Community Evolution," 30.
10. John Hope Franklin and Alfred A. Moss, Jr., *From Slavery to Freedom: A History of Negro Americans*, 6th ed. (Alfred A. Knopf, 1988), 206.
11. R. H. Woody, "The South Carolina Election of 1870," *North Carolina Historical Review*, 8, no. 2 (1931): 169. www.jstor.org/stable/23516336.
12. Simkins, "Ku Klux Klan," 608–9.
13. The probated will and estate documents of William Harleston, Probate Court, Charleston, SC, estate files 228-24/230-24 Pr-EF-037. In William Harleston's will, probated on January 11, 1875, only the name "Kate" appears, without a last name. In a June interview with Mrs. Whitlock, she stated that in researching her family history she discovered that Kate's maiden name was Wilson.
14. Recorded Inventory of the Estate of William Harleston, Probate Court, Charleston, SC, filed March 30, 1876, Book G, 507. In the will and other inventory records only the name "Kate" appears; yet, in the entry dated May 3, 1876, the mother of William Harleston's children is referred to as Kate Harleston.
15. Recorded Inventory of the Estate of William Harleston; Jervey, "Harlestons," 173. Although the exact date of William's death does not appear on the probate documents, the year 1874 is present. The accounting records show that in addition to a cash settlement Kate received ongoing financial support. On March 19, 1875, she received $13.35 for groceries and bacon. On August 9, 1875, she was given $15 in

cash and sent $24.23 worth of groceries. On August 12, she was given $600 in cash and $10.75 for groceries. This monetary support continued until February of 1876.

16. Mrs. Edwina H. Whitlock interview by M. Akua McDaniel, June 17, 1991, Charleston, SC.

17. Ball and Whitlock, *Sweet Hell*, 24–25.

18. "1870 United States Federal Census, St James Goose Creek, Charleston, SC," Ancestry.com, Roll M593_1488; p. 137A.

19. Kristina A. Shuler and Ralph Bailey, Jr., "A History of the Phosphate Mining Industry in the South Carolina Lowcountry" (Brockington and Associates, 2004), 1.

20. Shuler and Bailey, "Phosphate Mining," xvii.

21. Whitlock interview by McDaniel.

22. Ball and Whitlock, *Sweet Hell*, 33.

23. General Orders No. 8, "Marriage Rules," August 11, 1865, Headquarters Assistant Commissioner, Bureau of Refugees, Freedmen, and Abandoned Lands, South Carolina, Georgia, and Florida, in 39th Congress, 1st Session, serial vol. 1256, House Ex. Doc. No. 70. "Report of Commissioners of Freedmen's Bureau," March 1866, 108–11, quoted in: Tera W. Hunter, *Bound in Wedlock: Slave and Free Black Marriage in the Nineteenth Century* (Harvard University Press, 2017), 233, 236.

24. Josephine Harreld Love, *Edwin A. Harleston: Painter of an Era: 1882–1931* (Your Heritage House, 1983), 9.

25. Dale Rosengarten et al., *Between the Tracks: Charleston's East Side During the Nineteenth Century* (The Charleston Museum and Avery Research Center, 1987), 81.

26. Powers, "Community Evolution," 32.

27. Ta-Nehisi Coates, *We Were Eight Years in Power: An American Tragedy* (One World, 2017), XIII–IV.

28. Burchill Richardson Moore, "A History of the Negro Public Schools of Charleston, South Carolina: 1867–1942" (unpublished master's thesis, University of South Carolina, 1942), 19.

29. Moore, "History of the Negro Public Schools," 19–23.

30. William G. Whitford, *An Introduction to Art Education* (Appleton, 1929), 10.

31. Green, *Educational Ideas*, 119.

32. F. H. Hayward, *The Educational Ideas of Pestalozzi and Frobel* (Ralph, Holland, 1904; repr., Greenwood Press, 1979), 43.

33. *Painter of an Era*, 10.

34. *Painter of an Era*, 10.

35. *Painter of an Era*, 10.

36. "Who's Who in Colored America Questionnaire," Edwina H. Whitlock Papers, Charleston, SC, hereafter referred to as the Whitlock Papers, 1928; and I. A. Newby, *Black Carolinians: A History of Blacks in South Carolina from 1895 to 1968* (University of South Carolina Press, 1973), 158.

37. Moore, "Negro Public Schools," 46.

38. Moore, 46.

39. Moore, 46.

40. Thomas A. Barlow, *Pestalozzi and American Education* (Este Es Press, 1977), 16.

41. Hayward, Educational Ideas *of Pestalozzi*, 42.

42. Barlow, *Pestalozzi*, 13.

43. Barlow, *Pestalozzi*, 82, 86.

44. *Avery Normal Institute Catalogue 1906–1907*, Maude Smith's private papers, Winston-Salem, NC, 17.

45. *Avery Normal Institute Catalogue*, 17.

46. Booker T. Washington, *Up from Slavery*, 3rd ed. (Doubleday, Page, 1924), 220.

47. Edmund L. Drago, *Initiative, Paternalism and Race Relations: Charleston Avery Normal Institute* (University of Georgia Press, 1990), 85.

48. Drago, *Initiative*, 45.

49. *Avery Normal Institute Catalogue*, 20.

50. Whitlock interview by McDaniel, February 17, 1992, Charleston, SC.

51. Whitlock interview by McDaniel, June 14, 1991, Charleston, SC.

52. Maurine A. McDaniel, "Edwin Augustus Harleston, Portrait Painter, 1882–1931" (PhD diss. Emory University, 1994), 18. C. W. Harvard, ed., *Black's Medical Dictionary* (Savage, Barns & Noble Books, 1990), 23.

53. Whitlock interview by McDaniel, December 5, 1991, Charleston, SC.

54. *Commencement 1900 Avery Normal Institute*, unpaginated booklet, Archives, Avery Research Center for African American History & Culture at the College of Charleston, Charleston, SC.

55. Holzer, Boritt, and Neely, *Lincoln Image*, 125; The print was published by D. Hensel & Co. and Goff & Bros. of Philadelphia, PA.

56. George Brown Tindall, *South Carolina Negroes 1877–1900* (University of South Carolina Press, 1952), 288–89.

57. Harry T. Peters, *Printmakers to the American People* (Doubleday, Doran, 1942), 35.

58. Mark Edward Thistlethwaite, *The Image of George Washington: Studies in Mid-Nineteenth- Century American History Painting* (Garland, 1979), 21.

Chapter 2: Gate City of the New South

1. *Catalogue of the Officers and Students of Atlanta University 1902–1903* (Atlanta University Press, 1902), 19.

2. Stone Hall was designed by Godfrey Leonard Norman, a Swedish American architect who designed buildings for The Cotton States and International Exchange Exposition located in what is now Piedmont Park and several other buildings in Atlanta. *Catalogue of the Officers and Students*, 22.

3. *Catalogue of the Officers and Students*, 20.

4. Clarence Albert Bacote, *The Story of Atlanta University: A Century of Service, 1865–1965* (Atlanta University Press, 1969), 104. Bumstead insisted that the University include all levels of learning because most of the education for Black people, throughout the South, was so poor.

5. *Bulletin of Atlanta University* (hereafter referred to as BAU), May 1890, 4–5 and 105–6; and Horace Bumstead, "Some Mistakes Concerning Education in the South," speech, 1890, repr., BAU, November 1891, 5, Woodruff Library, Special Collections, Clark Atlanta University, Atlanta, GA.

6. Louis R. Harlan, "The Secret Life of Booker T. Washington." *Journal of Southern History* 37, no. 3 (1971): 393.

7. Bacote, *Story of Atlanta*, 137.

8. Bacote, *Story of Atlanta*, 115.

9. *BAU*, May 1890, 4–5,

10. *BAU*, May 1890, 4–5, 106.

11. *Atlanta University Catalogue 1900–1901* (Atlanta University Press, 1900), 25–26.

12. Bacote, *Story of Atlanta*, 129. Adrienne McNeil Herndon was married to Alonzo Herndon, the owner of three of the largest barber shops in the city of Atlanta catering exclusively to white patrons. He would later become the founder and president of Atlanta Life Insurance Company and one of the first African American millionaires in the country.

13. *Scroll* vol.6, no. 5 (1901): 63, Woodruff Library, Special Collections, Clark Atlanta University, Atlanta, GA.

14. *Scroll* 7, no. 6 (1903): 85.

15. *Scroll* 7, nos. 6 and 12 (1903): 85.

16. *Scroll* 7, no. 6 (1903): 85.

17. Bacote, *Story of Atlanta*, 132.

18. *Scroll*, 8, no. 6 (1904): 103.

19. W. E. B. Du Bois, "The Art and Art Galleries of Modern Europe," an unpublished essay appearing in *Against Racism*, ed. Herbert Apthehem (University of Massachusetts Press, 1985), 34–35.

20. Dewey F. Mosby, *Henry Ossawa Tanner* (Philadelphia Museum of Art, 1991), 94.

21. Carlyn Gaye Crannell, "In Pursuit of Culture: A History of Art Activity in Atlanta, 1847–1926" (PhD diss., Emory University, 1981), 83.

22. Crannell, "In Pursuit of Culture," 83.

23. Bacote, *Story of Atlanta*, 219.

24. "John Adams, Negro Artist, Has Won Great Success," *Constitution* (Atlanta, GA), June 23, 1902, Woodruff Library, Emory University, Atlanta, GA. Adams created images of his ideal African American man and women for the *Voice of the Negro* magazine and the NAACP's *The Crisis*.

25. Whitlock interview by McDaniel, September 19, 1991, Charleston, SC.

26. Whitlock interview by McDaniel, September 19, 1991, Charleston, SC.

27. Letter from "Little Bit" to Edwin Augustus Harleston, May 18, 1905, and letter from Inez Canty to Edwin Harleston, undated, Edwin A. Harleston and Edwina Harleston Whitlock Family Papers, Stuart A. Rose Manuscript, Archives, and Rare Book Library, Emory University.

28. Mamie Cole to Edwin Harleston, photocopied letter in the hand of Mamie Cole, June 11, 1902, Edwin A. Harleston and Edwina Harleston Whitlock Family Papers, Stuart A. Rose Manuscript, Archives, and Rare Book Library, Emory University.

29. "Some Negro Members of Reconstruction Conventions and Legislatures and of Congress," authored by Monroe N. Work, Thomas S. Staples, H. A. Wallace, Kelly Miller, Whitefield McKinlay, Samuel E. Lacy, R. L. Smith, and H. R. McIlwaine, *Journal of Negro History* 5, no. 1 (1920): 63–119; published by University of Chicago Press on behalf of the Association for the Study of African American Life and History Stable, https:// www.jstor.org/Stable/2713503." Edward Charles Mickey served in the state legislature from 1868 until 1870.

30. "Mickey Funeral Home (50 Cannon Street)," inventory of the Mickey Funeral Home Papers, Avery Research Center, *Historic Charleston Foundation/Preservation Advocacy in Charleston, SC*, www.historiccharleston.org.

31. Suzanne E. Smith, *To Serve, To Serve the Living: Funeral Directors and the African American Way of Death* (Harvard University Press, 2010), 20–21.

32. Smith, *To Serve*, 21. Kara Ann Morrow, "Bakongo Afterlife and Cosmological Direction: Transition of African Culture into North Florida Cemeteries," *Florida Online Journals*, 2002, 105.

33. Smith, *To Serve*, 28.

34. Smith, *To Serve*, 32, 38–39.

35. Whitlock interview by McDaniel. September 19, 1991, Charleston, SC.

36. "U.S. City Directories, 1822–1995," *Ancestry: Genealogy, Family Trees & Family History Records*, Charleston City Directory, 1903–1904, Ancestry.com, www.ancestry.com, 470.

37. *Scroll* 9, no. 1 (1904): 14.

38. *Atlanta University Catalogue*, 1903–04, 45.

39. George W. Carn's acceptance letter to Edwin A. Harleston, 11 May 1905, Whitlock papers. The letter was in response to Harleston's application of April 26, 1905. Along with his notice of admission, the correspondence informed Harleston that he would have to pass "five approved courses each year."

40. In the lower portion of a 1901 photograph of Edwin Harleston taken in New York, he notes that he worked the Hudson River Day Line, which ran between New York City and Albany, to earn tuition money, Whitlock Papers.

Chapter 3: Boston and the School of the Museum of Fine Arts

1. Stephen Thernstrom, *The Other Bostonians: Poverty and Progress in the American Metropolis 1870–1970* (Harvard University Press, 1973), 23

2. Mattie Marsh, Charleston, SC, to Edwin Harleston, Boston, MA, March 30, 1912, transcript in the hand of Mattie Marsh, Whitlock Papers. This letter expresses Marsh's regret that Harleston did not choose to enter the field of teaching but congratulates him on his decision to become an artist.

3. Edwin A. Harleston, Boston, MA, to Elise Forrest Harleston, Charleston, SC, December 3, 1923, transcript in the hand of Edwin Harleston, Whitlock Papers, Official Register of Harvard University, 1905–1906, 2nd ed. (Harvard University Press, 1905), 53, iii.lib.harvard.edu.

4. *A Guide to Boston* (Macular, 1907), 27.

5. Frederick Coburn, "Edmund C. Tarbell," *International Studio* 32, no. 127 (1907): 125.

6. Trevor J. Fairbrother, *The Bostonians: Painters of an Elegant Age, 1870–1930* (Museum of Fine Arts, 1986), 1.

7. David M. Lubin, *Act of Portrayal: Eakins, Sargent, James* (Yale University Press, 1985), 6.

8. Charles H. Caffin, "Some American Portrait Painters," *Critic* 44, no. 1 (1904): 32.

9. Archives of American Art, "Marie Danforth Page papers, 1826–2016," http://www.aaa.si.edu/collections/marie-danforth-page-papers-8891.

10. SMFA Admissions Catalogue 1906–1907, p. 3, SMFA Archives, Boston, MA.

11. Whitlock interview by McDaniel, July 5, 1992, Charleston, SC. Westmoreland Company receipt dated 1906, Whitlock Papers.

12. *Museum of Fine Arts Boston* (*Newsweek Inc.* & Arnoldo Mondadori Editore, 1969), 166.

13. *SMFA Admissions Catalogue 1906–1907*, 6.

14. *SMFA Catalogues and Reports 1912–1921*, table showing student demographics, SMFA Archives, Boston, MA, 18–19.

15. According to James D. Anderson in *The Education of Blacks in the South 1860–1935* (University of North Carolina Press, 1988), 245, from a Black population of 10 million, there were approximately three thousand African American college and professional graduates in 1906.

16. "School of the Museum of Fine Arts," newspaper clipping, *Boston Transcript*, October 13, 1906, SMFA Scrapbook 1906–1909, no. 3.

17. Bernice Kramer Leader, "The Boston Lady as a Work of Art: Painting by the Boston School at the Turn of the Century" (PhD diss., Columbia University, 1980), 5.

18. Henry F. May, *The End of American Innocence: The First Years of Our Time 1912–1917* (Oxford University Press, 1959), 9, 20, 30.

19. Martha J. Hoppin, *William Morris Hunt: A Memorial Exhibition* (Museum of Fine Arts, 1979), 13.

20. Martha A. S. Shannon, *Boston Days of William Morris Hunt* (Marshall Jones, 1923), 21.

21. H. Winthrop Peirce, *The History of the School of the Museum of Fine Arts, Boston, 1877–1927* (Museum of Fine Arts, 1930), 17.

22. Leader, "Boston Lady," 15.

23. Philip Leslie Hale Papers, Archives of American Art, Washington, DC, D99:1620, quoted in Leader, "Boston Lady," 15.

24. Hoppin, *William Morris Hunt*, 26. Although Hunt received his training in Germany and Paris, the American artist Washington Allston was also an inspiration and model for Hunt.

25. SMFA Scrapbook 1906–1909, no. 3, "Many Students Fail to One who Succeeds...," newspaper clipping, n.p.; and Lois Marie Fink and Joshua C. Taylor describe the academic tradition based upon Italian models and refined by the French in *Academic Tradition in American Art* (Smithsonian Institution Press, 1975), 16.

26. Edwin A. Harleston, Perspective notebook, 1906, Whitlock Papers. This notebook contains perspective exercises which are based, in part, on the theories of mathematicians Brook Taylor and Johann Jacob Schubler as well as perspectivists Paul Heineken and Giacomo Fantana. Pierre Descargues and Ellyn C. Allison, *Perspective* (Harry N. Abrams, 1977), 134, 135, 138, 173.

27. Nikolaus Pevsner, *Academies of Art Past and Present* (Cambridge University Press, 1940), 202.

28. Fink and Taylor, *Academy*, 17; Albert Boiem, *The Academy and French Painting in the Nineteenth Century* (Yale University Press, 1971), 27.

29. Walter Muir Whitehill, *Museum of Fine Arts, Boston: A Centennial History* (Belknap Press, 1970), 198–199.

30. Fairbrother, *Bostonians*, 221.

31. R. H. Gammell, *The Boston Painters 1900–1930* (Parnassus Imprints, 1986), 110.

32. SMFA Record Book 1902–1907, 197, SMFA Archives, Boston MA, n.p.

33. *SMFA Thirty-first Annual Report, 1906–1907*, 16, SMFA Archives.

34. SMFA Register of Pupils, 521, SMFA Archives.

35. Faith A. Bedford et al., *Frank W. Benson: A Retrospective* (Berry-Hill Galleries, 1989), 40, citing letter from Frank W. Benson to Albert Kennedy, Salem, May 20, 1932, Hale Papers Roll 103, Archives of American Art.

36. Patricia Jobe Pierce, *The Ten* (Rumford Press, 1976), 64 and SMFA Scrapbook 1906–1909, no. 3, SMFA Scrapbook 1902–1906, no. 2, "Gay Art Students Quit Old Museum," newspaper clipping, 197.

37. Perspective notebook, 1906, Whitlock Papers.

38. Whitlock interview by McDaniel, December 5, 1991, Charleston, SC; *Edwin A. Harleston: Painter of an Era*, 12.

39. Whitlock interview by McDaniel, 5 December 1991, Charleston, SC. Whitlock interview by McDaniel; *Edwin A. Harleston: Painter of an Era*, 12; Boston, Crew Lists, 1811–1921, Ancestry.com, https://familysearch.org/ark:/61903/1:2:Q2JY-7HTT.

40. Whitlock interview by McDaniel. Ball and Whitlock, *Sweet Hell*, 88.

41. Inez Canty, Atlanta, GA, to Edwin Harleston, Boston, MA, August 17, 1908, transcript in the hand of Inez Canty, Whitlock Papers.

42. John Daniels, *In Freedom's Birthplace: A Study of Boston Negroes.* (Houghton Mifflin, 1914), 148–49.

43. Daniels, *Freedom's Birthplace*, 108.

44. "Today in Georgia History: Henry Grady," Georgia Historical Society, Georgia Public Broadcasting, 2024, www.todayingeorgiahistory.org/HenryGrady. In his image of the New South, Henry Grady, a white supremacist, advocated for northern investment to spur southern industrial and agricultural growth using cheap Black labor as a means of reconciliation.

45. Daniels, *Freedom's Birthplace*, 121. Millington W. Bergeson-Lockwood, "'We Do Not Care Particularly about the Skating Rinks': African American Challenges to Racial Discrimination in Places of Public Amusement in Nineteenth-Century Boston, Massachusetts," *Journal of the Civil War Era* 5, no. 2 (2015): 254–88, http://www.jstor.org/stable/26070303.

46. Fink and Taylor, *Academy*, 59.

47. SMFA Scrapbook 1909–1911, no. 4, "New Studio School Opens Monday," SMFA Archives, Boston, MA, 2.

48. SMFA Scrapbook 1909–1911, no. 4, "New Studio School Opens Monday," 2; "New Art Museum," August 11, 1908, newspaper clipping, n.p.

49. SMFA Scrapbook 1906–1909, no. 3, "Gay Art Students Quit Old Museum," newspaper clipping, n.p.

50. SMFA Scrapbook 1909–1911, no. 4, "Passing of Old Art Museum is. . . ," February 3, 1909, newspaper clipping, n.p.

51. "Gay Art Students Quit Old Museum," newspaper clipping, n.p.

52. "Passing of Old Art Museum is. . . ," newspaper clipping, n.p.

53. SMFA Scrapbook 1906–1909, no. 3, Photograph of Moving Day, SMFA Archives, n.p.

Chapter 4: From Amateur to Fine Artist

1. SMFA Scrapbook 1909–1911, no. 4. "Students Masquerade: Housewarming at New School of Museum of Fine Arts," March 4, 1909, n.p.
2. SMFA Scrapbook 1909–1911, no. 4. "Students Masquerade: Housewarming at New School of Museum of Fine Arts," March 4, 1909, n.p.
3. Lerone Bennett, Jr., *Before the* Mayflower: *A History of Black America* 5th ed. (Penguin Books, 1984), 271.
4. Bennett, *Before the* Mayflower, 271.
5. "Celebrations of the Fiftieth Anniversary of the Public Murder of John Brown," program, December 2, 1909, Edwin Harleston Papers, South Carolina Historical Society, Charleston, SC. The National Independent Political League was similar to the NAACP but without the political power and financial backing of sympathetic white liberals.
6. Benjamin Quarles, ed., *Blacks on John Brown* (University of Illinois Press, 1972), 83.
7. Kenneth Haley, "The Ten American Painters: Definition and Reassessment" (PhD diss., State University of New York at Binghamton, 1875), 16. Boulanger and Lefebvre were both graduates of the École des Beaux-Arts and winner of the Prix de Rome.
8. Gammell, *Boston Painters*, 82; and Richard J. Boyle, *American Impressionism* (New York Graphic Society, 1974), 31.
9. Pierce, *Ten*, 86.
10. E.B.L., "Advice on Painting from F.W.B.," January 28, 1939, typescript [photocopy], 5, Essex Institute, Salem, MA.
11. Alice F. Brooks, Boston, to Edwin Harleston, Boston, April 11, 1911, transcript in the hand of Alice F. Brooks, Whitlock Papers.
12. SMFA scholarship program, Admission Catalogue, 1906–07, 8–10.
13. Pierce, *Ten*, 57.
14. Leader, "Boston Lady," 137.
15. Tonalism is closely associated with late nineteenth century landscape painting. However, the term can be applied to any work, regardless of subject matter, that is worked in tones that are usually warm and produces in subject matter and color a quiet, somber mood. *McGraw-Hill Dictionary of Art*, ed. Bernard S. Myers, vol. 5 (McGraw-Hill Book, 1969), 333.
16. Samuel Isham, *The History of American Painting* (MacMillian, 1905), 374.
17. John Walker, *Portraits: 5,000 Years* (Harry N. Abrams, 1983), 231.
18. Neil Harris, ed., *The Land of Contrasts, 1880–9101* (George Braziller, 1970), 17.
19. John E. D. Trask, "About Tarbell," *American Magazine of Art*, no. 6 (April 1918), 228.
20. Pierce, *Ten*, 40.
21. *Painter of an Era*, 49.
22. Hoppin, William Morris Hunt, 14.
23. Pierce, *Ten*, 46.
24. SMFA Scrapbook 1906–1909, no. 3, "Art Museum School Students," n.p.
25. *Handbook of The Museum of Fine Arts* (Museum of Fine Arts, 1911), 159.
26. SMFA School Council Records 1909–1913, meeting of March 13, 1912, SMFA Archives.

27. SMFA Annual Meeting Minutes, May 22, 1912, SMFA Archives.
28. SMFA Scrapbook 1911–1913, no. 5, "Heads Art Museum School," *Boston Transcript*, December 2, 1912. SMFA School Council Records 1907–1913, May 7, 1912, 83, SMFA Archives.
29. SMFA Scrapbook 1911–1913, no. 5, "Heads Art Museum School," *Boston Transcript*, December 2, 1912. SMFA School Council Records 1907–1913, May 7, 1912, 83, SMFA Archives; *Boston Transcript*, December 2, 1912. SMFA School Council Records 1907–1913, January 15, 1913, 178.
30. SMFA Scrapbook 1911–1913, "Criticizes Museum Trustees" Letter to the Editor, 9 February 1913, 101.
31. SMFA School Council Records 1907–1913, 178.
32. Gammell, *Boston Painters*, 87.
33. *U.S. City Directories, 1822–1995 (1913)*, Ancestry.com.
34. Whitlock interview by McDaniel, July 5, 1992, Charleston, SC.
35. United States Federal Census, Year 1900; Census Place: Charleston Ward 11, Charleston, SC, 6; Enumeration District: 0110; FHL microfilm: 1241521.
36. Ball and Whitlock, *Sweet Hell*, 61.
37. Whitlock interview by McDaniel, July 5, 1992, Charleston, SC. New York State Archives; Albany, NY; State Population Census Schedules, 1915; Election District: 18; Assembly District: 21; City: New York, County: New York; 45.
38. Whitlock interview by McDaniel, July 5, 1992, Charleston, SC. New York State Archives; Albany, New York; State Population Census Schedules, 1915; Robert W. Habenstein and William M. Lamers, *The History of American Funeral Directing* (Bulfin, 1955), 348–49, 509, 511.
39. Ball and Whitlock, *Sweet Hell*, 63.

Chapter 5: The Homecoming

1. Walter J. Fraser Jr., *Charleston! Charleston! The History of a Southern City* (University of South Carolina Press, 1989), 327.
2. Fraser, *Charleston!*, 352.
3. John Joseph Duffy, "Charleston Politics in the Progressive Era" (PhD diss., University of South Carolina, 1963), 31.
4. Theodore Hemmingway, "Prelude to Change: Black Carolinians in the War Years, 1914–1920," *Journal of Negro History* 65, no. 3 (Summer 1980), 212.
5. Hemmingway, "Prelude to Change," 213.
6. C. Vann Woodward, *The Strange Career of Jim Crow* (Oxford University Press, 1966), 98; The segregation of workers was formalized by the South Carolina code of 1915.
7. Woodward, *Strange Career*, 336.
8. A.V. Huff, "The Democratization of Art: Memorializing the Confederate Dead in South Carolina, 1866–1914," in *Art in the Lives of South Carolinians: Nineteenth-Century Chapters* (Carolina Art Association, 1979), AH-2; and Francis W. Bilodeau, ed., *Art in South Carolina 1670–1970* (South Carolina Tricentennial Commission, 1970), 185.
9. Mae Whitlock Gentry, "Elise Forrest Harleston," University of South Carolina Aiken, May 12, 2006, www.usca.edu/aasc/EliseForrestHarleston.htm.

10. Ball and Whitlock, *Sweet Hell*, 109.

11. Terence Samuel, Terence, "A New Political Gospel" *U.S. News and World Report*, 2003. David H. Jackson Jr., "Booker T. Washington in South Carolina, March 1909." *South Carolina Historical Magazine* 113.3 (July 2012): 192–220.

12. Harlan Greene and James Hutchins, eds., *Renaissance in Charleston: Art and Life in the Carolina Low Country, 1900–1940* (University of Georgia Press, 2003), 192.

13. "A Colored Man's Enterprise," unidentified, undated newspaper clipping, Whitlock Papers. "Harleston Funeral Home" brochure, unpaginated, Box 6, Edwin A. Harleston and Edwina Harleston Whitlock Family Papers, Stuart A. Rose Manuscript, Archives, and Rare Book Library, Emory University.

14. "A Colored Man's Enterprise," unidentified.

15. H. C. Dugas, Augusta, GA, to Edwin Harleston, Charleston, SC, January 25, 1915, typewritten letter, Whitlock Papers.

16. Note in the hand of Edwin Harleston to Elise F. Harleston with sketch, undated, Box 1, Folder 1, Edwin A. Harleston and Edwina Harleston Whitlock Family Papers, Stuart A. Rose Manuscript, Archives, and Rare Book Library, Emory University.

17. Student identification card for the Renouard Training School for Embalmers, dated January 2, 1917, Whitlock Papers.

18. Student identification card for the Renouard Training School, Whitlock Papers, 511; Whitlock interview by McDaniel, September 19, 1991, Charleston, SC. Mrs. Whitlock stated that one reason for Harleston's success was his ability to make such accurate drawings of the various body parts studied in class.

19. Rob Frydiewicz, "Weather Highlights of the 1910s in New York," New York City Weather Archives, www.starryeye.typepad.com/weather/2018/12/weather-highlights-of-the-1910s.html.

20. *Painter of an Era*, 15.

21. Forrest to Harleston, September 2, 1918.

22. Works by William M. Farrow, a successful African American printmaker who taught at the Art Institute of Chicago, appeared in the novel. Information about Farrow is included in James A. Porter, *Modern Negro Art* (Arno and *New York Times* Press, 1969), 159.

23. Western Book Supply Company, Lincoln, NE, to Edwin A. Harleston, Charleston, SC, undated, Whitlock Papers. The book company sent a request for the name of a "Negro artist" to an anonymous source in a letter dated January 26, 1917. Evidently, the person to whom the letter was sent forwarded it to Harleston requesting that he submit an illustration. The author of the letter, Oscar D. Micheaux, would later become one of the most important African American film producers of the 1920s.

24. Mae Gentry, text message to author, May 15, 2024.

25. This conclusion has been reached because the signature on this painting is very different when compared with the signature that appears on the *Portrait of Aaron Douglas*, indicating that it was probably signed by Elise after Edwin's death. Because Harleston usually signed works that he considered finished, it is possible that he continued to work on the face in his spare time to recapture the level of technical excellence exhibited in his earlier portraits.

26. Truman K. Gibson, Atlanta, GA, to Edwin A. Harleston, Charleston, SC, October 16, 1917, typewritten letter, Whitlock Papers.

27. "Centennial Celebration: The Odd Fellows Building," *Atlanta Daily World*, April 29, 2013.

28. Gibson to Harleston, October 16, 1917.

29. Dan Moore, Clarissa Myrick, and Carolyn Seals, *Sweet Auburn Street of Pride: A Pictorial History* (The APEX, 1988), 23, quoting "Ben Davis, Atlanta's Leading Colored Citizen, and the Great Work He Is Doing for His Race," *Atlanta Independent*, November 20, 1915. Davis was not only the leader of the Georgia Odd Fellows but he was also publisher of the *Atlanta Independent*, a local African American newspaper.

30. Elise Forrest, Asheville, NC, to Edwin A. Harleston, Charleston, SC, September 2, 1918, transcript in the hand of Elise Forrest, Whitlock Papers.

31. Gibson to Harleston, October 30, 1917; and "Membership Prizes," *Atlanta Independent*, October 20, 1917, 2.

32. "Prize Winners," *Atlanta Independent* February 9, 1918, 2.

33. Application for the Charter of Charleston Branch of the National Association for the Advancement of Colored People, approved by Committee on Branches, March 23, 1917, Whitlock Papers, photocopied from the collections in the Manuscript division, Library of Congress.

34. Charles Flint Kellogg, *NAACP: A History of the National Association for the Advancement of Colored People* (Johns Hopkins University Press, 1967), 134.

35. Newby, *Black Carolinians*, 157.

36. James W. Johnson, New York, NY, to Edwin A. Harleston, Charleston, SC, April 20, 1917, typewritten letter, Whitlock Papers.

37. Kellogg, *NAACP*, 134.

38. Johnson to Harleston, April 20, 1917.

39. Application for the Charter of Charleston Branch of the NAACP.

40. Richard A. Mickey, Charleston Branch secretary, Charleston, SC, to Mr. Roy Nash, National Secretary of the NAACP, New York, NY, April 11, 1917, typewritten letter, Whitlock Papers.

41. This conclusion is because less than a month after Du Bois's visit an article concerning the need for "Negro" teachers to teach "Negro" students in the Charleston, SC, school system appeared in "Awake," *The Crisis*, April 1917, 270.

42. Thomas E Miller, John M. Thompson, William H. Johnson, Edwin A. Harleston and Charles O. Jacobs, "Charleston, S.C., School Petition," January 18, 1919, photocopy, Whitlock Papers.

43. "Colored Teachers in Charleston Schools," *Crisis*, June 1, 1921, 58, https://modjourn.org/issue/bdr513685/.

44. Reverend L. F. Alston, "A Just Appeal," *Charleston America*, January 16, 1916, news clipping, Whitlock Papers.

45. "Awake," *Crisis*, April 1917.

46. Richard Mickey, Charleston, SC, to the board of directors of the NAACP, New York, NY, December 21, 1917, typewritten, Whitlock Papers.

47. Walter F. White, assistant secretary, New York, NY, to Richard Mickey, Charleston, SC, December 21, 1917, typewritten letter, Whitlock Papers.

48. Chad Williams, *Torchbearers of Democracy: African American Soldiers in the World War I Era* (University of North Carolina Press, 2010).

49. Fred Silva, ed. *Focus on The Birth of a Nation* (Prentice Hall, 1971), 83.

50. Silva, *Focus*, 83.

51. Silva, *Focus*, 83, https://a.co/31RXBd3.

52. Silva, *Focus*, 83, https://a.co/3zEEluC, quoted in "Messages" from the *Messenger*, an African American Socialist magazine founded by labor activist, A. Phillip Randolph and economist, Chandler Owen, *Messenger*, November 1917.

53. Silva, *Focus*, 83, https://a.co/3zEEluC, quoted in "Messages" from the *Messenger*, November 1917.

54. "Editorial: World War and the Color Line," *Crisis*, November 1914.

55. Amy Helene Kirschke, "For the Privilege of Dying: The Crisis Takes on The War," in *World War I and American Art*, ed. Robert Cozzolino, Anne Classen Knutson, and David Lubin (Pennsylvania Academy of the Fine Arts, 2016), 74.

56. Augustus Granville Dill to Edwin A. Harleston, January 31, 1919, transcript in the hand of A. G. Dill. In Dill's letter he thanks Harleston for his willingness to help with *The Crisis*. During this period, the magazine was one of the largest patrons of African American artists.

57. Arthur E. Barbeau and Florette Henri, *The Unknown Soldiers: Black American Troops in World War I* (Temple University Press, 1974), 7.

58. "The Black Soldier," *Crisis*, June 1918, 60.

59. "Editorial," *Crisis*, June 1917, 60.

60. Robert Cozzolino et al., eds., *World War I and American Art* (Princeton University Press, 2016), 75.

61. Hal S. Chase, "Struggle for Equality: Fort Des Moines Training Camp for Colored Officers," *Phylon* 39, no. 4 (1960), 297–98.

62. Joyce Ross, *J.E. Spingarn and the Rise of the NAACP 1911–1939* (Athenaeum, 1972), 85–86.

63. Hal S. Chase, "Struggle for Equality," 299, 305–6.

64. Chase, "Struggle for Equality," 305–6.

65. Chase, 305–6.

66. W. E. B. Garney, first lieutenant, infantry, War Department headquarters, Charleston, SC, to Edwin A. Harleston, Charleston, SC, May 1917, Whitlock Papers.

67. *Painter of an Era*, 49; Whitlock interview by McDaniel, September 19, 1991, Charleston, SC.

68. Chase, "Struggle for Equality," 306. John L. Thompson, *History and Views of Colored Officers Training Camp: For 1917 at Des Moines, Iowa, Bystander*, 1917, Birmingham-Southern College Library Data Base, catalogue hathitrust.org/api /volumes/ocic/3879374.html, 84, 96.

69. Williams, *Torchbearers*, 45.

70. Williams, *Torchbearers*, 49.

71. Hemmingway, "Prelude to Change," 215.

72. Barbeau and Henri, *Unknown Soldiers*, 62; Only 629 of the original 1,250 became commissioned officers. The other recruits were allowed to return home or continue as noncommissioned officers.

73. Williams, *Torchbearers*, 16.

74. Hemmingway, "Prelude to Change," 216.

75. Edwin A. Harleston, *The War Cross*, typewritten manuscript, 1918, Whitlock Papers. While Harleston was a student in Boston, he wrote a one-act play, *Stage Struck*, which was performed on Tuesday, May 21, 1911, at the Palm Garden in Boston. The production also included a series of musical performances, supper for twenty-five cents and dancing from ten at night until two in the morning. *Stage Struck* flyer, Box 6, Edwin A. Harleston and Edwina Harleston Whitlock Family Papers, Stuart A. Rose Manuscript, Archives, and Rare Book Library, Emory University.

76. Whitlock interviewed by McDaniel, September 19, 1991.

77. "*U.S. World War I Draft Registration Cards (1917–1918)*," Ancestry.com.

78. Gentry, "Elise," 3.

79. Hemmingway "Prelude to Change," 216; Williams, *Torchbearers*, 191.

80. Edwin A. Harleston, Charleston, SC, to Dr. Myron Adams, Atlanta, GA, undated, transcript in the hand of Edwin Harleston, Whitlock Papers. In this letter to Adams, Harleston is asking for a personal reference for the war work program sponsored by the YMCA.

81. W. E. B. Du Bois, "Opinion," *Crisis*, May 1919, 14.

82. Williams, *Torchbearers*, 190.

83. Madeline G. Allison, "Harleston! Who is E. A. Harleston?" *Opportunity* (January 1924): 21; and Elise F. Harleston, Charleston, SC, to Edwin A. Harleston, Philadelphia, PA, January 13, 1924, transcript in the hand of Elise Harleston, Whitlock Papers.

84. Edwin A. Harleston, president, Charleston Branch of the NAACP, Charleston, SC, to Walter White, assistant secretary of the NAACP, New York, NY, May 20, 1918, transcript in the hand of E. A. Harleston, Whitlock Papers.

85. Hemmingway, "Prelude to Change," 220.

86. "Negro Teachers For Negro Race," unidentified newspaper clipping, January 16, 1919, n.p. Whitlock Papers. Hemmingway, "Prelude to Change," 221.

87. Rayford W. Logan and Michael R. Winston, eds., *Dictionary of American Negro Biography* (W.W. Norton & Company, 1982), s.v. "Thomas E. Miller," outlines Miller's involvement in South Carolina government. In 1874 he was elected as a state representative to the SC General Assembly and in 1880 he was elected to the state senate. During that same year he was nominated for and lost the race for lieutenant governor of the state. In 1890 Miller was elected to the US House of Representatives; however, he served only a small portion of his term because his election was contested. When he ran for the position again Miller was voted out of office. Miller continued to serve his community and in 1896 he became the first president of Claflin College, in Orangeburg, SC, a position he held until 1911.

88. "Negro Teachers for Negro Race."

89. "Colored Teachers in Charleston Schools," 58.

90. "Negroes Petition General Assembly," clipping from *The Columbia State*, January 23, 1919, n.p., Whitlock Papers.

91. "Colored Teachers in Charleston Schools," 60. "Affidavit by Chairman of Board of Registers," undated clippings from *The Columbia State*, n.p.; and "Charleston, S.C. School Petition," Whitlock Papers.

92. "Colored Teachers in Charleston Schools," 60.

93. August Kohn, "Colored Teachers' Bill," *News and Courier*, January 22, 1919, n.p., Whitlock Papers. In February 1919, a similar resolution was passed by the Board of School Commissioners of the City of Charleston, as stated in the resolution from A. B. Rhett, Supt., and George H. Moffett, vice chairman of the school board, February 1919, Whitlock Papers.

94. Edward T. Ware, Atlanta University, Atlanta, GA, to Edwin A. Harleston, Charleston, SC, May 12, 1919, Whitlock Papers.

95. Mary White Ovington, New York, NY, to Edwin A. Harleston, Charleston, SC, undated letter, Whitlock Papers.

96. W. E. B. Du Bois, New York, NY, to Edwin A. Harleston, Charleston, SC, February 10, 1920, typewritten letter, Whitlock Papers.

97. "Thomas E. Miller." Rayford W. Logan and Michael R. Winston, eds., *Dictionary of Negro Biography* (W.W. Norton, 1982).

98. "Atlanta University in the Fine Arts," *Crimson and Gray* 8, no. 2 (1918): 2–3; "Presentation of Dean Adams' Portrait," *Crimson and Gray* 9, no. 2 (1919): 2. Adams served as acting president of Atlanta University during the 1922–23 academic year and president from 1923 to 1929.

99. "Atlanta University in the Fine Arts," 2–3; "Presentation of Dean Adams' Portrait," 2. Adams served as acting president of Atlanta University during the 1922–23 academic year and president from 1923 to 1929.

100. "A. F. Herndon Honored in Remarkable Way," unidentified newspaper clipping, Whitlock Papers.

101. William H. Gerdts, Diana Dimodica Sweet, and Robert R. Preato, *Tonalism: An American Experience* (Grand Central Art Galleries Art Education Association, 1982), 39.

102. Isham, *American Painting*, 479.

103. Charles H. Caffin, *Story of American Painting: The Evolution of Painting in America from Colonial Times to the Present* (Frederick A. Stokes, 1907), 254.

104. Edwin A. Harleston, *Sketch of the George A. Hearn Portrait*, pencil on paper, 1919, Whitlock Papers.

105. Edwin A. Harleston, Charleston, SC, to Elise Forrest, New York, NY, March 2, 1920, transcript in the hand of Edwin Harleston, Whitlock Papers.

106. Harleston to Forrest, January 1920.

107. "Two Hearts that Beat as One in the City by The Sea," unidentified newspaper clipping, Whitlock Papers.

108. Harleston to Elise Forrest, December 1919.

109. "A. F. Herndon Honored in Remarkable Way."

110. Harleston, Charleston, SC, to Elise, New York, NY December 1919.

111. Forrest, New York, to Harleston, Charleston, April 1919.

112. E. Brunel Training School of Photography, Inc. contract agreement with Elise B. Forrest, Whitlock Papers.

113. *American Magazine*, no. 4E, vol.87, 1919. Brunel Training School of Photography ad., New York Institute of Photography web site, nyip.edu/about/history.

114. Edwin A. Harleston, Charleston, SC, to Elise B. Forrest, New York, NY, undated letter, transcript in the hand of Edwin Harleston, Whitlock Papers.

115. Forrest to Harleston, September 15, 1919.
116. Harleston to Forrest, January 1920.
117. Harleston to Forrest, December 1919 and 20.
118. Elise B. Forrest, New York, NY, to Edwin Harleston, Charleston, SC, March 2, 1920, transcript in the hand of Elise Forrest, Whitlock Papers; Valencia Hollins Coar, *A Century of Black Photographers: 1840–1960* (Rhode Island School of Design, 1983), 184.
119. Edwin A. Harleston, Charleston, SC, to Elise B. Forrest, New York, NY, undated letter, transcript in the hand of Edwin Harleston, Edwin A. Harleston and Edwina Harleston Whitlock Family Papers, Stuart A. Rose Manuscript, Archives, and Rare Book Library, Emory University.
120. Mrs. Forrest, Charleston, SC, from Edwin A. Harleston, Charleston, SC, July 1920, transcript in the hand of Edwin Harleston, Whitlock Papers.
121. Forrest to Harleston, undated letter.
122. Harleston to Forrest, September 5, 1920.
123. "Two Hearts That Beat as One."
124. Forrest to Harleston, undated letter.
125. Notes from the personal diary of Elise Forrest Harleston, September 20, 1920, Whitlock Papers.

Chapter 6: The Emergence of the New Negro

1. Forrest to Harleston, undated letter. In this correspondence, Elise gives the times and dates for their wedding, honeymoon, and reception.
2. Marie Forrest Harleston, Charleston, SC, to Elise B. Forrest, New York, NY, undated letter, transcript in the hand of Marie Harleston, Edwin A. Harleston and Edwina Harleston Whitlock Family Papers, Stuart A. Rose Manuscript, Archives, and Rare Book Library, Emory University.
3. Marion M. Torchia, "The Tuberculosis Movement and the Race Question, 1890–1950," *Bulletin of the History of Medicine* 49, no. 2 (1975): 162, http://www .jstor.org/stable/44450215.
4. "Summerville," Town of Summerville, SC, November 18, 2005, http://www.summer ville.sc.us/.
5. Marie F. Harleston, Summerville, SC, to Elise B. Forrest, New York, N.Y. undated letter, transcript in the hand of Marie Harleston, Edwin A. Harleston and Edwina Harleston Whitlock Family Papers, Stuart A. Rose Manuscript, Archives, and Rare Book Library, Emory University. Marie's letter is written on stationary from the Harleston Funeral Home in Summerville, SC.
6. Whitlock interview by McDaniel, July 23, 1993, Atlanta, GA.
7. There are several photographs in the SMFA archives of exhibitions featuring student work; however, there are no catalogues or programs listing students' names. The same is true for the various meetings and conventions during which Harleston exhibited his work upon his return to Charleston.
8. Truman K. Gibson, Chicago, IL, to Edwin A. Harleston, Charleston, SC, May 8, 1921, typewritten letter, Whitlock Papers.
9. Edwin A. Harleston, Atlanta, GA, to Elise F. Harleston, Charleston, SC, August 11, 1921, transcript in the hand of Edwin Harleston, Whitlock Papers.

10. Edwin Harleston to Elise Harleston, August 22, 1921.
11. *"Oh! Freedom: Cornelius M Battey," Oh! Freedom: Teaching African American Civil Rights through American Art*, Smithsonian Museum of American Art, https://american.si.edu/education/oh-freedom/cornelius-m-battey. Pictorialism was influenced by impressionism. Photographers often put Vaseline on the camera lens to create the desired soft focus and manipulated the negative to give the image a painterly quality. The result was a portrait that gave the subject a more "artistic sophistication."
12. Deborah Willis and Howard Dodson, *Black Photographers Bear Witness: 100 Years of Social Protest* (Williams College Museum of Art, 1989), 26.
13. Willis and Dodson, *Black Photographers Bear Witness*, 26; Coar, *Black Photographers*, 181; quoted in *Tuskegee Messenger*, Tuskegee Institute, AL, March 12–26, 1927; *Opportunity: Journal of Negro Life*, National Urban League, NY, vol. 5, May 1927, 126.
14. Edwin Harleston to Elise Harleston, August 22, 1921.
15. Edwin A. Harleston, Atlanta, GA, to whom it may concern, Atlanta, GA, August 23, 1921, typewritten letter, Whitlock Papers.
16. Edwin A. Harleston, Charleston, SC, to Elise F. Harleston, Tuskegee, AL, November 18, 1921, transcript in the hand of Edwin Harleston, Whitlock Papers.
17. Edwin Harleston to Elise Harleston, November 2, 1921.
18. Edwin Harleston to Elise F. Harleston, December 2, 1921.
19. *Painter of an Era*, 18. Whitlock interviewed by McDaniel, May 22, 1992, Charleston, SC.
20. Michael Francis Blake: 1912–1934, Repository Collections & Archives, Duke University, www.repository.duke.edu.
21. Whitlock interviewed by McDaniel.
22. Ernestine Rose, New York, NY, to Edwin A. Harleston, Charleston, SC, July 9, 1923, typewritten letter, Special Collections, South Carolina Historical Society, Charleston, SC (hereafter shall be referred to as SCHS).
23. Augustus Grandville Dill, New York, NY to Edwin A. Harleston, Charleston, SC, July 28, 1921, typewritten letter, Whitlock Papers; and *Catalogue of The Negro Arts Exhibit*, August 1 to September 30, 1921. The executive committee for the exhibition included W. E. B. Du Bois, James Weldon Johnson, and Atlanta University alumnus Albert A. Edwards.
24. Lawrence Rubin, "Washington and the Negro Renaissance," *Crisis*, April–May 1971, 80.
25. Nathan Irvin Huggins, *Harlem Renaissance* (Oxford University Press, 1971), 14.
26. Huggins, *Harlem Renaissance*, 13, 18, 22.
27. Wilfred Russell, New York, NY, to Edwin A. Harleston, Charleston, SC, September 18, 1923, typewritten letter, Special Collections, SCHS; and *Painter of an Era*, 48.
28. Whitlock interview by McDaniel, December 28, 1993, Atlanta, GA; *World War I Draft Registration Card:* State: Georgia; Registration County: Richmond; Ancestry.com.
29. Gary A. Reynolds and Beryl J. Wright, *Against the Odds: African-American Artists and the Harmon Foundation* (Newark Museum, 1989), 73.

30. Host De La Croix, Richard G. Tansey, and Diane Kirkpatrick, *Gardner's Art Through the Ages*, 9th ed. (Harcourt Brace Jovanovich, 1991), 607. Agnolo di Casimo Branzino was a sixteenth-century Florentine who painted in the Mannerist style.

31. Frances Weitzenhoffer, *The Havemeyers: Impressionism Comes to America* (Harry N. Abrams, 1986), 223. Harry Havemeyer, one of the nation's sugar barons, and his wife, Louisine, were collectors of Impressionist paintings as well as works by the old masters. Although the couple purchased the Bronzino portrait in the early 1900s, it did not go on public display until April 6, 1915.

32. *Catalogue of The Negro Arts Exhibit.*

33. Russell to Harleston, September 18, 1923.

34. Russell to Harleston, September 6, 1923.

35. Russell to Harleston.

36. Russell to Harleston, September 18, 1923.

37. Solicitation letter draft, October 1923, photocopy of transcript in the hand of Edwin A. Harleston, Edwin A. Harleston and Edwina Harleston Whitlock Family Papers, Stuart A. Rose Manuscript, Archives, and Rare Book Library, Emory University.

38. Edwin A. Harleston, New York City, NY, to Elise F. Harleston, Charleston, SC, November 7, 1923, transcript in the hand of Edwin Harleston, Whitlock Papers.

39. David Levering Lewis, *When Harlem Was in Vogue* (Random House, 1979) 50.

40. Charles S. Johnson, New York City, NY, to Edwin Harleston, Charleston, SC, October 26, 1923, typewritten letter, Whitlock Papers.

41. Edwin A. Harleston, New York City, NY, to Elise F. Harleston, Charleston, SC, November 7, 1923. In this letter, Harleston mentions that he went to see the "Negro musical revue *Runnin' Wild*" written by African American playwrights F. E. Miller and Aubrey Lyles. A new song and dance were introduced called "The Charleston . . . closing the first act in a whirlwind amid great applause."

42. Milton W. Brown et al., *American Art: Painting, Sculpture, Architecture, Decorative Arts, Photographs* (Harry N. Abrams, 1979), 443.

43. Houston A. Baker Jr., *Modernism and the Harlem Renaissance* (University of Chicago Press, 1967), 11.

44. Baker, *Modernism*, 11.

45. Mary Church Terrell, "History of the High School for Negroes in Washington," *Journal of Negro History* 2, no. 3 (1917), 252.

46. Edwin A. Harleston, Canton, MA, to Elise F. Harleston, Charleston, SC, December 12, 1923, transcript in the hand of Edwin Harleston, Whitlock Papers.

47. Exhibition announcement for the Edwin A. Harleston Exhibition at Dunbar High School, Washington, DC, November 20–28, 1923, 9 AM to 10 PM, SCHS.

48. Flyer, typewritten, published by Tanner Student Art League, November 1923, Paul Lawrence Dunbar High School.

49. Edwin Harleston, Canton, MA, to Elise Harleston, Charleston, SC, November 15, 1923.

50. Edwin Harleston, New York City, NY, to Elise Harleston, Charleston, SC, November 10, 1923.

51. Edwin A. Harleston, Boston, MA, to Elise F. Harleston, Charleston, SC, December 3, 1923, transcript in the hand of Edwin Harleston, Whitlock Papers. The

arrangements were made by Harleston's close friend Dr. William Augustus Hinton, a graduate of Harvard Medical School and member of the faculty.

52. Edwin Harleston, Canton, MA, to Elise Harleston, Charleston, SC, November 18, 1923.

53. Edwin Harleston to Elise Harleston, December 12, 1923.

54. Edwin Harleston to Elise Harleston, December 22, 1923.

55. Allison, "Harleston!," 21.

56. Dick Mickey, Chicago, IL, to Edwin A. Harleston, Charleston, SC, March 13, 1924, transcript in the hand of Dick Mickey, Whitlock Papers. Dick Mickey was a cousin of Harleston's who worked for Jesse Binga; and Carl R. Osthaus, "The Rise and Fall of Jesse Binga, Black Financier," *Journal of Negro History* 58, no. 1 (1973): 39.

57. Dick Mickey, Chicago, IL, to Edwin A. Harleston, Charleston, SC, May 14, 1924.

58. Edwin A. Harleston, Charleston, SC, to Mr. Jesse Binga, Chicago, IL, May 28, 1924, typewritten letter, Whitlock Papers.

59. "Harleston! Who is E. A. Harleston?," promotional brochure, Harleston Studio, 1924, unpaginated. Whitlock Papers.

60. Edwin A. Harleston, Chicago, IL, to Elise F. Harleston, Charleston, SC, July 1924, transcript in the hand of Edwin Harleston, SCHS. In this letter, Harleston mentions the possibility of going to Washington, DC.

61. Paige Smith, *Redeeming the Time: A People's History of the 1920s and the New Deal* (New York: McGraw-Hill Book Company, 1987), 71; and John Hope Franklin and Alfred A. Ross, Jr. *From Slavery to Freedom: A History of Negro Americans*, 6th ed. (Alfred A. Knopf, 1988), 311–12.

62. "Washington and the Negro Renaissance," *Crisis*, April–May 1971, 80.

63. Edwin Harleston, Washington, DC, to Elise Harleston, Charleston, SC, July 1924. This letter indicates that Harleston's research into the qualifications for teaching in the Washington, DC, public school system was already well under way.

64. Edwin Harleston, Washington, DC, to Elise Harleston, Charleston, SC, July 1924. In this section of the letter, Harleston mentions visiting the superintendent and being overwhelmed by "the politics at work in the system."

65. Edwin A. Harleston, Charleston, SC, to Martin W. Hawkins, Atlanta, GA, February 1, 1924, typewritten letter, Whitlock Papers. This letter was written in response to a request from a Morehouse student about art schools.

66. Turman K. Gibson, Chicago, IL, to Edwin A. Harleston, Charleston, SC, June 1924, transcript in the hand of T. K. Gibson, Edwin A. Harleston and Edwina Harleston Whitlock Family Papers, Stuart A. Rose Manuscript, Archives, and Rare Book Library, Emory University.

67. Turman Gibson to Edwin Harleston.

68. Edwin Harleston, Chicago, IL, to Elise Harleston, Charleston, SC, July 7, 1924.

69. Edwin Harleston to Elise Harleston.

70. Edwin Harleston to Elise Harleston, July 1924; and *School of the Art Institute of Chicago Student Records*, Summer 1925.

71. Edwin Harleston to Elise Harleston; and *School of the Art Institute of Chicago Student Records*, Summer 1925.

72. Ester Sparks, "A Biographical Dictionary of Painters and Sculptors in Illinois 1808–1945" (PhD diss., Northwestern University, 1971), 258.

73. Edwin Harleston, Chicago, IL, to Elise Harleston, Charleston, SC, July 7, 1924.

74. Edwin A. Harleston, Chicago, IL, to Elise F. Harleston, Charleston, SC, August 22, 1925.

75. Sparks, "Biographical," 389.

76. Edwin A. Harleston, Chicago, IL, to Elise F. Harleston, Charleston, SC, July 20, 1924.

77. Don Hayner, *Binga: The Rise and Fall of Chicago's First Black Banker* (Northwestern University Press, 2019), 157.

78. Elise F. Harleston, Charleston, SC, to Edwin A. Harleston, Chicago, IL, undated, transcript in the hand of Elise Harleston, Edwin A. Harleston and Edwina Harleston Whitlock Family Papers, Stuart A. Rose Manuscript, Archives, and Rare Book Library, Emory University.

79. Edwin A. Harleston, Chicago, IL, to Elise F. Harleston, Charleston, SC, August 10, 1924.

80. Elise F. Harleston, Charleston, SC, to Edwin A. Harleston, Chicago, IL, July 1924.

81. Ball and Whitlock, *Sweet Hell*, 234.

82. Hayner, *Binga*, 8. Many white people saw Binga's success as an unwanted symbol of the change, especially in northern cities. Living under constant threat, he traveled around Chicago with a bodyguard and had guards stationed around his home. Despite these measures, vandals were still able to bomb his residence, located in a predominantly white neighborhood, more than six times and yet, he refused to relocate.

83. "The Negro in Art Week, Exhibition of Primitive African Sculpture/Modern Paintings, Sculpture, Applied Art, and Books." Art Institute of Chicago (November 16–23, 1927), https://www.artic.edu/exhibitions/3240/children-s-museum-school-show-1927.

84. "The Negro in Art Week," Art Institute of Chicago (November 16–23, 1927).

85. Edwin A. Harleston, Chicago, IL, to Elise F. Harleston, Charleston, SC, July 20, 1924.

86. E.I. Du Pont De Nemours, *Du Pont: The Autobiography of an American Enterprise,* (Charles Scribner's Sons, 1952), 84.

87. "Colored Artist Painting a Picture of Man who Gave Millions for Education," *Philadelphia Tribune*, November 15, 1924, 1.

88. "Colored Artist Painting," *Philadelphia Tribune*, November 15, 1924, 1.

89. George Towns, Atlanta, GA, to Edwin A. Harleston, Charleston, SC, September 12, 1924, transcript in the hand of George Towns, SCHS.

90. Edmund T. Ware, Montclair, NJ, to Edwin A. Harleston, Charleston, SC, September 12, 1924, transcript in the hand of Edmund Ware, SCHS.

91. Pierre S. DuPont, Wilmington, DE, to Edwin A. Harleston, Philadelphia, PA, November 12, 1924, typewritten letter, Whitlock Papers.

92. Edwin A. Harleston, Philadelphia, PA, to Elise F. Harleston, Charleston, SC. November 1924, transcript in the hand of Edwin Harleston, SCHS.

93. H. V. Holloway, state superintendent of Public Instruction, Dover, DE, to The Colored Teachers of the State of Delaware, November 29, 1924, typewritten memo, Whitlock Papers.

94. Pierre S. DuPont to Edwin Harleston, November 1924.

95. Executive Committee DuPont Testimonial Association, Dover, DE, to Edwin A. Harleston, Charleston, SC, February 23, 1925, typewritten letter, Whitlock Papers.

96. "Colored Artist Painting a Picture of a Man Who Gave Millions for Education," *Philadelphia Tribune*, November 15, 1924.

97. Because it was the party of Lincoln, most African Americans claimed membership in the Republican Party until the election of Franklin D. Roosevelt in 1933. The Coolidge Republican Club of Boston was an African American political club whose members included Atlanta University graduates and several of Harleston's personal acquaintances.

98. The veteran's hospital was considered a possible location for the portrait because Coolidge had become friends with Robert Russa Morton, the successor to Booker T. Washington as principal of Tuskegee Institute. Coolidge officially supported Morton's efforts to hire African Americans for positions at the veteran's hospital in spite of local opposition by white citizens. Maceo Crenshaw Dailey, Jr. "Calvin Coolidge's Afro-American Connection," *Contributions in Black Studies* 8, article 7 (1986): 80.

99. William M. Butler, Chicago, IL, to Dr. Benjamin E. Robinson, Boston, MA, September 24, 1924, typewritten letter, Whitlock Papers.

100. Donald R. McCoy, *Calvin Coolidge: The Quiet President* (New York: Macmillan, 1967), 254.

101. Edwin A. Harleston, Montclair, NJ, to Elise Harleston, Charleston, SC, November 24, 1924.

102. Edwin A. Harleston, Montclair, NJ, to Elise Harleston, Charleston, SC, November 24, 1924.

103. Edwin A. Harleston to Elise Harleston, November 24,1924.

104. Edmund Twichell Ware, Montclair, NJ, to Edwin A. Harleston, Charleston, SC, January 1, 1925, transcript in the hand of Ware, South Carolina Historical Society (SCHS).

105. George B. Towns, Atlanta, GA, to Edwin Harleston, Charleston, SC, May 27, 1925.

106. Letter, Executive Committee Du Pont Testimonial Association, February 1925; Elise Harleston, Charleston, SC, to Edwin A. Harleston, Philadelphia, PA, November 25, 1925, transcript in the hand of Elise Harleston, Whitlock Papers; James Weldon Johnson, New York, NY, to Edwin A. Harleston, Charleston, SC, December 15, 1924, typewritten letter, SCHS.

107. "Unveil Memorial to Late Music Master," *Chicago Defender*, December 10, 1925, newspaper clipping, Whitlock Papers.

108. Edwin A. Harleston, Chicago, IL, to Elise F. Harleston, Charleston, SC, August 7, 1925.

109. Elisa Honig Fine, *The Afro-American Artist: A Search for Identity* (Holt, Rinehart and Winston, 1973), 78.

110. Edwin A. Harleston, Chicago, IL, to Elise F. Harleston, Charleston, SC, August 17, 1925.

111. Tony Kail, "Hoodoo and Hairdo: The Remarkable Story of Madame Hightower," Medium.com, https:/memphishoodoo.medium.com/hoodoo-and-hairdo-the-remarkable-story-of-madame-hightower-abe9400340d8.

112. Edwin A. Harleston, Chicago, IL, to Elise F. Harleston, Charleston, SC, August 1, 1925.
113. Edwin A. Harleston to Elise F. Harleston.
114. Madame Mamie Hightower, Memphis, TN, to Edwin A. Harleston, Charleston, SC, August 14, 1925, typewritten letter, Whitlock Papers; Martha H. Patterson, ed. *The American New Woman Revisited: A Reader* (Rutgers University Press, 2008), 271.
115. Edwin A. Harleston, Chicago, IL, to Elise F. Harleston, Charleston, SC, August 17, 1925.
116. Reynolds and Wright, *Against the Odds*, 14.
117. "The Amy Spingarn Prize in Literature and Art," Robert S. Cox Special Collections & University Archives Research Center, http://scua.library.umass.edu/tag/s/.
118. Jervis Anderson, *This Was Harlem: 1900–1950* (Noonday Press, 1982), 201; and Huggins, *Harlem Renaissance*, 59.
119. Martina Mallocci, "'All Art Is Propaganda': W. E. B. Du Bois's *The Crisis* and the Construction of a Black Public Image," *Journal of American History and Politics*, 1 (2018), 19, http://usabroad.unibo.it/article/view/177/7504.
120. Mae Gentry, "Re: 1925 Spingarn Prize," email received by M. Akua McDaniel, April 29, 2022. Mae Gentry, Edwin Harleston's great-niece, has concluded that Elise was the model for *Portrait of a Woman.*
121. Paul E. Teed and Barbara A. Gannon. *Army History*, no. 91 (2014): 46–47. http://www.jstor.org/stable/26300206. Established in 1866, the Grand Army of the Republic was primarily an organization of white Union veterans of the Civil War. However, there was a large contingent of African American soldiers who formed their own posts in an effort to preserve their experiences and memories of the war.
122. Whitlock interview by McDaniel, July 23, 1993, Atlanta, GA.
123. Elise F. Harleston, Charleston, SC, to Edwin A. Harleston, Chicago, IL, August 19, 1925.
124. Mallocci, "All Art," 1, 3.
125. Mallocci, "All Art," 15, 19.
126. W. E. B. Du Bois, "Criteria of Negro Art," *Crisis*, October 1926, 296.
127. "Spingarn Art Prize Is Awarded to E. A. Harleston," unidentified newspaper clipping, Whitlock Papers; and Elise F. Harleston, Charleston, SC, to Edwin A. Harleston, Chicago, IL, October 28, 1925.
128. Edwin A. Harleston, Chicago, IL, to Elise F. Harleston, Charleston, SC, August 12, 1925.
129. Elise F. Harleston, Charleston, SC, to Edwin A. Harleston, Chicago, IL, August 28, 1925.
130. Edwin A. Harleston, Chicago, IL, to Elise F. Harleston, Charleston, SC, August 30, 1925.

Chapter 7: Hopes Crushed to Earth

1. Edwin A. Harleston, New York, NY to Elise F. Harleston, Charleston, SC, November 4, 1925.
2. Edwin A. Harleston, New York, NY, to Elise F. Harleston, Charleston, SC, November 4, 1925. Transcript in the Hand of Edwin Harleston, Whitlock Papers.

3. Alain Locke, "The Legacy of the Ancestral Arts," *The New Negro*. New York: Albert and Charles Boni, 1925; reprint, Atheneum, 1968, 266.

4. Reynolds and Wright, *Against the Odds*, 75.

5. Fine, *Afro-American Artist*, 75.

6. Ada Hinton, Canton, MA, to Elise F. Harleston, Charleston, SC, December 27, 1923, transcript in the hand of Ada Hinton, Whitlock Papers; and Meta V. W. Fuller, Framingham, MA, to Edwin A. Harleston, Charleston, SC, November 12, 1925, transcript in the hand of Meta Fuller, SCHS.

7. J. B. Randolph, Orangeburg, SC, to Edwin Harleston, Charleston, SC, December 15, 1925, typewritten letter, SCHS.

8. Thomas P Stoney, Charleston, SC, to Laura M. Bragg, Charleston, SC, March 31, 1926, typewritten letter, Whitlock Papers.

9. Reynolds and Wright, *Against the Odds*, 28.

10. Stoney to Bragg, March 31, 1926.

11. Louise Anderson Allen, *A Bluestocking in Charleston: The Life and Career of Laura Bragg* (University of South Carolina Press, 2001), 9–11.

12. Fraser, *Charleston!*, 372.

13. Laura M. Bragg, Charleston, SC, to Thomas P. Stoney, Charleston, SC, April 2, 1926, typewritten letter, Whitlock Papers.

14. Fraser, *Charleston!*, 370.

15. Bragg to Stoney, April 2, 1926. This quote appeared on the letterhead of The Charleston Museum's stationary.

16. Allen, *Bluestocking*, 13, 27.

17. Edwin A. Harleston, Charleston, SC, to Laura Bragg, Charleston, SC, April 28, 1926, handwritten letter, transcript in the hand of Edwin Harleston, Whitlock Papers.

18. Stephanie E. Yuhl, *A Golden Haze of Memory: The Making of Historic Charleston* (University of North Carolina Press, 2005), 57.

19. Elise Harleston, Charleston, SC, to Edwin A. Harleston, St. Augustine, FL, September 14, 1929, handwritten letter, transcript in the hand of Elise Harleston, Whitlock Papers.

20. Laura M. Bragg, Charleston, SC, to Edwin A. Harleston, St. Augustine, FL, September 14, 1929, Typewritten letter, Whitlock Papers.

21. Edwin A. Harleston, Charleston, SC, to Laura M. Bragg, Charleston, SC, April 22, 1926.

22. Laura M. Bragg, Charleston, SC, to Edwin A. Harleston, Charleston, SC, April 29, 1926, typewritten letter, Whitlock Papers.

23. Edwin A. Harleston, Charleston, SC, to Laura M. Bragg, Charleston, SC, May 7, 1926.

24. Greene and Hutchisson, *Renaissance*, 36.

25. Greene and Hutchisson.

26. Yuhl, *Golden Haze*, 37.

27. Clelia P. McGowan, Columbia, SC, to Edwin A. Harleston, Charleston, SC, April 30, 1926, typewritten letter, Edwin A. Harleston and Edwina Harleston Whitlock Family Papers, Stuart A. Rose Manuscript, Archives, and Rare Book Library, Emory University.

28. Clelia P. McGowan, Columbia, SC, to Edwin A. Harleston, Charleston, SC, May 24, 1926, Typewritten letter, SCHS.

29. Harmon is given credit for inventing the concept of subdivisions real estate. He also developed large real estate projects in Boston and New York that included much of Brooklyn and Staten Island. Reynolds and Wright, *Against the Odds: African American Artists and the Harmon Foundation*, 27.

30. Reynolds and Wright, *Against the Odds*, 28–29.

31. David Driskell, *Harlem Renaissance Art of Black America* (Harry N. Abrams, 1987), 39.

32. Mary Beattie Brady, New York, NY, to Edwin A. Harleston, Charleston, SC, June 15, 1926, typewritten letter, Edwin A. Harleston and Edwina Harleston Whitlock Family Papers, Stuart A. Rose Manuscript, Archives, and Rare Book Library, Emory University.

33. Edwin A. Harleston, Charleston, SC, to Elise F. Harleston, Washington, DC, June 9, 1926, transcript in the hand of Edwin Harleston, Edwin A. Harleston and Edwina Harleston Whitlock Family Papers, Stuart A. Rose Manuscript, Archives, and Rare Book Library, Emory University. During this visit Harleston mentioned his cousin, Edmond Jenkins, a composer who had studied at the Royal Academy of Music in London, as a possible candidate in the music category.

34. Mary Beattie Brady, New York, to William E. Harmon, New York, June 17, 1926, typewritten memorandum, SCHS.

35. Reynolds and Wright, *Against the Odds*, 31, quoted in "Five Year Report," Harmon Foundation Papers, Library of Congress, Manuscript Division, Washington, DC. According to the *Macmillan Encyclopedia of Architects* (Free Press, 1982), 3, 241, William Boring (1859–1937) was one of the designers of the United States Immigration Station on Ellis Island, NY. Grosvenor Atterbuty (1869–1956), a contemporary of Frank Lloyd Wright trained in the beaux arts, is responsible for designing the Forest Hills Gardens in Queens, NY. Critics consider this community to be the "archetypal" American middle-class neighborhood of the early twentieth century.

36. Allan M. Gordon, *Palmer C. Hayden* (Museum of African American Art, 1988), 12–13.

37. Winifred Stoelting, "The Atlanta Years: A Biographical Sketch," *Hale Woodruff: 50 Years of His Art* (The Studio Museum in Harlem, 1979),10.

38. Reynolds and Wright, *Against the Odds: African American Artists and the Harmon Foundation*, 31.

39. Winifred Stoelting, "The Atlanta Years," 10. Winifred Stoelting has identified four of the five paintings that Woodruff sent to the Harmon competition as landscapes.

40. Reynolds and Wright, *Against the Odds*, 31; and Allan M. Gordon, *Palmer C. Hayden*, 12–13.

41. Reynolds and Wright, *Against the Odds*, 32, quoted in letter from Mary B. Brady to George E Hayes, November 5, 1926, Harmon Foundation Papers, Library of Congress, Manuscript Division, Washington, DC.

42. Reynolds and Wright, *Against the Odds*, 32, quoted in a letter from Laura Wheeler Waring to George E. Hayes, November 23, 1926, Harmon Foundation Papers, Library of Congress, Manuscript Division, Washington, DC.

43. Reynolds and Wright, *Against the Odds*, 32, quoted in a letter from Grosvenor Atterbury to George E. Haynes, November 23, 1926, Harmon Foundation Papers, Library of Congress, Manuscript Division, Washington, DC.

44. Reynolds and Wright, *Against the Odds*, 32. The works of Hayden and Woodruff went on display at the foundation headquarters at 140 Nassau Street in New York City for four days during the month of December.

45. William E. Harmon, New York, to Edwin A. Harleston, Charleston, SC, December 9, 1926, typewritten letter, SCHS.

46. "Who's Who in Artists of Exhibit," SIA 2016-011415, Record Unit 311, Box 35, Folder 3, Smithsonian Institute Archives.

47. Anderson, *Education of Blacks*, 197.

48. According to the *Constitution and By-Laws of the Unity and Friendship Society* (Furlong Printing House, 1909), 1, the Unity and Friendship Society was an organization designed to give support during illness and provide burial plots to family members after death.

49. Edwin A. Harleston, St. Augustine, FL, to Elise F. Harleston, Charleston, SC, February 8, 1927, transcript in the hand of Edwin Harleston, SCHS.

50. Eleanor Jewett, "Exhibition Review." *Chicago Daily Tribune*, November 15, 1927. Asa H. Gordon, Industrial College, GA, to Edwin A. Harleston, Charleston, SC, September 10, 1927, typewritten letter, SCHS.

51. Augusta Savage, New York, NY, to Edwin A. Harleston, Charleston, SC, July 6, 1927, quoted in *Painter of an Era*, 42.

52. H. C. Gauss, Washington, DC, to Edwin A. Harleston, Charleston, SC, February 18, 1928, typewritten letter, SCHS.

53. W. E. B. Du Bois, New York, NY, to Edwin A. Harleston, Charleston, SC, February 18, 1928, transcript in the hand of Du Bois, SCHS.

54. J. B. Randolph, Orangeburg, SC, to Edwin A. Harleston, Charleston, SC, February 14, 1929.

55. Edwin A Harleston to J. B. Randolph, Orangeburg, SC, undated, draft of letter in the hand of Edwin A Harleston, Whitlock Papers.

56. *Exhibit of Fine Arts: Work of Negro Artists*, exhibition prospectus (Harmon Foundation and Commission on the Church and Race Relations Federal Council of Churches, 1927), unpaginated.

57. George Towns, Atlanta, GA, to Edwin A. Harleston, Charleston, SC, December 17, 1927.

58. Edwin A. Harleston, St. Augustine, FL, to Elise F. Harleston, Charleston, SC, August 30, 1929.

59. Richard J. Powell, *Homecoming: The Art and Life of William H. Johnson* (Rizzoli International Publications, 1991), 41.

60. Edwin A. Harleston, St. Augustine, FL, to Elise F. Harleston, Charleston, SC, August 30, 1929.

61. Paula Giddings, *When and Where I Enter: The Impact of Black Women on Race and Sex in America* (William Morrow, 1984), 200.

62. Edwin A. Harleston, St. Augustine, FL, to Elise F. Harleston, Charleston, SC, September 8, 1929.

63. Whitlock interview by McDaniel, August 12, 1993, Atlanta, GA.

64. *Painter of an Era*, 25.

65. Sue Bailey, New York, NY, to Edwin A. Harleston, Charleston, SC, December 23, 1929, transcript in the hand of Sue Bailey, Whitlock Papers.

66. Undated note from Edwina Harleston Whitlock, typewritten, Box 10, File 15, Edwin A. Harleston and Edwina Harleston Whitlock Family Papers, Stuart A. Rose Manuscript, Archives, and Rare Book Library, Emory University.

67. Alain Locke, Washington, DC, to Edwin A. Harleston, Charleston, SC, December 7, 1929, transcript in the hand of Alain Locke, Whitlock Papers.

68. Edwin A Harleston, "Building A Picture" form letter, January 21, 1930, typewritten, Whitlock Papers.

69. Benjamin Brawley, Raleigh, NC, to Edwin A. Harleston, Charleston SC, January 24, 1930, transcript in the hand of Benjamin Brawley, SCHS. A. B. Cooper, Jacksonville, FL, to Edwin A. Harleston, Charleston SC, January 27, 1930, transcript in the hand of A. B. Cooper, SCHS. W. J. Trent, Talladega, AL, to Edwin A. Harleston, Charleston SC, January 28, 1930, transcript in the hand of W. J. Trent, SCHS. And James P. O'Brien, New Orleans, LA, to Edwin A. Harleston, Charleston SC, February 10, 1930, transcript in the hand James P. O'Brien, SCHS.

70. Truman K. Gibson, Chicago, IL, To Edwin A. Harleston, Charleston, SC, March 10, 1930.

71. Edwin A. Harleston, Charleston, SC, to Walter White, New York, NY, May 12, 1930, typewritten letter, Whitlock Papers.

72. Walter White, New York, NY, to Edwin A. Harleston, Charleston, SC, May 19, 1930, typewritten letter, Whitlock Papers.

73. Edwin A. Harleston, King's Mountain, NC, to Elise F. Harleston, Charleston, SC, transcript in the hand of Edwin Harleston June 8, 1930, Whitlock Papers.

74. Frances Johnson Tyler, Dudley, NC, to Edwina H. Whitlock, Charleston, SC, February 23, 1982, transcript in the hand of Frances Tyler, Whitlock Papers.

75. *Harlem Renaissance Art*, 110.

76. Porter, *Modern Negro Art*, 114.

77. Aaron Douglas interview by Dr. L. M. Collins, July 16, 1971, transcript, p. 27, Fisk University Oral History Collection, Fisk University Library, Nashville, TN. Douglas had obtained the Fisk University commission through Charles S. Johnson, editor of *Opportunity* magazine, who was aware that Dr. Thomas Elias Jones, president of Fisk, was looking for an artist to design and execute the library mural project.

78. Douglas interview by Collins.

79. Aaron Douglas, Nashville, TN, to Edwin A. Harleston, Charleston, SC, July 12, 1930, transcript in the hand of Aaron Douglas, SCHS. Eventually, Douglas would be hired as head of the Art Department at Fisk University where he taught classes until his retirement in 1966.

80. Edwin A. Harleston, Nashville, TN, to Elise F. Harleston, Charleston, SC, August 3, 1930, transcript in the hand of Edwin Harleston, Whitlock Papers.

81. Edwin A. Harleston, Nashville, TN, to Elise F. Harleston, Charleston, SC, August 11, 1930.

82. Harleston to Harleston.

83. Douglas interview by Collins, 29.

84. Edwin A. Harleston, Nashville, TN, to Elise F. Harleston, Charleston, SC, August 11, 1930.

85. Harleston to Harleston; "Biographical Information on Those for whom Fisk University Buildings were Named," 1977, Special Collections, Fisk University, Nashville, TN.; Aaron Douglas interview by Dr. L. M. Collins, 30; Fletcher F. Moon, "So "Fisk" dictated Ladies and Gentlemen: Highlights From 150 Years of Fisk University's Musical Tradition, Impact, and Influence" (2016). Library Faculty and Staff Publications and Presentations. 12-15. https://digitalscholarship.tnstate.edu/lib/15.

86. Dedication of Fisk University Library Program, Fisk Memorial Chapel, November 20, 1930, Special Collections, Fisk University, Nashville, TN.

87. Edwin A. Harleston, "The New Fisk Library," draft of an unpublished article, 1930, transcript in the hand of Edwin Harleston, Whitlock Papers.

88. Aaron Douglas, "*Mural Decoration-Build Thee More Stately Mansions*," n.d. a description of the murals, Special Collections, Fisk University, Nashville, TN.

89. Edwin A. Harleston, Nashville, TN, to Elise Harleston, Charleston, SC, August 3, 1930.

90. Edwin A. Harleston to Elise Harleston, August 11, 1930.

91. Edwin A. Harleston to Elise Harleston, August 11, 1930.

92. Edwin A. Harleston, Nashville, TN, to Elise Harleston, Charleston, SC, August 25, 1930; and Edwin A. Harleston to Elise Harleston, September 2, 1930.

93. Edwin A. Harleston to Elise Harleston, September 7, 1930.

94. Edwin A. Harleston to Elise Harleston, August 25, 1930.

95. Edwin A. Harleston to Elise Harleston, October 4, 1930.

96. *Painter of an Era*, 26.

97. Edwin A. Harleston, Nashville, TN, to Elise Harleston, Charleston, SC, August 25, 1930.

98. Elise F. Harleston, Charleston, SC, to Edwin A. Harleston, Nashville, TN, August 19, 1930, transcript in the hand of Elise Harleston, Whitlock Papers.

99. Elise F. Harleston to Edwin A. Harleston, September 12, 1930.

100. James V. Herring, Washington, DC, to Edwin A. Harleston, Nashville, TN, September 12, 1930, typewritten letter, Whitlock Papers.

101. J. T. Carter, Talladega, AL, to Edwin A. Harleston, Nashville, TN, September 29, 1930, typewritten letter, Whitlock Papers.

102. Edwin A. Harleston, Nashville, TN, to Elise Harleston, Charleston, SC, August 11, 1930.

103. Hannah Motiarta, New York, NY, to Edwin A. Harleston, Charleston, SC, June 13, 1930, typewritten letter, SCHS. When the awards and exhibition program was originally designed, the committee decided that at the end of the fifth year the project would be evaluated to see if it should continue.

104. The task of identifying African American artists had been the primary responsibility of D. George E. Haynes, director of the Federal Council of Churches. However, the Harmon Foundation and those working in this behalf felt that Haynes had received undeserved credit for the success of the awards and exhibition program. This conclusion led to the termination of the Harmon Foundation's contract with the council at the end of the 1930–31 exhibition season. Reynolds and Wright, *Against the Odds*, 35.

105. Edwin A. Harleston, Nashville, TN, to Elise Harleston, Charleston, SC, October 4, 1930.
106. Harleston to Harleston.
107. Elise F. Harleston, Charleston, SC, to Edwin A. Harleston, Nashville, TN, October 6, 1930.
108. Aaron Douglas, New York, NY, to Edwin A. Harleston, Charleston, SC, undated, transcript in the hand of Aaron Douglas, Whitlock Papers. In this letter Douglas thanks Harleston for sending the photo and states he found it interesting comparing it to the painting.
109. Elise F. Harleston, Charleston, SC, to Edwin A. Harleston, Nashville, TN, September 26, 1930. Transcript in the hand of Elise Harleston, Whitlock Papers. Evidently, Harleston sent his wife a photograph of himself with Douglas for in her letter she states "that Mr. D is larger than you. Hasn't he a palette and smock . . . or did you just want him to use your things? Elise recognized the smock because she made it for him. Daniel J. Fuller, "Aaron Douglas Murals, 1930 Cravath Hall Fisk University, Nashville," https://danieljfuller.com/aaron-douglas-murals -1930-cravath-hall-fisk-university-nashville/. This section shows a kneeling figure holding a torch under a planet-filled sky. The microscope at his feet and the column behind him underscores the connection between ancient and modern scientific worlds.
110. Douglas to Harleston, undated letter.
111. Whitlock interview by McDaniel, September 9, 1993, Atlanta, GA.
112. Mary Ann Calo, "African American Art and Critical Discourse between World Wars," *American Quarterly* 51, no. 3 (1999): 583, http://www.jstor.org/stable /30042183.
113. Edwin A. Harleston, Charleston, SC, to Hannah Motiarta, New York, NY, March 11, 1931, transcript in the hand of Edwin Harleston, Whitlock Papers.
114. Greene and Hutchisson, *Renaissance*, 45.
115. Mathew Baigell, *A History of American Painting* (Praeger, 1971), 227.
116. Mae Gentry to M. Akua McDaniel, *Some News*, July 26, 2024, email. Mae received an email from Harlan Greene identifying the honey man as Ralph Bennett, a 1920s Charleston street vendor.
117. Whitlock, interview by McDaniel, August 12, 1993.
118. Hannah Motiarta, New York, NY, to Edwin A. Harleston, Charleston, SC, December 30, 1930.
119. Reynolds and Wright, *Against the Odds*, 35.
120. Mary Beattie Brady, New York, NY, to Edwin A. Harleston, Charleston, SC, February 14, 1931, typewritten letter, Whitlock Papers.
121. The other artists in the competition with Harleston for the Locke Prize included Robert Savon Pious, O. Richard Reid, Vivian Schyuler Key, J. H. D. Robinson, Lillian A. Dorsey, and Sargent Claude Johnson. James Lesesne Wells was the gold-medal prize winner in 1931. "*Exhibition of the Work of Negro Artists*" catalogue was produced by the Harmon Foundation and the Federal Council of Churches.
122. Edwin A. Harleston, Charleston, SC, to W. Burke Harmon, New York, NY, March 7, 1931, typewritten letter, SCHS.

123. Douglas to Harleston, undated letter.
124. Reynolds and Wright, *Against the Odds*, 115.
125. "Exhibit Raises Question Whether Negro Should Paint "White," *Art Digest*, February 15, 1931: 7; and Reynolds and Wright, *Against the Odds*, 114.
126. "Negro Art, Art Center," *The Art News*, February 15, 1931:12.
127. Edwin Harleston, Charleston, SC to W. Burke Harmon, New York, NY, March 7, 1931, typewritten letter, SCHS.
128. *Painter of an Era*, 27.
129. *Painter of an Era*, 27.
130. Elise F. Harleston, Charleston, SC, to Alain Locke, Washington, DC. May 10, 1931, telegram, Alain Locke no. 164, Box 33, Manuscript Division, Mooreland-Spingarn Research Center, Washington, DC.

Epilogue

1. "Mr. Edwin A. Harleston Passed Away," unidentified newspaper clipping, Whitlock Papers.
2. Ball and Whitlock, *Sweet Hell*, 288.
3. Alain Locke, Washington, DC, to Elise F. Harleston, Charleston, SC, May 12, 1931, transcript in the hand of Alain Locke, Whitlock Papers.
4. Ball and Whitlock, *Sweet Hell*, 288.
5. "E. A. Harleston Impressively Funeralized," unidentified newspaper clipping, Box 6, Stuart A. Rose Manuscript, Archives, and Rare Book Library, Emory University.
6. Edwina Harleston Whitlock, "Edwin A. Harleston: A Biographical Sketch," in *Painter of an Era*: 27.
7. Locke, "Legacy," 266; Alain Locke, "The American Negro as Artist," *American Magazine of Art* 23, no. 3, (1931): 215, http://www.jstor.org/stable/23936618.
8. Whitlock interview by McDaniel, September 20, 1991, Charleston, SC.
9. Ball and Whitlock, *Sweet Hell*, 292. Conversation with Mae Gentry, Charleston, SC, October 31, 2023.
10. *Exhibition of Works by Negro Artists* (1933), Smithsonian Institute, Washington, DC, Sponsored by the Association for the Study of Negro Life and History, on display October 31 to November 6, 1933. Numerous artworks by Edwin Harleston appeared in this exhibition, including the following: paintings: *Portrait Study* (loaned by Elise Harleston Wheeler), *Magnolia Gardens, The Pool, Entrance to Magnolia Gardens, Old Church*; drawings: *Old Lady with Bandana* (loaned by Elise Harleston Wheeler), *Old War Veteran, A Charlestonian, The Artist's Father, Head of Child*. Exhibition catalogue, Box 10, File 15, Stuart A. Rose Manuscript, Archives, and Rare Book Library, Emory University.
11. Porter, *Modern Negro Art*, 86.
12. Carby, *Race Men*, 46.
13. *Painter of an Era*, 42, quoted in correspondence from Augusta Savage to Edwin A. Harleston, July 6, 1927. In a letter to the artist, Savage stated that "in my estimation your work ranks next to Tanner." This well-known sculptor, who came to prominence during the Harlem Renaissance, sent Harleston information concerning exhibitions and other artist activities during the 1920s.

14. Dewey F. Mosby and Darrel Sewell, *Henry Ossawa Tanner* (Philadelphia Museum of Art, 1991), 116.
15. Richard A. Long, "Edwin A. Harleston and W. H. Johnson: A Study in Contrasts," unpublished essay, n.d. Richard Long Papers, Auburn Avenue Research Library, Atlanta, GA.
16. Huggins, *Harlem Renaissance*, 157.
17. Porter, *Modern Negro Art*, 108.
18. Mae Gentry, email message "Your Mom," to author, September 14, 2023.
19. Mae Gentry, email message.
20. Mae Gentry, email message. Bridget R. Cooks, *Exhibiting Blackness: African Americans and the American Art Museum* (University of Massachusetts Press, 2011), 87. David Driskell was a graduate of Howard University and a student of James A. Porter, and at the time of the exhibition, Driskell was the chair of the Art Department at Fisk University.
21. Cooks, *Exhibiting Blackness*, 87. Edwin Harleston Whitlock, "Edwin A. Harleston: A Biographical Sketch, *Painter of an Era*, 9–27.
22. Nancy S. Smith, "Harleston surprising exhibit," *News & Courier/The Evening Post*, December 11, 1983, sec. 14–E Sunday, newspaper clipping, Box 6, Stuart A. Rose Manuscript, Archives, and Rare Book Library, Emory University.
23. Reynolds and Wright, *Against the Odds*, 281.
24. Dr. Martin Luther King Jr. preached his final Sunday sermon, "Remaining Awake Through a Great Revolution," at the National Cathedral, Washington, DC, March 31, 1968.

SELECTED BIBLIOGRAPHY

Archives

Avery Research Center for African American History & Culture. Charleston, SC. Clark Atlanta University Special Collections, Atlanta, GA.

Edwin A. Harleston and Edwina Harleston Whitlock Family Papers. Stuart A. Rose Manuscript, Archives, and Rare Book Library, Emory University, Atlanta, GA.

Edwin Augustus Harleston. Papers. Edwina Harleston Whitlock Collection. South Carolina Historical Society, Charleston, SC. Note: A major portion of the Whitlock Papers were transferred to the Rose Manuscript Archives at Emory University.

School of the Museum of Fine Arts Special Collection. Tufts University, Medford, MA.

Interview

Edwina Augusta Harleston Whitlock. Interviews conducted by M. Akua McDaniel (author). Atlanta, GA, and Charleston, SC.

Publications

Adams, Myron Whitlock. *A History of Atlanta University*. Atlanta University Press, 1930.

Allen, Louise Anderson. *A Bluestocking in Charleston: The Life and Career of Laura Bragg*. University of South Carolina Press, 2001.

Allison, Madeline G. "Harleston: Who Is E. A. Harleston?" *Opportunity* (January 1924): 21–23.

Anderson, James D. *The Education of Blacks in the South 1860–1935*. University of North Carolina Press, 1988.

Archives of American Art. "Marie Danforth Page papers, 1826–2016." http://www .aaa.si.edu/collections/marie-danforth-page-papers-8891.

Bacote, Clarence Albert. *The Story of Atlanta University: A Century of Service, 1865–1965*. Atlanta University Press, 1969.

Baker, Houston A., Jr. *Modernism and the Harlem Renaissance*. University of Chicago Press, 1967.

Ball, Edward, and Edwina Harleston Whitlock. *The Sweet Hell Inside: A Family History*. HarperCollins, 2001.

Barbeau, Arthur E. and Florette Henri. *The Unknown Soldiers: Black American Troops in World War I*. Temple University Press, 1974.

Barlow, Thomas A. *Pestalozzi and American Education*. Este Es Press, 1977.

Bedford, Faith A., Susan C. Faxon and Bruce W. Chambers. *Frank W. Benson: A Retrospective*. Berry-Hill Galleries, 1989.

Berlin, Ira. *Slaves Without Masters: The Free Negro in the Antebellum South*. Pantheon Books, 1974.

Bilodeau, Francis W., ed. *Art in South Carolina 1670–1970*. South Carolina Tricentennial Commission, 1970.

Blum, John Morton. *Woodrow Wilson and the Politics of Morality*. Little, Brown, 1956.

Boiem, Albert. *The Academy and French Painting in the Nineteenth Century*. Yale University Press, 1971.

Boyle, Richard J. *American Impressionism*. New York Graphic Society, 1974.

Burnie, C. W. "Education of the Negro in Charleston, S.C. Prior to the Civil War." *Journal of Negro History* 12 (January 1927): 15–16.

Caffin, Charles H. "The Art of Frank W. Benson." *Harper's Monthly Magazine* 119 (June 1909): 109.

Caffin, Charles H. "Some American Portrait Painters." *The Critic* 44, no. 1 (1904): 32.

Calo, Mary Ann. "African American Art and Critical Discourse between World Wars." *American Quarterly* 51, no. 3 (1999).

Carby, Hazel V. *Race Men*. Harvard University Press, 1998.

Chandler, Alfred D., and Stephen Salsbury. *Pierre S. du Pont and the Making of the Modern Corporation*. Harper & Row, 1971.

Charleston, South Carolina: The Centennial Incorporation, 1883. News and Courier Book Presses, 1884.

Chase, Hal S. "Struggle for Equality: Fort Des Moines Training Camp for Colored Officers." *Phylon* 39, no. 4 (1960): 297–98.

Coar, Valencia Hollins. *A Century of Black Photographers: 1840–1960*. Rhode Island School of Design, 1983.

Coates, Ta-Nehisi. *We Were Eight Years in Power: An American Tragedy*. One World, 2017.

Coburn, Frederick. "Edmund C. Tarbell." *International Studio* 32, no. 127 (1907): 125–37.

Coburn, Frederick. "Edmund C. Tarbell, Painter." *World Today* 2 (1906): 1077–85.

Coburn, Frederick. "Philip L. Hale, Artist and Critic." *World Today* 14, no. 1 (1908): 59–67.

Coke, Van Deren. *The Painter and the Photographer*. University of New Mexico Press, 1954.

"Colored Teachers in Charleston Schools." *Crisis* 22, no. 2 (1921): 58. https://modjourn .org/issue/bdr513685/.

Corn, Wanda M. *The Color of Mood: American Tonalism 1880–1910*. M. H. De Young Memorial Museum and California Palace of the Legion of Honor, 1972.

Cozzolino, Robert, Anne Classen Knutson, and David Lubin, eds. *World War I and American Art*. Princeton University Press, 2016.

Crannell, Carlyn Gaye. "In Pursuit of Culture: A History of Art Activity in Atlanta, 1847–1926." PhD diss., Emory University, 1981.

Cross, Anson K. *Light and Shade*. Ginn, 1897.

Daniels, John. *In Freedom's Birthplace: A Study of Boston Negroes*. Houghton Mifflin, 1914.

Downs, William Howe. "Boston Painters and Painting." *Atlantic Monthly* 3 (July–December 1888): 6.

Drago, Edmund L. *Initiative, Paternalism and Race Relations: Charleston Avery Normal Institute*. University of Georgia Press, 1990.

Drake, St. Clair, and Horace Cayton. *Black Metropolis: A Study of Negro Life in a Northern City*. Harcourt, Brace, 1945.

du Bois, Guy Pène. "The Boston Group of Painters: An Essay on Nationalism in Art." *Arts & Decoration* 5 (October 1915): 457–60.

Du Bois, W. E. B. *The Black North in 1901: A Social Study*. Arno Press and *New York Times* Press, 1969.

Du Bois, W. E. B., and Herbert Aptheker. *Against Racism: Unpublished Essays, Papers, Addresses, 1887–1961.* University of Massachusetts Press, 1985.

Duffy, John Joseph. "Charleston Politics in the Progressive Era." PhD diss., University of South Carolina, 1963.

Fairbrother, Trevor J. *The Bostonians: Painters of an Elegant Age, 1870–1930*. Museum of Fine Arts, 1986.

Fink, Lola Harris, and Joshua C. Taylor. *Academy: The Academic Tradition in American Art*. Smithsonian Institution Press, 1975.

Frankenstein, Alfred V., and Ann C. Van Devanter. *American Self-Portraits*. International Exhibition Foundation, 1974.

Fraser, Walter J., Jr., *Charleston! Charleston! The History of a Southern City*. University of South Carolina Press, 1989.

Frazier, E. Franklin. *The Free Negro Family*. Fisk University Press, 1932.

Frederickson, Geroge M. *The Black Image in the White Mind: The Debate on Afro-American Character and Destiny 1817–1914*. Harper & Row, 1971.

Gammell, R. H. *The Boston Painters 1900–1930*. Parnassus Imprints, 1986.

Gentry, Mae Whitlock. "Elise Forrest Harleston." University of South Carolina Aiken, 2006.

Gerdts, William H. *American Impressionism*. Henry Art Gallery and University of Washington, 1980.

Gordon, Asa H. *Sketches of Negro Life and History in South Carolina*. 2nd. University of South Carolina Press, 1971.

Green, J. A. *The Educational Ideas of Pestalozzi*. W. B. Clive, 1914. Reprint, Greenwood Press, 1969.

Greene, Harlan, and James M. Hutchisson, eds. *Renaissance in Charleston: Art and Life in the Carolina Low Country, 1900–1940*. University of Georgia Press, 2003.

Habenstein, Robert W. and William M. Lamers. *The History of American Funeral Directing*. Bulfin, 1955.

Hale, Nancy. *The Life in the Studio*. Little, Brown, 1957.

Harlan, Louis R. "The Secret Life of Booker T. Washington." *Journal of Southern History*, no. 3, JSTOR, Aug. 1971, 393–416.

Hayner, Don. *Binga: The Rise and Fall of Chicago's First Black Banker*. Northwestern University Press, 2019.

Hayward, F. H. *The Educational Ideas of Pestalozzi and Frobel*. Ralph, Holland, 1904. Reprint, Greenwood Press, 1979.

Hemmingway, Theodore. "Prelude to Change: Black Carolinians in the War Years, 1914–1920." *Journal of Negro History* vol. 65, no. 3 (Summer 1980): 212–27.

Herlihy, Elizabeth, ed. *Fifty Years of Boston: A Memorial Volume Issued in Commemoration of the Tercentenary of 1930*. Subcommittee on the Memorial History of Boston Tercentenary Commission, 1932.

Holzer, Harold, Gabor S. Boritt, and Mark E. Neely. *The Lincoln Image: Abraham Lincoln and the Popular Print*. Scribner, 1984.

Hoppin, Martha J. *William Morris Hunt: A Memorial Exhibition*. Museum of Fine Arts, 1979.

Horton, James Oliver. *Black Bostonians: Family Life and Community Struggle in the Antebellum North*. Homes & Meier, 1979.

Huggins, Nathan Irvin. *Harlem Renaissance*. Oxford University Press, 1971.

Hunter, Tera W. *Bound in Wedlock: Slave and Free Black Marriage in the Nineteenth Century*. Harvard University Press, 2017.

Jackson, David H., Jr., "Booker T. Washington in South Carolina, March 1909." *South Carolina Historical Magazine* 113, no. 3 (July 2012): 192–220.

Jervey, Theodore D. "The Harlestons." *South Carolina Historical and Genealogical Magazine* 3 (July 1902): 150–73.

"John Adams, Negro Artist, Has Won Great Success," *The Constitution*, 23 (June 1902): 5.

Johnson, Michael P. and James L. Roark. *Black Masters: A Free Family of Color in the Old South*. W.W. Norton, 1984.

Kantrovitz, Nathan. "Racial and Ethnic Residential Segregation in Boston, 1830–1970." *Annals of the American Academy of Political and Social Sciences* 44 (January 1979): 41–54.

Kellogg, Charles Flint. *NAACP: A History of the National Association for the Advancement of Colored People*. Johns Hopkins University Press, 1967.

Keys, Ronald D. *The Genteel Tradition*. Rollins College, 1985.

Lack, Richard, ed. *Realism and Revolution: The Art of the Boston School, 1864–1960*. Taylor, 1985.

Lander, Ernest McPherson. *A History of South Carolina, 1865–1960*. University of North Carolina Press, 1960.

Lander, Ernest McPherson, and Robert K. Ackerman. *Perspective in South Carolina History: The First 100 Years*. University of South Carolina Press, 1973.

Lanes, Jerrold. "Boston Painting 1880–1930." *Artforum* 10 (January 1972).

Leader, Bernice Kramer. "The Boston Lady as a Work of Art: Painting by the Boston School at the Turn of the Century." PhD diss., Columbia University, 1980.

Lee, Ellen Wardwell. *William McGregor Paxton 1884–1941*. Indianapolis Museum of Art, 1979.

Lewis, David Levering. *When Harlem Was in Vogue*. Random House, 1979.

Locke, Alain. *The New Negro: An Interpretation*. Simon and Schuster, 1997.

Long, Richard A. "Edwin A. Harleston and William H. Johnson: A Study in Contrasts." Auburn Avenue Research Library, n.d.

Long, Richard A. "Introduction: Artists of the Harlem Renaissance." *In Selected Essays: Art and Artists from the Harlem Renaissance to the 1980s*. National Black Arts Festival, 1998.

Love, Josephine Harreld. *Edwin A. Harleston: Painter of an Era: 1882–1931*. Your Heritage House, 1983.

Lubin, David M. *Act of Portrayal: Eakins, Sargent, James*. Yale University Press, 1985.

Macanic, James. "History of the Charleston Chapter of the NAACP." *Charleston Inquirer*, May 22, 1964.

Mallocci, Martina. "'All Art is Propaganda': W. E. B. Du Bois's *The Crisis* and the Construction of a Black Public Image." *Journal of American History and Politics* 1, no. 1 (2018): 1–12.

May, Henry F. *The End of American Innocence: The First Years of Our Time 1912–1917*. Oxford University Press, 1959.

Mazyck, Authur, and Gene Waddell. *Charleston in 1883*. Southern Historical Press, 1983.

Meier, August. *Negro Thought in American, 1880–1915: Racial Ideologies in the Age of Booker T. Washington*. University of Michigan Press, 1963.

"Mickey Funeral Home Papers." Inventory of the Mickey Funeral Home Papers, Avery Research Center. Historic Charleston Foundation/Preservation Advocacy in Charleston, SC.

Moltke-Hansen, David. *Art in the Lives of South Carolinians*. Carolina Art Association, 1978.

Moore, Burchill Richardson. "A History of the Negro Public Schools of Charleston, South Carolina 1876–1942." Master's thesis, University of South Carolina, 1942.

Morrow, Kara Ann. "Bakongo Afterlife and Cosmological Direction: Transition of African Culture into North Florida Cemeteries." *Florida Online Journals*, 2002.

Mosby, Dewey F. *Henry Ossawa Tanner*. Philadelphia Museum of Art, 1991.

Mumford, Lewis. *The Brown Decades: A Study of the Arts in America 1865–1895*. Harcourt, Brace, 1931.

Museum of Fine Arts Boston. Newsweek Inc. and Arnoldo Mondadori Editore, 1969.

Myrdal, Gunnar. *An American Dilemma: The Negro Problem and Modern Democracy*. Harper & Brothers, 1944.

Neils, Christensen. "Fifty Years of Freedom: Conditions in the Sea Coast Region." *Annals of the American Academy of Political and Social Sciences* 49 (September 1913): 58–66.

Newby, I. A. *Black Carolinians: A History of Blacks in South Carolina from 1895 to 1968*. University of South Carolina Press, 1973.

Novak, Barbara. *American Painting of the Nineteenth Century: Realism, Idealism and American Experience*. Praeger, 1961.

Osthaus, Carl R. "The Rise and Fall of Jesse Binga: Black Financier." *Journal of Negro History* 58, no. 1 (1973): 39–60.

Patterson, Martha H., ed. *The American New Woman Revisited: A Reader*. Rutgers University Press, 2008.

Peirce, H. Winthrop. *The History of the School of the Museum of Fine Arts, Boston, 1877–1927*. Museum of Fine Arts, 1930.

Peters, Harry T. *Printmakers to the American People*. Doubleday, Doran, 1942.

Pevsner, Nikolaus. *Academies of Art Past and Present*. Cambridge University Press, 1940.

Pierce, Patricia Jobe. *Edmund C. Tarbell and the Boston School of Painting 1889–1980*. Pierce Galleries, 1980.

Pierce, Patricia Jobe. *The Ten*. Rumford, 1976.

Porter, James Amos. *Modern Negro Art*, 2nd ed., Arno and *New York Times* Press, 1969.

Powell, Richard J. *Homecoming: The Art and Life of William H. Johnson*. National Museum of American Art, Smithsonian Institution, 1991.

Quarles, Benjamin, ed. *Blacks on John Brown*. University of Illinois Press, 1972.

Quick, Michael. *American Portraiture in the Grand Manner, 1720–1920*. Los Angeles Museum of Art, 1981.

Rabinowitz, Howard N. *Race Relations in the Urban South, 1865–1900*. Oxford University Press, 1978.

Reynolds, Gary A., and Beryl J. Wright. *Against the Odds: African-American Artists and the Harmon Foundation*. Newark Museum, 1989.

Rose, Barbara. *American Art Since 1900: A Critical History*. Frederick A. Praeger, 1967.

Rosengarten, Dale, Martha Zierden, Kimberly Grimes, Ziyadah Owusu, Elizabeth Alson, and Will Williams. *Between the Tracks: Charleston's East Side During the Nineteenth Century*. Charleston Museum and Avery Research Center, 1987.

Ross, Joyce. *J. E. Spingarn and the Rise of the NAACP 1911–1939*. Athenaeum, 1972.

Shannon, Martha A. S. *Boston Days of William Morris Hunt*. Marshall Jones, 1923.

Silva, Fred, ed. *Focus on The Birth of a Nation*. Prentice Hall, 1971.

Smith, Minna C. "The Work of Frank W. Benson." *International Studio* 35 (October 1908): cii.

Smith, Page. *America Enters the World*. McGraw-Hill Book, 1985.

Smith, Suzanne E. *To Serve the Living: Funeral Directors and the African American Way of Death*. Harvard University Press, 2010.

Sparks, Ester. "A Biographical Dictionary of Painters and Sculptors in Illinois, 1880–1945." PhD diss., Northwestern University, 1971.

St. James, Warren D. *The National Association for the Advancement of Colored People: A Case Study in Pressure Groups*. Exposition Press, 1958.

Stuart, Evelyn Marie. "Finished Impressions of a Portrait Painter." *Fine Arts Journal* 32, no. 1 (1918): 150–58.

Taylor, Alrutheus Ambush. *The Negro in South Carolina During Reconstruction*. Association for the Study of Negro Life and History, 1924.

Teall, Gardner. Catalogue. "Paxton: A Painter of Things Seen." St. Botolph Club, 1916.

Thernstrom, Stephen. *The Other Bostonians: Poverty and Progress in the American Metropolis 1870–1970*. Harvard University Press, 1973.

Thistlethwaite, Mark Edward. *The Image of George Washington: Studies in Mid-Nineteenth- Century American History Painting*. Garland, 1979.

Tindall, George Brown. *South Carolina Negroes 1877–1900*. University of South Carolina Press, 1952.

The Scroll, 1900–1904. Woodruff Library, Special Collections, Clark Atlanta University, Atlanta, GA.

Trask, John E. D. "About Tarbell." *American Magazine of Art*, no. 6 (April 1918), 228.

Troyen, Carol. *The Boston Tradition: American Painting from the Museum of Fine Arts*. The Federation, 1980.

Wade, Richard C. *Slavery in the City: The South 1820–1860*. Oxford University Press, 1964.

Washington, Booker T. *Up From Slavery*, 3rd ed. Doubleday, Page, 1924.

Weber, Nicolas Fox. "Rediscovering American Impressionists." *American Review* (January/February 1976).

Weitzenhoffer, Frances. *The Havemeyers: Impressionism Comes to America*. Harry N. Abrams, 1986.

Whitford, William G. *An Introduction to Art Education*. Appleton, 1929.

Wikramanayake, Maria. *A World in Shadow: The Free Black in Antebellum South Carolina*. University of South Carolina Press, 1973.

Williams, Chad. *Torchbearers of Democracy: African American Soldiers in the World War I Era*. University of North Carolina Press, 2010.

Williamson, Joel. *After Slavery: The Negro in South Carolina During Reconstruction 1861–1877*. University of North Carolina Press, 1965.

Willis, Deborah. *Reflections in Black: A History of Black Photographers, 1840 to the Present*. W.W. Norton, 2000.

Willis, Deborah, and Howard Dodson. *Black Photographers Bear Witness: 100 Years of Social Protest*. Williams College Museum of Art, 1989.

Wilmerding, John. *American Art*. Spanierman Gallery, 1988.

Wilmerding, John, Sheila Dugan, and Williams Gerdts. *Frank W. Benson: The Impressionist Years*. Spanierman Gallery, 1988.

Woodward, C. Vann. *The Strange Career of Jim Crow*. Oxford University Press, 1966.

Yuhl, Stephanie E. *A Golden Haze of Memory: The Making of Historic Charleston*. University of North Carolina Press, 2005.

INDEX